More Dreamers of the Golden Dream

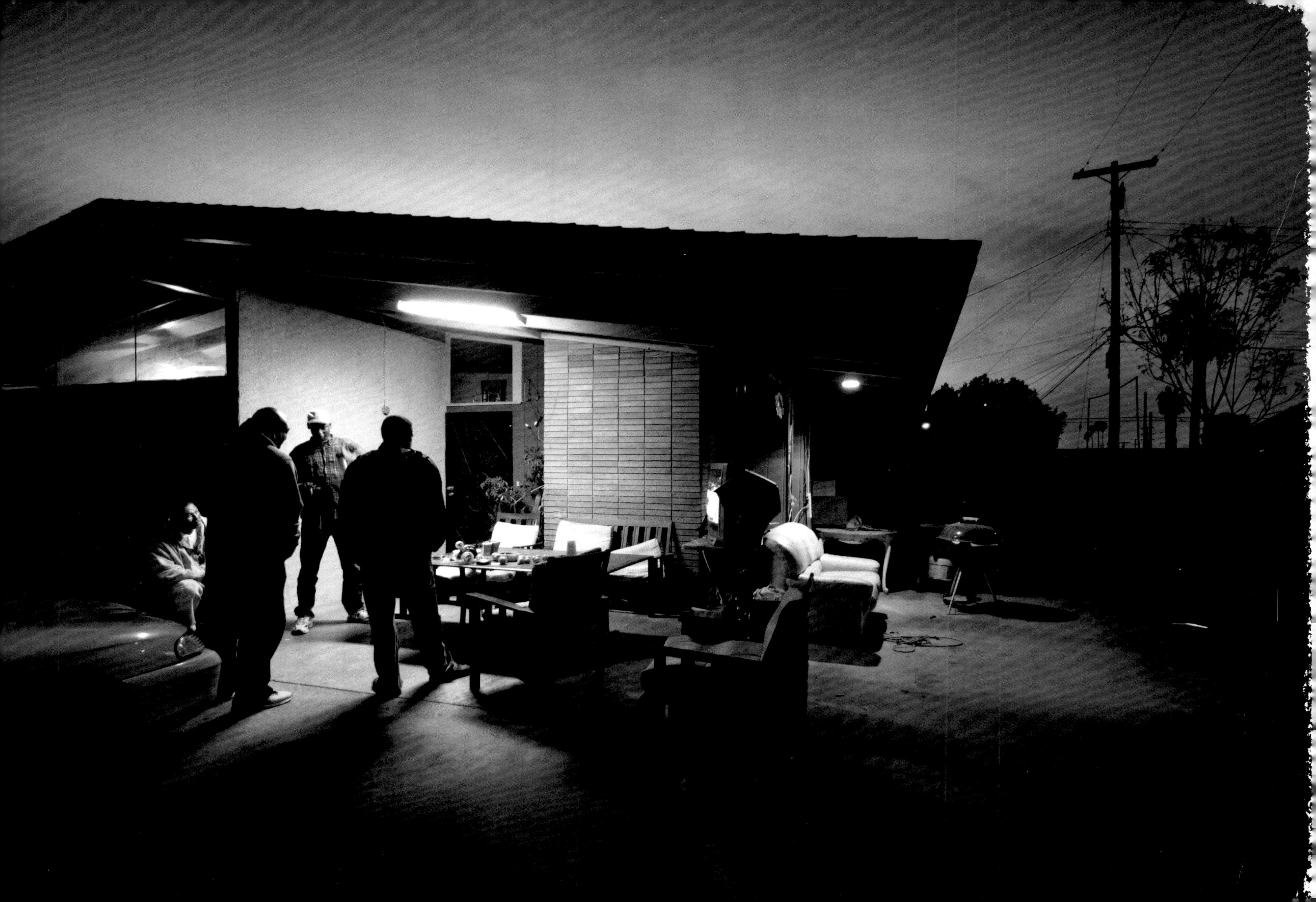

More Dreamers of the Golden Dream

Susan Straight ▪ Douglas McCulloh

Introduction and Essay by Delphine Sims

First published in the United States in 2021 by Inlandia Institute.

Orders, inquiries, and correspondence should be addressed to:

Inlandia Institute
4178 Chestnut Street
Riverside, California 92501
951.790.2458
www.inlandiainstitute.org

Inlandia Books are distributed to the trade by Itasca Books Distribution and Fulfillment.

ISBN: 978-1-955969-00-0

The Library of Congress has cataloged this edition as follows:

Names: Straight, Susan, author. | McCulloh, Douglas, author. | Sims, Delphine, author.
Title: More Dreamers of the Golden Dream / Susan Straight, Douglas McCulloh, Delphine Sims.
Description: Riverside, California : Inlandia Institute, 2021.
Identifiers: LCCN 2021033450 | ISBN 9781955969000 (paperback)
Subjects: LCSH: Riverside (Calif.) | LCGFT: Essays.
Classification: LCC PS3569.T6795 M67 2021 | DDC 814/.54--dc23
LC record available at https://lccn.loc.gov/2021033450

Printed in the United States of America.

10 9 8 7 6 5 4 3 2 1

More Dreamers of the Golden Dream

Eternal Dances of Home, Love, and Rememory

SUSAN STRAIGHT

When I first stepped onto the driveway at 4289 Michael Street, my life was changed by Alberta and General Sims, the royalty who held court at the community gatherings in that ribbon of cement leading to a carport under which the stories of six generations flowed out with laughter and shouting. Once Alberta said to me, "You know, everything stays in your rememory." And when my daughters were born, and Dwayne Sims and I brought them to the driveway, they learned what true loyalty and kinship meant.

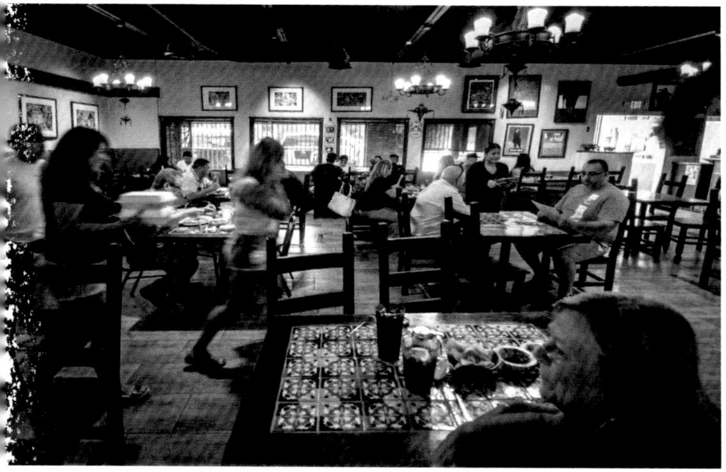

Zacatecas Café's new location — bigger and brighter — with the Medina family twirling behind other counters, July 2021

All of the places in *More Dreamers of the Golden Dream* mean that to the people whose stories and images are here — whether it's the iconic Zacatecas Café and the Medina family that feeds thousands; the parishioners at Our Lady of Guadalupe tracing ashes onto the foreheads of the faithful; the boxers in the ring housed inside the old kindergarten building of Lincoln School, once Irving School, where Alberta stood with her friend Susan Strickland; the sidewalk in front of Orange Valley Lodge #13 set with folding chairs and narrative.

When Douglas McCulloh and I first shared this show at the Riverside Art Museum, in 2013, so many of the people featured came to the opening that the building was full of surprises and shared histories. Now, after recent years of pandemic and violence, hardship and isolation, and new movements for racial reconciliation, looking at these images and text makes me even more grateful for shared community like ours. We have lost many of these storytellers since 2013 — Dorella Anderson, Clarice and Jesse Lee Collins, Rita Butts, Karen Lark, Rosie Morris Burns, and Jesse Wall, among others. Zacatecas Café has moved to a new location — bigger and brighter — with the Medina family twirling behind other counters.

The driveway on Michael Street is eternal, as long as there are chairs to unfold, a lighter to a grill, the huge smoker as sculpture behind us, the bend of knees when we lean toward each other to whisper something of rememory, and right now.

People say no one is from southern California, but we know better. As Robert Anderson says, "We grew up trading biscuits for tacos when we were little. And we ate them all." The pepper trees and bougainvillea shade our porches, and the palm tree in front of Orange Valley Lodge grows closer to the sky. There were family reunions at Fairmount Park in the 1880s in photographs saved by Dorella Anderson, and the Sims family reunions gather hundreds every year on that same ground, even now.

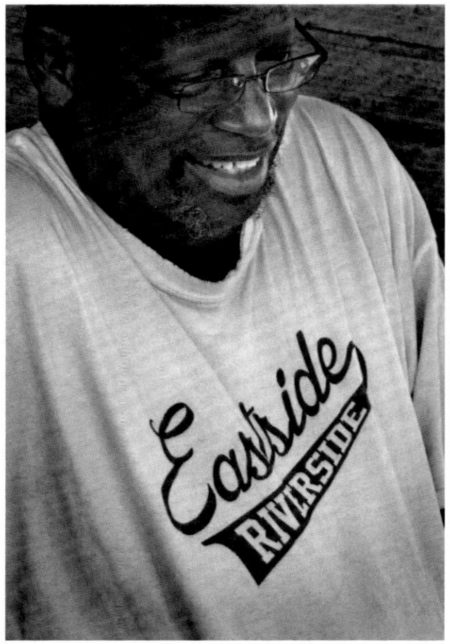

Trent Chatham in the Michael Street driveway wearing the T-shirt he had custom screenprinted for himself and friends, June 2021

These dreamers and their dreams are eternal, as long as there is smoke and laughter, hymnals and ringing, hands lifted to spirits and hands holding disks of ground corn, when all feels golden. As long as there are hands slamming dominoes onto a shaking table, lacing gloves and considering how to duck and move, and someone calling out a story, we are eternal. Let the circle be unbroken, as the new generations of dreamers walk on our sidewalks, enter into our doors, and tell their own stories of rememory and love. ■

Mediating Riverside Time

DELPHINE SIMS

Radiant light draws us into the casual driveway communion in the frontispiece of this catalogue. The illumination continually surprises me, because despite years of visiting my family at this precious Sims locus, I do not truly know Michael Street — our name for our family home – at night. The creeping darkness that frames the luminous cement of this Sims microcosm appears different to me (the third of four generations of Sims that know this house). I am of this driveway, the same one my mother, writer Susan Straight, has so lovingly returned to over and over again through her decades of writing, and yet it is both familiar and unfamiliar. In my memory, the driveway is sunlit (like photograph 22). Yet in this opening image, sunset hovers beyond the hour when those like me have to leave to return to the various locales where we live now. This experience of the driveway at night is telling, however, because it captures the relationship between the co-conspirators of *More Dreamers of the Golden Dream*, Douglas McCulloh and Susan Straight, their artistry and their cherished Riverside.

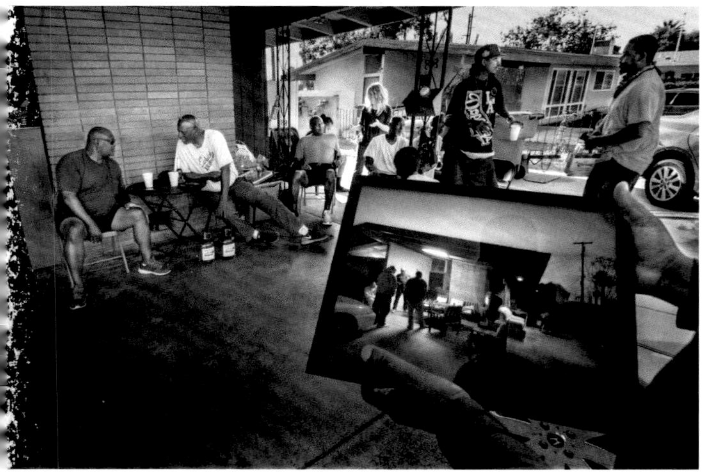

A sunny afternoon in the driveway: General Sims III holds a photo of a nighttime gathering in the same place , June 2021

My mother (Susan) starts the second essay of this catalogue reliving the moment the driveway became the setting for her welcome into the Sims family. As with hundreds of people, first you become family with food and drink, and then with patience and time, carefully selected narratives (always be ready and willing to listen) are bestowed upon you. It is within this paved landscape that so many find themselves initiated into the Sims clan. Thus it was unsurprising that Douglas was quickly embraced by the Sims family and able to embark on an essential project with my mother to document and record versions of the Sims Eastside community experience(s). And because to declare someone a member of the Sims family does not require biological relation to the Simses, their project became an intricate web that extended across Riverside's Eastside and folded in many other families.

Within the academic photography community there is much discussion of the collaborative nature of photography, but in the land of more dreamers it's beyond collaborative, it is kinship-image-making. Even with a population of over 325,000, much of Riverside remains a place that is family: a deeply connected, supportive community. It is in part this inherited nature of Riverside residents that enabled Douglas and Susan, two white artists – a writer and a photographer – and longtime Riversiders, to traverse the segregated, the desegregated, and the resegregated neighborhoods of the predominantly Black and Hispanic Eastside and be greeted by eager storytellers. The other part of their exceptional ability to bring *More Dreamers* to the Riverside Art Museum both in 2013 and again in 2021 is the way these two receive and mediate southern California stories.

Susan and Douglas first met at the opening for Douglas's 2009 exhibition *Dream Street*. It is unsurprising that a celebration of a project produced through happenstance and the patience to let intersections and relationships unfold would draw these two together, especially as each in their respective arts have dedicated careers to underappreciated Southern California landscapes and peoples. Douglas's first book *Chance Encounters* and later *Dream Street* established a thoughtful and dedicated photographic process that relies on chance. But it's important to focus on the time it takes to arrive at serendipity. It isn't always instantaneous. Much of Douglas's practice relies on ambling down streets and being open to whoever and whatever is slowly revealed to him. His meticulous documentation of this process in *Chance Encounters* includes not only location, date, and car mileage but also the time elapsed while he was on site. Sometimes it was upwards of eight hours.

Human connection takes time. Being the daughter of a mother who sustains herself through such connection, particularly in her Riverside hometown, means waiting. I am often suspended in an extended pause as entire life stories unravel during what are meant to be brief family visits, short meals, timed ceremonies, or a quick succession of errands.

Within this practice of patience is the promise of release – stories that have been told countless times are told once more to be heard again by my mother's burning ears. But just as often, those not previously spoken suddenly come pouring out. My mother asks the right questions, and folks want to bequeath their narratives to her, but ultimately they do so because they trust her, and Douglas, as stewards of the truth of their stories and images. Across my mother's nonfiction and foundational to her fiction are the oral histories of thousands. Specifically, there are the original KCET posts which preceded and eventually became the *More Dreamers* exhibition; a cataloguing of vast, multigenerational lives, each of which is a testament to the human experience but equally rooted in such rich singularity that it is a gift to read and view adaptations of their biographies.

Collaboration implies a potential end to a project, but here it is evident that this project and the constellation of people involved in its existence are part of an ever-evolving story. The reinstallation of *More Dreamers* and our encounter with the images and texts is filled with the promise that new stories will arise but only if there are those willing to stay and be a patient audience. To hear and see them, one must invest the care to start at our own "Michael Street" in the early afternoon light only to finally arrive at the images and climax even when it takes us beyond twilight. ■

Table of Contents

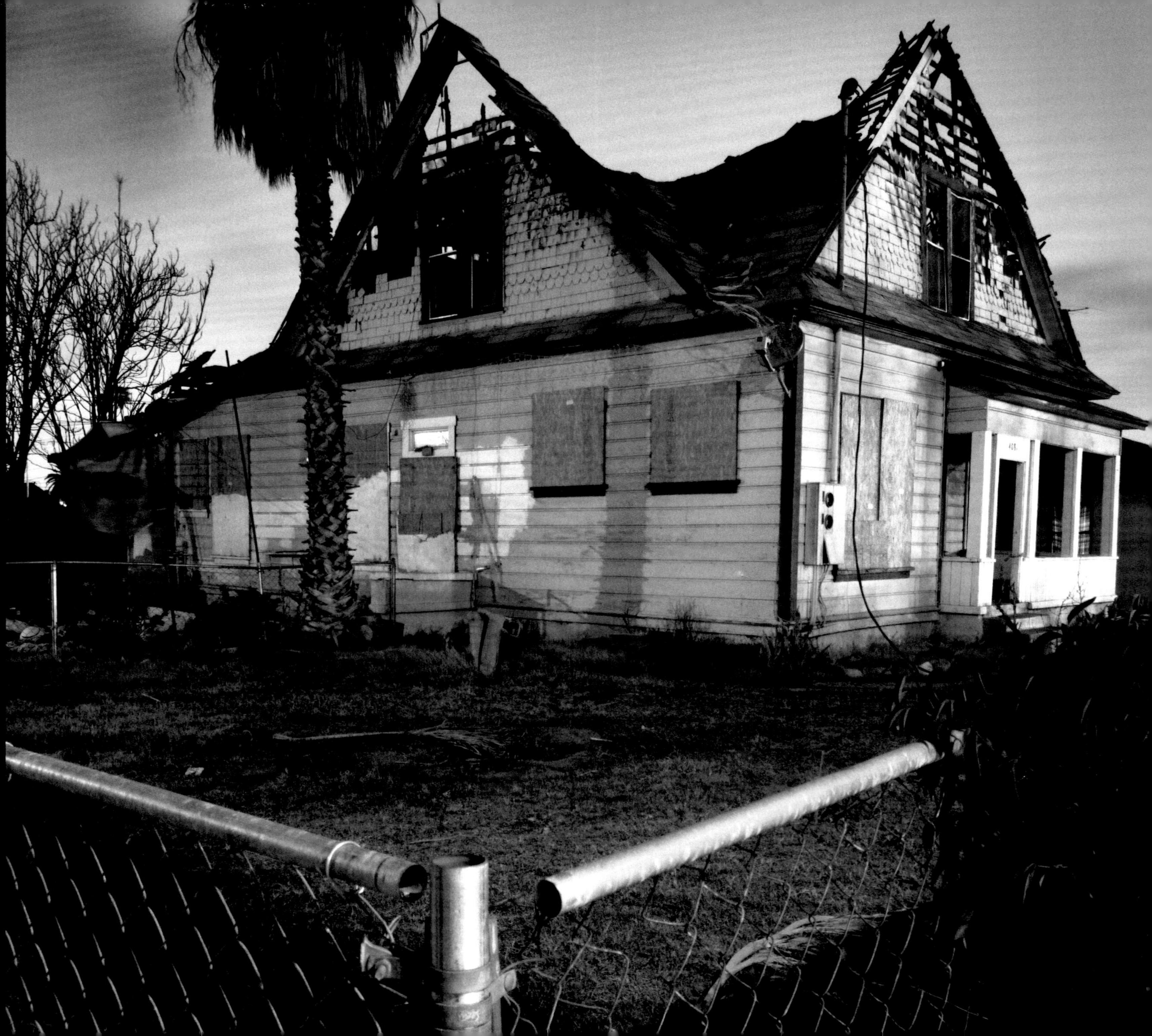

1.

Daisy Carter's House

Dwayne Sims called me one day in December, 2011. His voice was rough and clotted with pain. "Grandma's house is burning. Right now. I just drove by. There's people standing everywhere."

He parked past the two-story Victorian house – with cedar closets where he used to play, with windowsills where hundreds of sweet potato pies and teacakes had cooled until they were delivered by Daisy Carter's grandchildren to customers who wanted the best baked goods in the neighborhood, with a long upstairs bedroom where Daisy Carter's husband, one of the railroad's first Black armed security men, held court – burning in the way newspapers report as "spectacular." Flames were shooting out of the second story, collapsing onto the first floor in a huge sparking sag, the scalloped shingles and fretwork turning black.

A post-quinceaneara party had been in progress in the yard, with guests of the Mexican-born residents who rented the house. The crowd watched the fire burn. No one was inside. The flames appeared to have begun in the attic, where two teenagers were living.

This house was an icon on the Eastside. The next day, Dwayne couldn't believe there was no story in the newspaper. History erased. How many hundred-year-old Victorians burn in America, never to be replaced? Who can build a house like that now? And who would, in older neighborhoods like these in Detroit, or Albany, or Riverside, where empty foreclosed homes are everywhere?

Daisy's house somehow remained gracious even while sagging and charred. Maybe that's because Dwayne Sims and I stood there again and again while he told stories about the hundreds of adults and children passing through those rooms. Many of the older women of our childhood had come from the south, presiding over homes where kids were watched, fed, scolded, and bandaged after sliding into home. They told us their own Canterbury tales – heroic stories, terrifying ones, hilarious versions of the epic journeys they took to get to southern California. Mississippi is where Daisy Carter was born, and orphaned, and where she fled to remake herself on Kansas Avenue. But Daisy kept her journeys secret, even from her four daughters.

She is a fragment, Alberta. Bemused and regal and slightly mischievous, sitting beside her younger sister at a table where they are clearly out on the town. Are they with husbands? Are they with their older two sisters? It doesn't matter. They are both lovely, gazing at us.

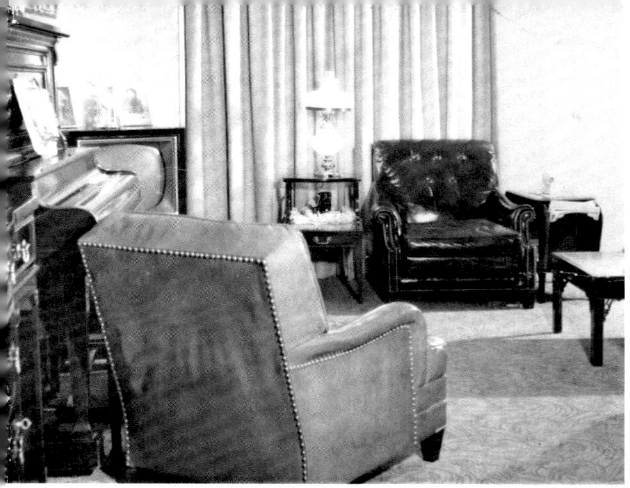

2.

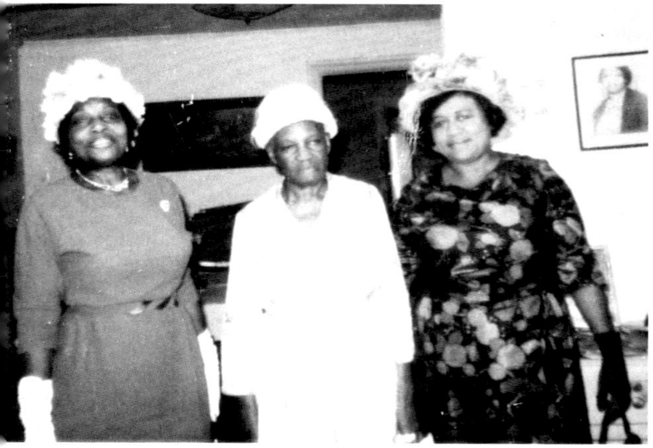

3.

No one ever knew where Alberta was born – it could have been Mississippi, Oklahoma, Arkansas, Texas or Calexico. Mysteries. When Daisy Morris arrived in California, she had nothing but four daughters, all with the same last name. "Oh, those girls!" people say even now. "I remember those sisters. Four of them. They were all beautiful."

Mary Louise, Myrtle, Alberta, and Rosie. Years later, my father-in-law told me, "Daisy never said a damn word about anything in the past. Never." But Alberta used to talk to me while we sat in her mother's old leather wing chairs trimmed with brass buttons, near the fireplace. I nursed my own daughters at lunchtime, before going back to work, and then Alberta held them close and bit their cheeks gently. That was her favorite thing to do. One day she said, "My grandmother was killed. Run down by a car on a dirt road, back in Mississippi. And my mother was so small. After that, she went from pillar to post, pillar to post."

I didn't understand that phrase then, but puzzled over it for weeks. All the different porches – Daisy moved from house to house. Rita Butts Sweeney, Mary Louise's oldest daughter, said, "What they told me was someone ran Daisy's mother down on purpose – no one knows why. But she knew – she threw the children over the embankment."

Aunt Dear, as she was known, was Daisy's mother's sister. After Mary was killed, and Daisy had grown up beautiful, "Aunt Dear took Daisy on the trek from Mississippi to California," according to Rita. "It was the turn of the century – women were migrating all over the country, and they made money however they could. I know she had my mom in Wewoka, Oklahoma. I know her husband was Mr. Morris. But that's it. They never told us anything more. They all kept secrets."

They came to Riverside to live with Margaret Henderson, Aunt Dear's sister. The girls went to Irving School, while Daisy worked during World War II in a munitions warehouse in Mira Loma. At night, her aunts watched the girls. In the day, they worked at the Turkey House, with many other women, plucking pinfeathers in the terrible smell. Daisy saved enough money to buy this house, a grand beacon to arriving immigrants from the Black South of the 1950s, which Eddie Chandler, her cousin, once called "a Third-World Country for us." She took in boarders, like Hattie Davis and her four children, who came from Georgia. Hattie married Reverend L.B. Moss, and moved into her new life. Daisy built a separate apartment for Floyd Walker's mother-in-law, known as Big Ma to the neighborhood kids. Originally from Georgia, Big Ma dipped snuff, and smoked out wasps from the eaves with a rolled newspaper lit on fire – she used the larvae to go fishing at the Salton Sea.

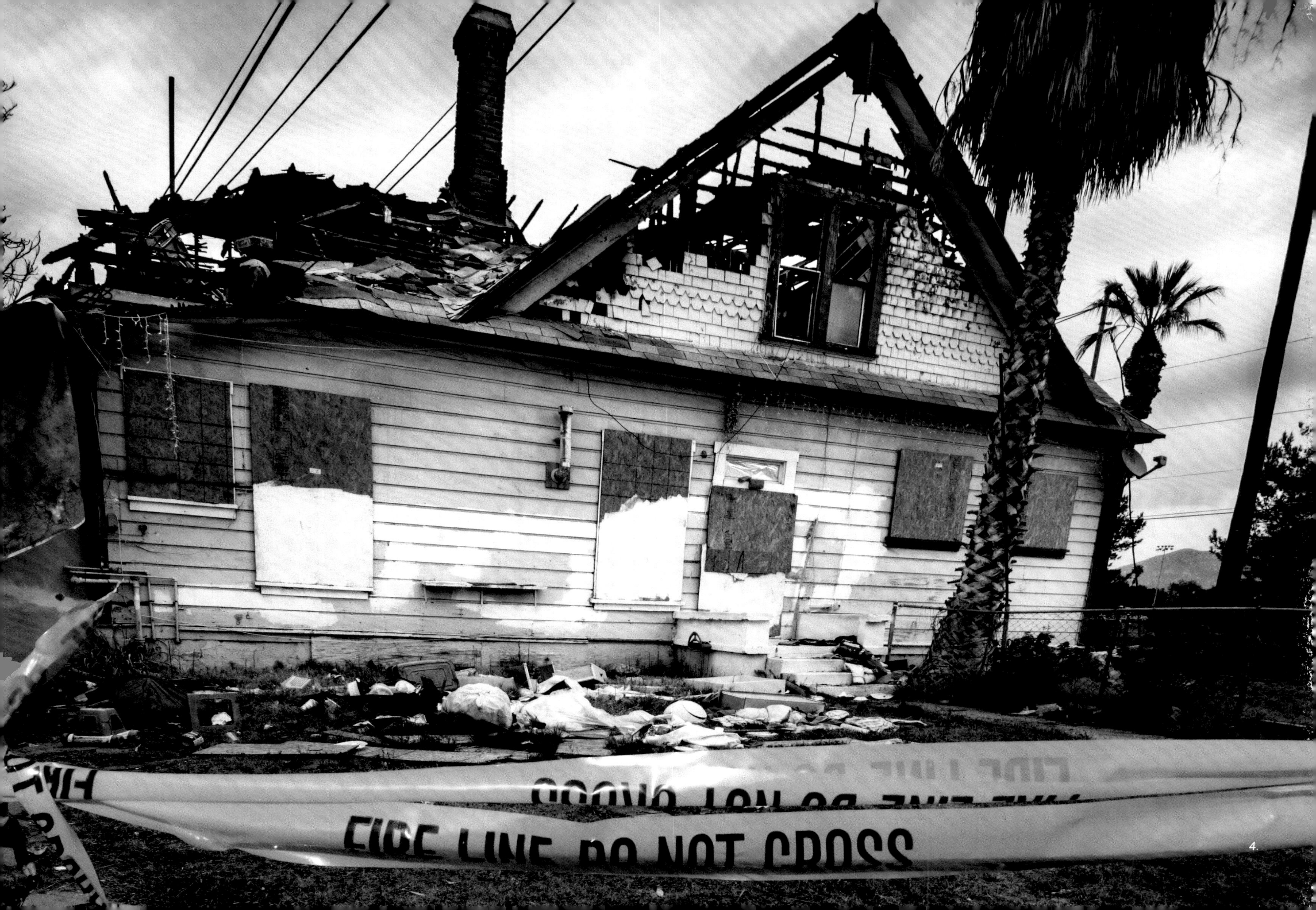

4.

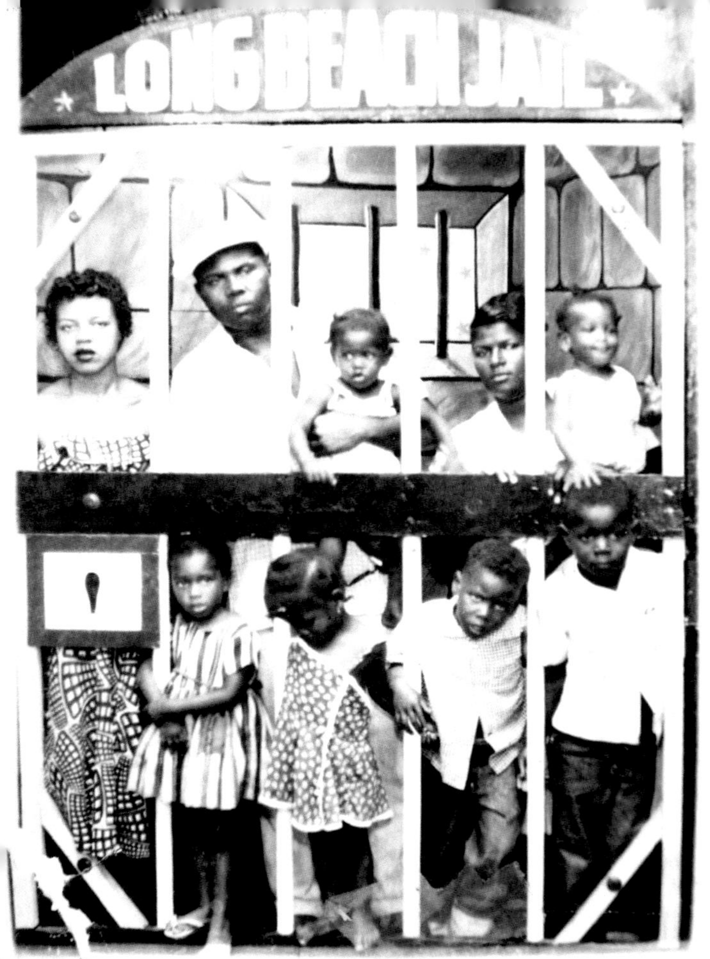

5.

6.

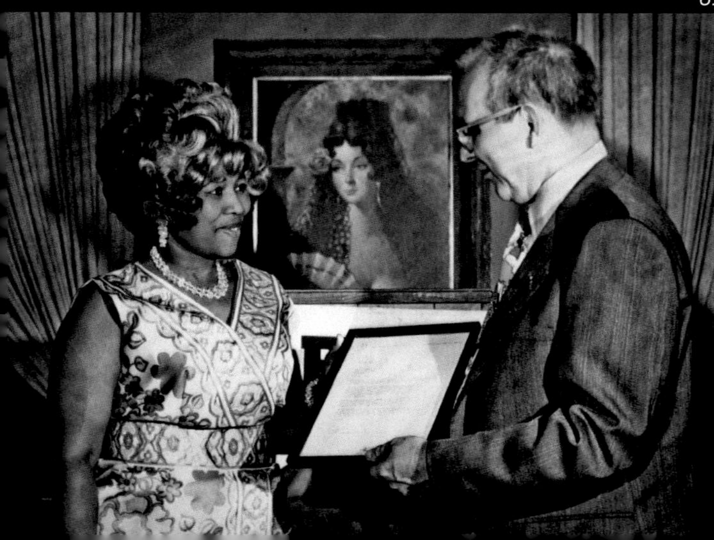

Once Daisy married Ernest Carter, who was much older and had worked for decades in San Bernardino for the Southern Pacific Railroad, "our whole family ascended into the middle class," as General put it. Mr. Carter – that's what everyone calls him even now – "treated Daisy like a queen. She was the style-setter for the whole Eastside," said Jesse Wall. They had a son – Ernest Carter, Jr., who used to laugh about accidentally shooting himself in the toe with one of his father's guns. She built a stucco bungalow next door, where her relatives could always live.

But she still sold those sweet potato pies. "Daisy could launder shirts like no one else in Riverside," Jesse Wall said. "Lawyers and businessmen all brought their shirts to her." I imagine the pies golden and the white shirts hanging starched. The four sisters were always there, working in the house, too. "They used to sit on that porch, two and two," Zerlie Aubert told me one day. "Everyone was in love with them."

"Oh, I loved Mary Louise," Leonard Walker, 84, told Dwayne and me another day, in his house on Park Avenue. "When I came to Riverside after I got out of the Marines, she was the most beautiful girl. But I had too much going on." Rita Butts said, "All the older men used to say that – they'd tell me, your daddy Gato got the prettiest one out the whole bunch. He had her face painted on a rice scroll when he was serving in Korea." Henderson Butts, nicknamed Gato, married Mary Louise and they had seven children.

After Robert Anderson recounted the story of his marriage to Mariko, his wife since 1969, he said offhandedly, "You know who my first love was, when I was only sixteen? Myrtle." I couldn't believe it. "Mr. Carter had the cleaning contract for Sage's Market, and he hired everybody – I worked down there with him. Myrtle was so beautiful, I wanted to talk to her all the time. But Aunt Dear, the one

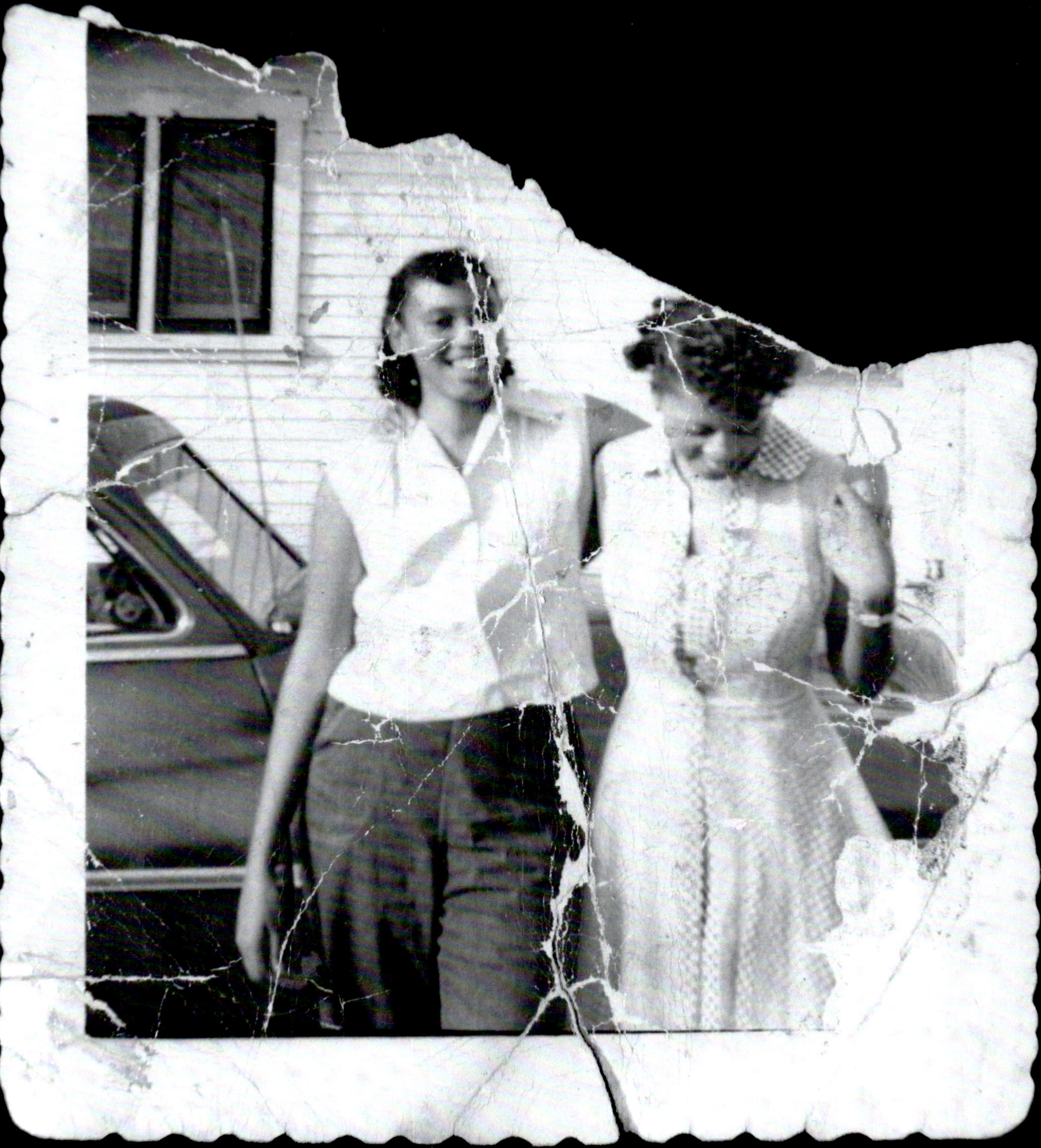

raising them, she was mean as a snake. She kept asking me, When are you gonna cut some cake? I was 16! I kept thinking, Where is this cake? Then I figured it out – she wanted me to get married!"

"Oh, I just kept trying to talk to Alberta, she was so fine," John Sims always told me. "I had just gotten here from Tulsa, with my mother, and when I got to Riverside Poly, Alberta was the one for me. But she just kept saying, Don't you have a brother named General?" He laughed regretfully every time.

In the Poly High yearbook, 1952, her gym teacher wrote, "Hope your married life will be happy and that the best will always be yours." Alberta and General Sims said their vows just after she graduated, and she had her first son in 1953.

Alberta and General bought a house on 11th Street, within sight of Daisy Carter's house. Then they bought the house on Michael Street, near the corner of 12th, and that is where Alberta lived until she died of a series of strokes, in 1995. (I was pregnant with my youngest daughter, who never met her grandmother, who has Alberta's elegant eyebrows and long legs.) She was only 61. Mary Louise had died in 1980 of leukemia, and Daisy passed away the following year, and in 1982, Myrtle died of liver disease, brought on, her family thought, by years of using harsh cleaners as a domestic worker. Her sister Rosie, who moved to Las Vegas with her two sons in the 1980s, remains there; her brother Ernest Carter Jr. lived in Seal Beach until recently, when he returned to Riverside, where he attends St. James Church. The house was sold to a rental company. For decades, when I drove past, different windows would be boarded up, and different faces looked out later from the apartments inside. People from Mexico were beginning their own life travels there, in the high-ceilinged rooms where the leather chairs once gleamed.

In the epic stories of migration, Daisy's life was classic – Mississippi to Oklahoma, Texas to Calexico, and finally Kansas Avenue. Pillar to post – a small house on Howard, then a Victorian. Alberta lived within a three-block radius for most of her life. Sensei Sims, standing on this corner, will have a son, Dustin, with Shaleah Thomas in a few months. If you add up the humans descended from Daisy and her daughters, children fed and clothed from the labors of plucked turkeys and starched shirts and rolled piecrusts, munitions for war and ministrations for love, there are more than 100 people in the world who exist solely because she made her way here, wearing those hats and gloves, her elegant cheekbones and winged eyebrows, her smile not dimmed. ■

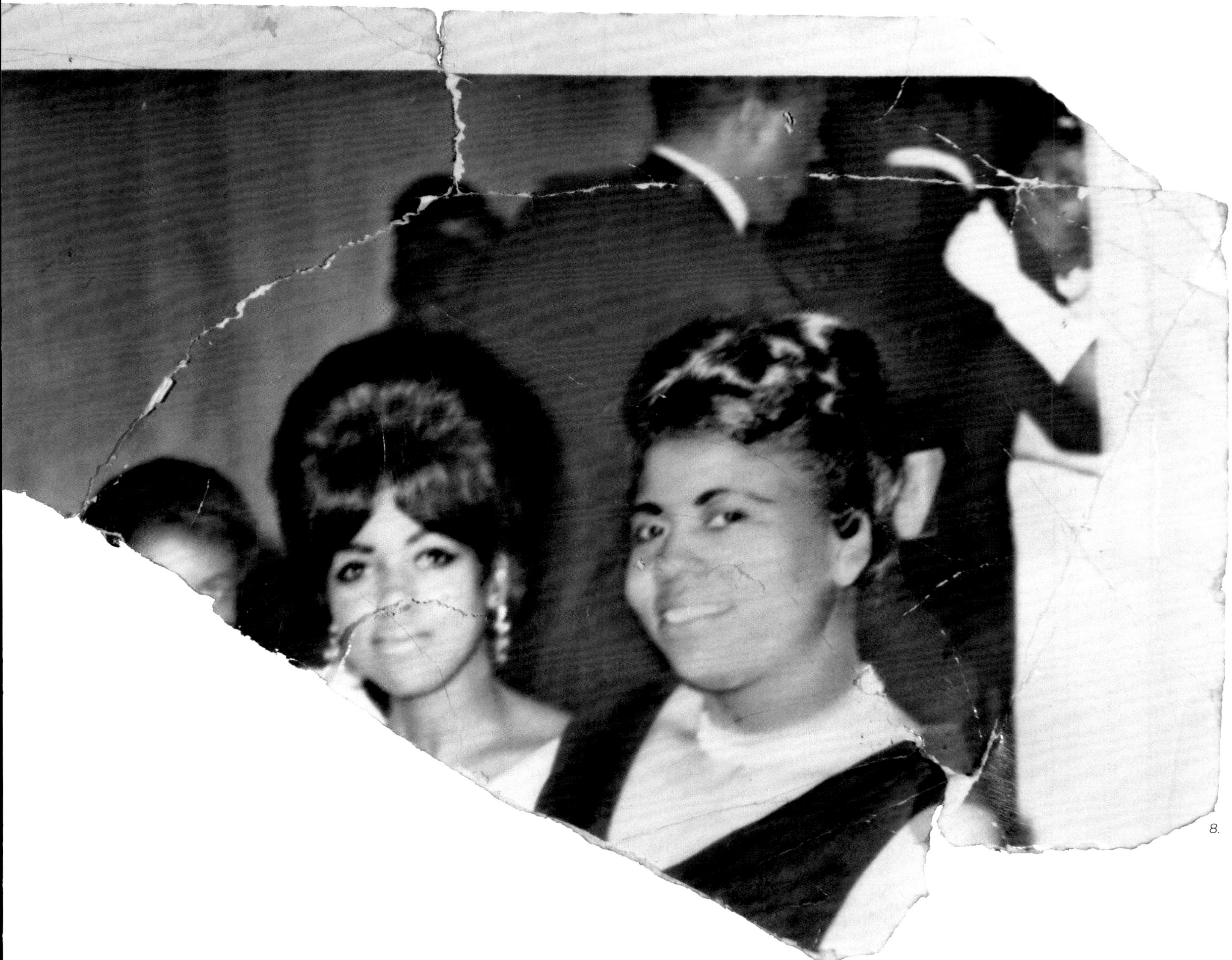

8.

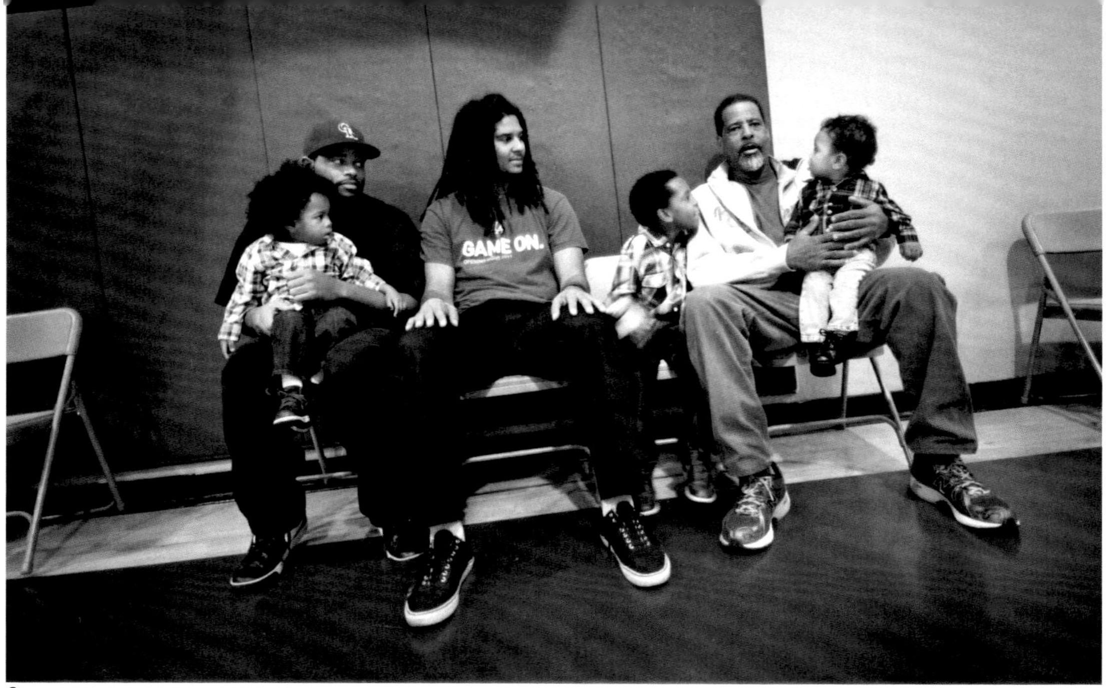

9.

1. *Daisy Carter's house on 11th Street and Kansas Avenue, after the fire, 2011*
2. *Daisy Carter's living room, with the leather chairs inherited by Alberta, then by Dwayne and Susan Sims, 1950s*
3. *Willie Frances Foster, Gertrude Luckett, and Daisy Carter, cousins, preparing for church at St. James Church of God in Christ, where Pastor James E. Wall, also a cousin, officiated, date unknown*
4. *Blackened shingles and fretwork: Daisy Carter's house on 11th Street and Kansas Avenue, after the fire, 2011*
5. *At the Long Beach Pike amusement park: Daisy's oldest daughter, Mary Louise Morris Butts, holding her twin daughter Judy, far right; Gregory Butts, Henderson Butts Jr., Rita Butts Sweeney, Riverside neighbors Kathy Nelson Barnes and her mother Lucille Nelson, and Henderson Butts holding the other twin, Jody, early 1960s*
6. *Myrtle Morris Samuel, receiving an award from the Riverside Heart Association, date unknown*
7. *Alberta Morris Sims and Loretta Preston, her sister-in-law, in front of Daisy Carter's house, 1950s*
8. *Alberta Morris Sims and Rosie Morris, out on the town, date unknown*
9. *Daisy Carter's legacy: Inside the gym at Bobby Bonds Sports Complex, Lennox Sims, General Sims IV, Sensei Sims, Cordae Sims, General Sims III holding Dustin Ozzy Sims*
10. *After the bulldozer removed the burned rubble of Daisy Carter's house: Dwayne Sims, Eddie Chandler Jr, General Sims III, Carnell Sims, Sensei Sims*

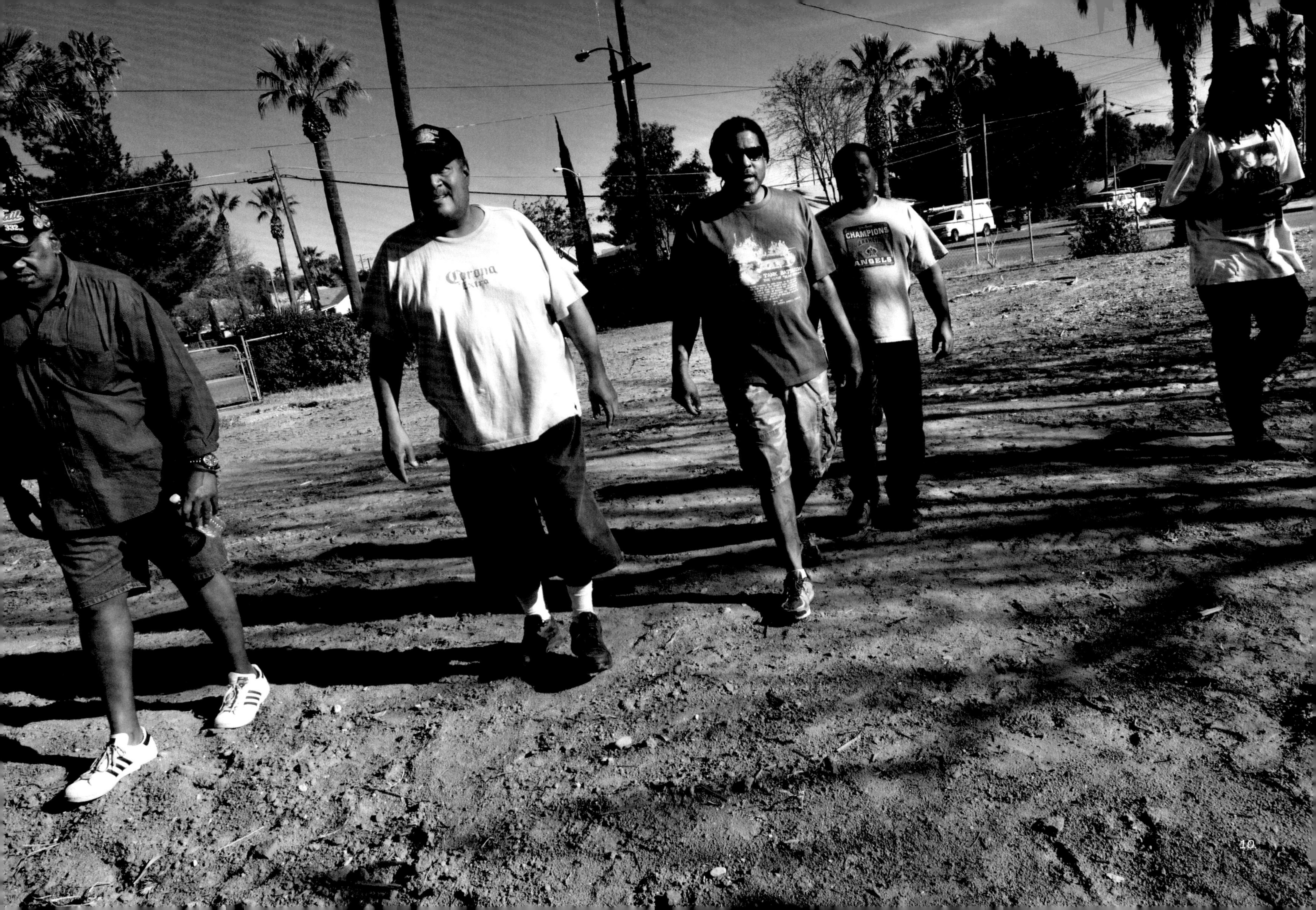
Corona
Extra
CHAMPIONS
ANGELS

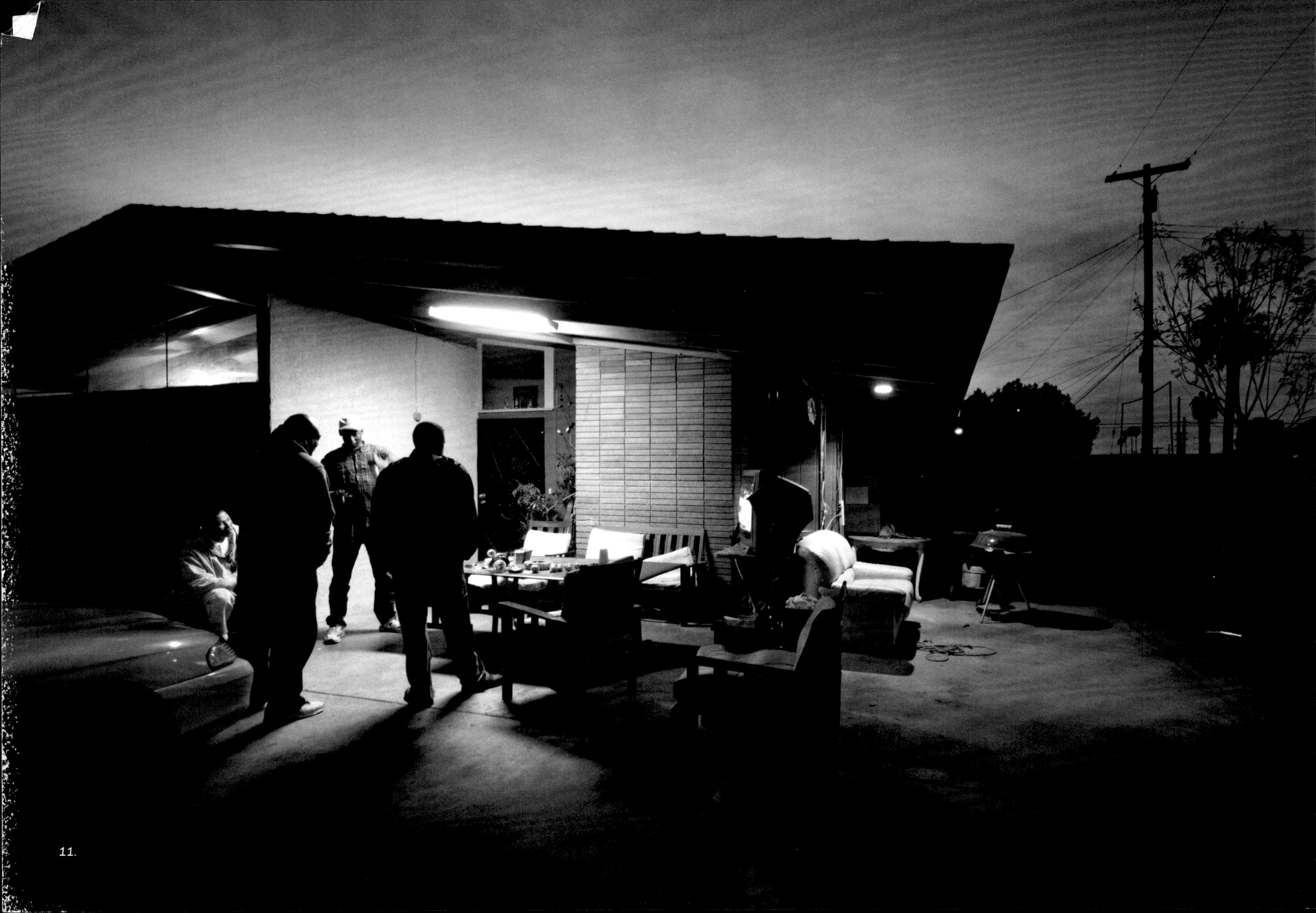

11.

The Driveway: A Love Story

The bricks. A massive chimney built of ochre bricks like a throne in the driveway of General Sims, on Michael Street, where for fifty years people have gathered. Every day – not just holidays or birthdays, but almost every afternoon and evening. General held court there with Ben Tyson, Dell Roberts, Tommie Chatham and Jesse Lee Collins and countless others. Now Jesse's son-in-law Keith Harris drops off bags of oranges and tangerines on the table near where the Lakers game plays on the massive television set outside near the rubber-tree plant which has somehow survived decades. Tommie Chatham's son Trent is here almost every day after work, working on a car with his brother-in-law Montrell Hamilton, sharing Coronas with Howard Fields and General III. Christine Sims Stuckey and Angela Sims arrive home from work and go inside.

There, the huge fireplace and built-in bookshelves dominate the other side – the living room. For as many years, Alberta Sims held her court here, from the red leather chair which came from her own mother's house on Kansas Avenue. The women sat around the fire on a winter day – Alberta and her sisters, Mary Louise, Myrtle and Rosie. General's sisters, Minerva and Loretta, and their own daughters. Clarice Collins, Dorella Anderson, Susan Strickland, Jean Taylor, Zerlie Aubert.

Those distinctive gold-toned bricks were brought to the tract home by Tony Chavarrias in the 1960s. He and General always worked out deals, traded labor and materials and beer and handshakes in the Eastside way, and the two of them built the fireplace and chimney where the carport stood, and then part of a wall along the driveway. General always sent his kids to buy food at Tony's Market, the store on Park Avenue owned for 50 years by Tony and his wife Mary.

General and Jesse Lee Collins left from the driveway every night to pick up Oscar Medina for their night shift servicing aircraft at Norton Air Force Base in San Bernardino. "We used to go over to Oscar's and his wife Josie would have to wake him up. We'd hear her calling him in Spanish – get up, get up! All the kids would be in the living room, and she would send one in there to get him," Jesse Collins said. Later, when both men were landscapers, they worked on lawnmower engines and lifted transmissions from trucks with a chain attached to the old ash tree nearby. Orchids raised from customers lined the wall, and collard green trees plucked into comical shapes by General.

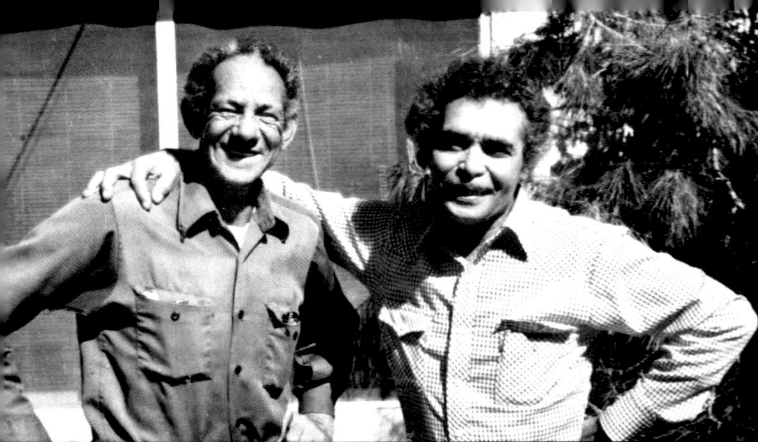

12.

13.

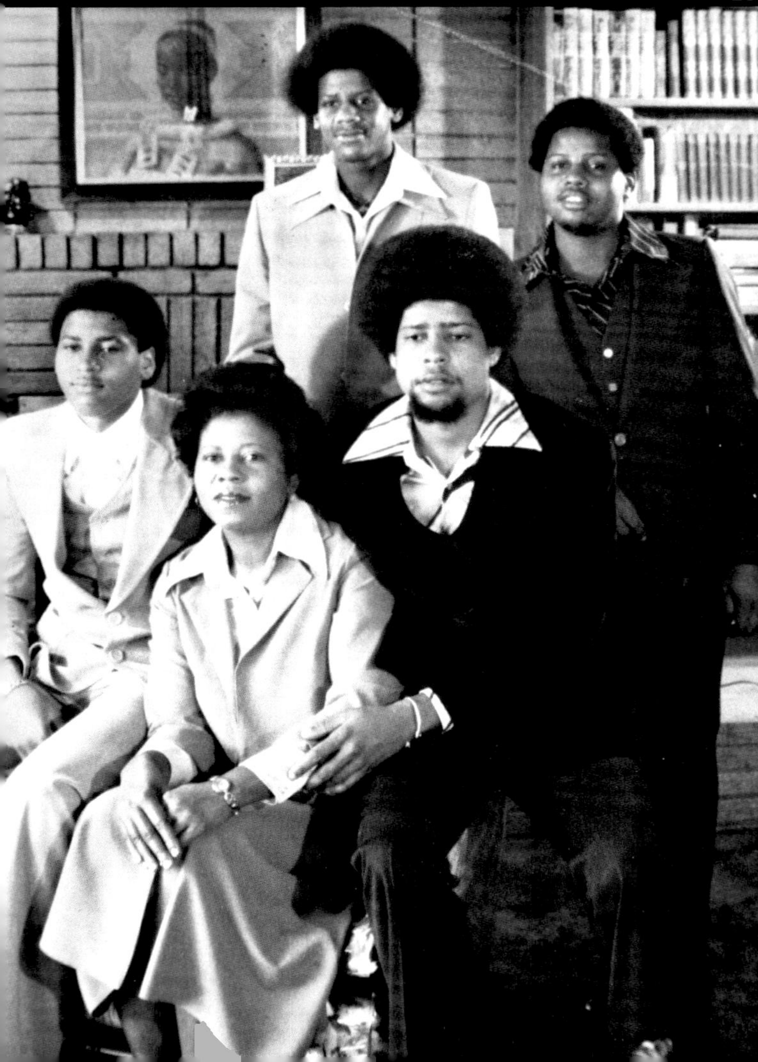

I walked down this driveway with much apprehension, wearing a halter dress when I was sixteen years old, in 1977. Dwayne Sims knew what might happen when he brought me on that Memorial Day. A small blonde girl being introduced to about a hundred family members, some of whom raised their eyebrows so high I winced and looked down. Some of the older people had watched Black Tulsa burn in 1921 from fires set by white mobs after a young man was accused of accosting a white woman in an elevator. Some had hidden under beds while the Klan wrecked their living rooms. And Dwayne led me toward Alberta, who said, “Come on inside and let me get you a plate.”

She gave everyone a plate, for her whole life. Strangers, new daughters-in-law (we were many!) and basketball player friends. That first day, after my plate was empty, I went into the kitchen and washed dishes, because I thought she might love me then. It worked. I cleaned the Formica counters, and learned how to clean chitlins (so hard!) with Alberta and her nieces and my sisters-in-law. Now, Marcella Vargas, Carnell’s wife, and I use a hatchet to cut long slabs of ribs into single pieces, and Margaret Chandler Cain puts a bowl of her potato salad on the counter.

Teri Andrews always brings peach cobbler from a recipe taught to her by her mother Minerva, General’s older sister. One of my favorite nights was Teri’s wedding reception. She was married at Allen Chapel, the historic African-American church downtown where Dwayne and I married as well. But after Teri’s wedding, we ate in the driveway from long tables covered with maroon cloths, and danced on the cement.

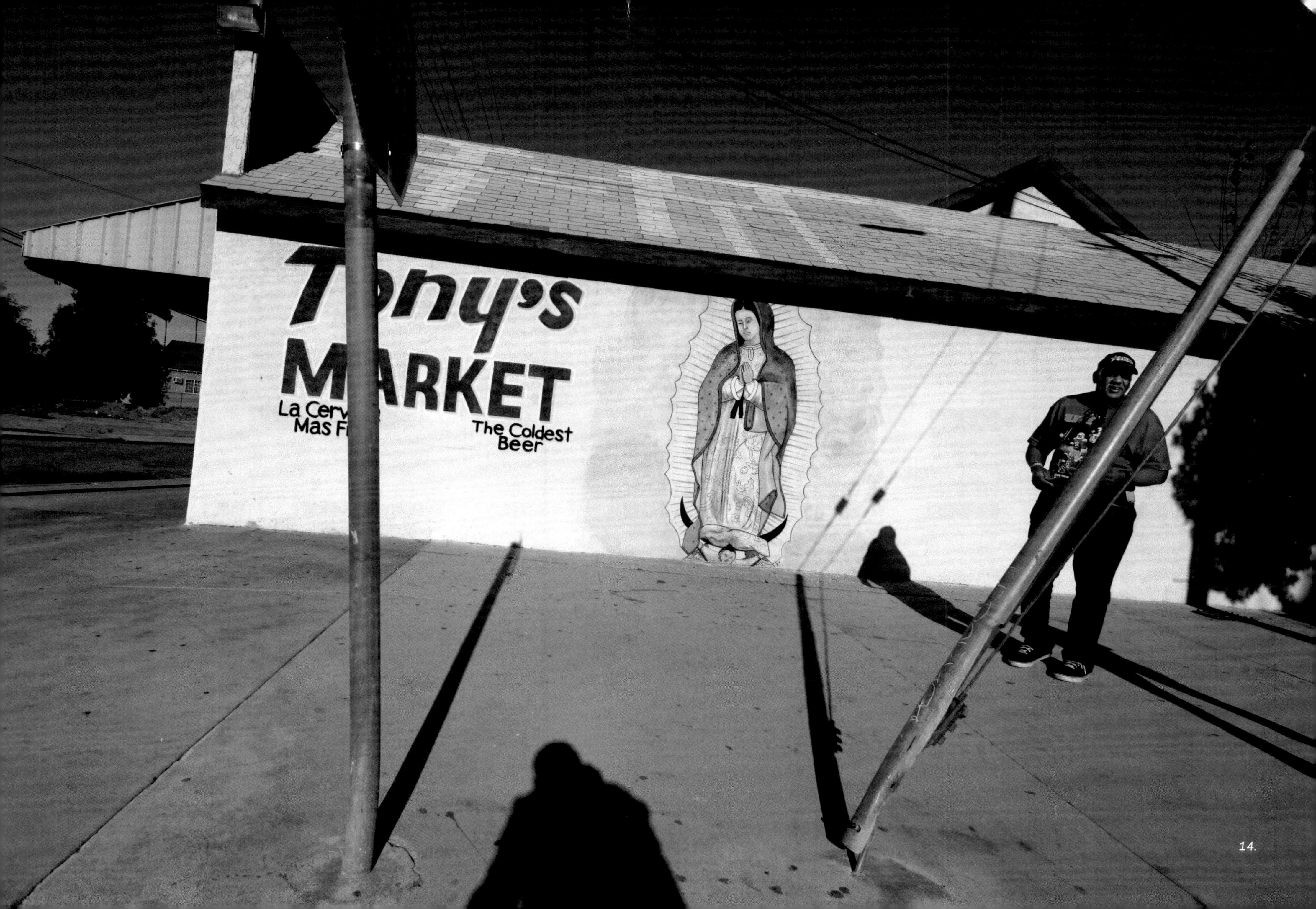
Tony's
MARKET
La Cerv
Mas F
The Coldest
Beer

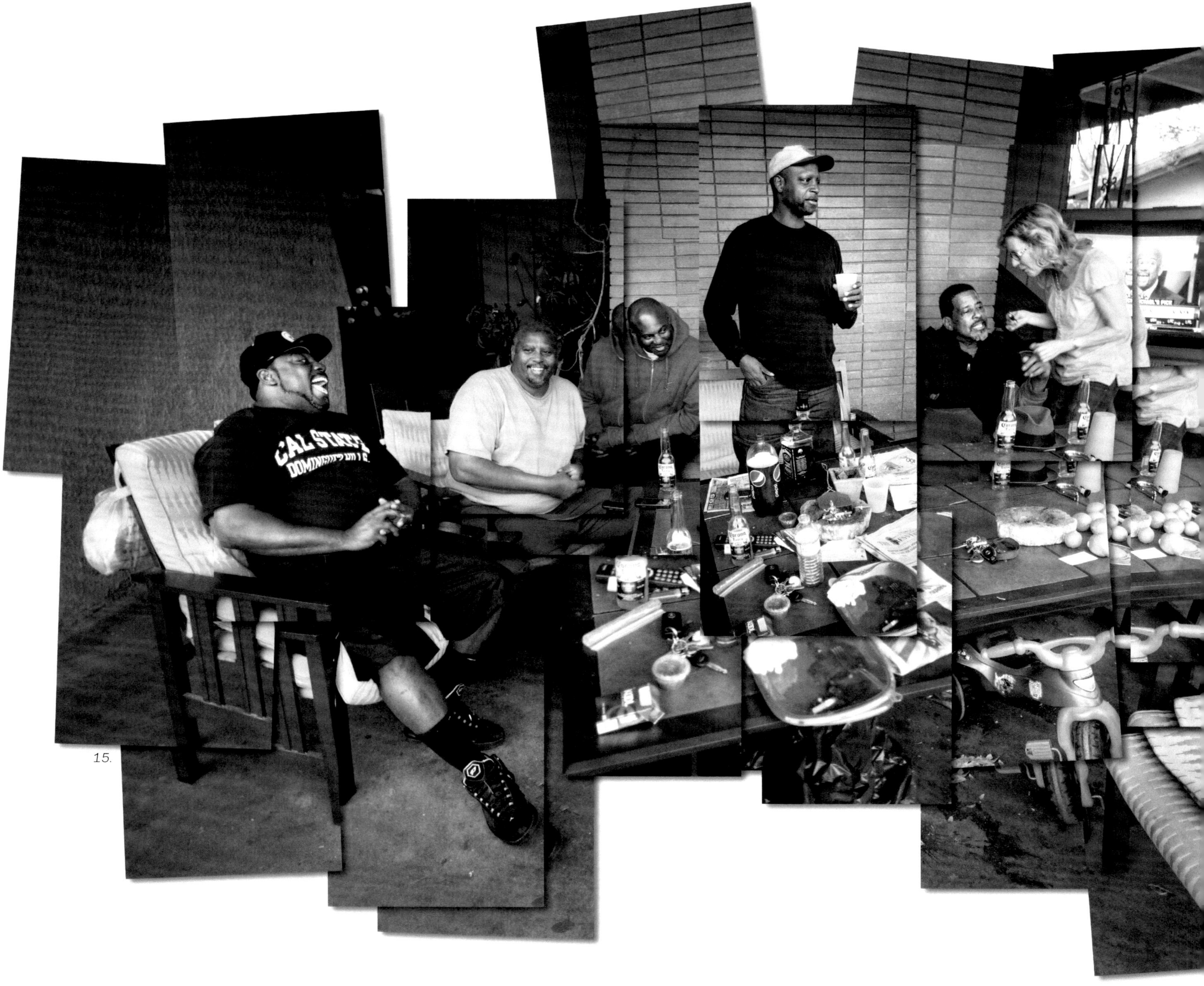

15.

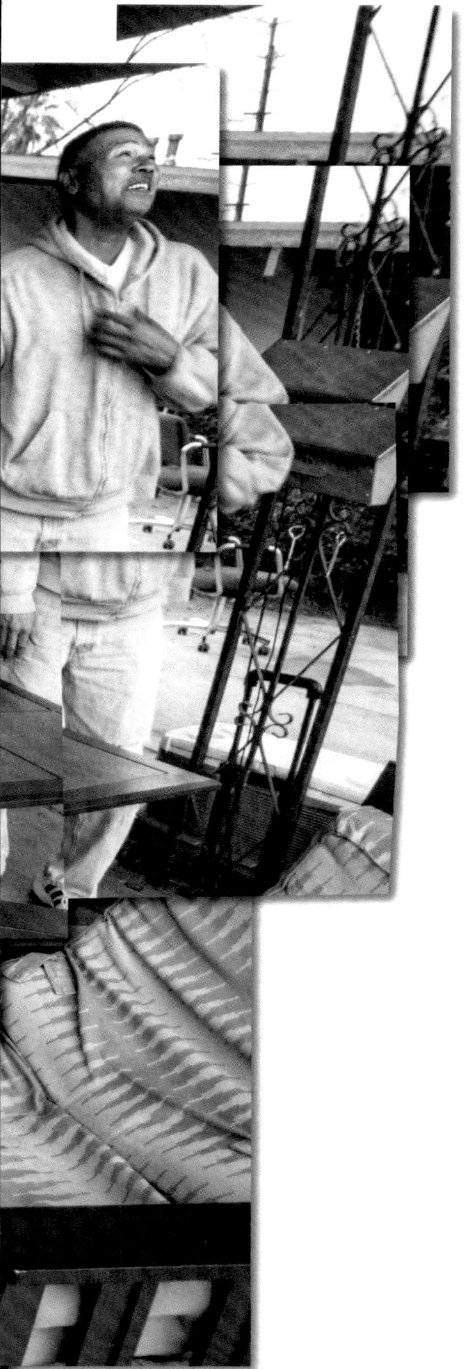

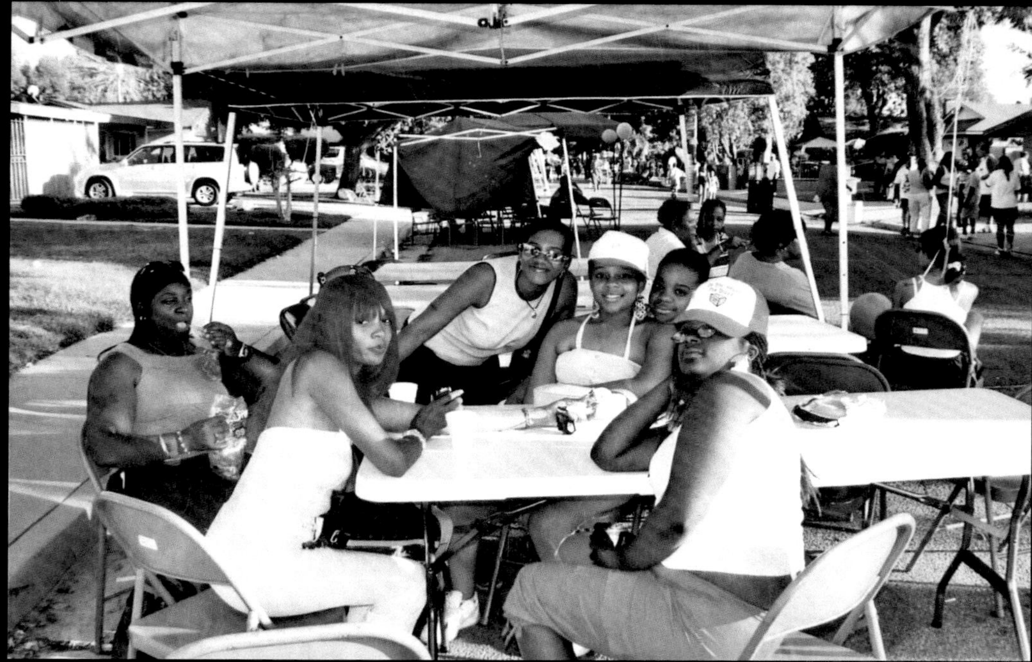

16.

17.

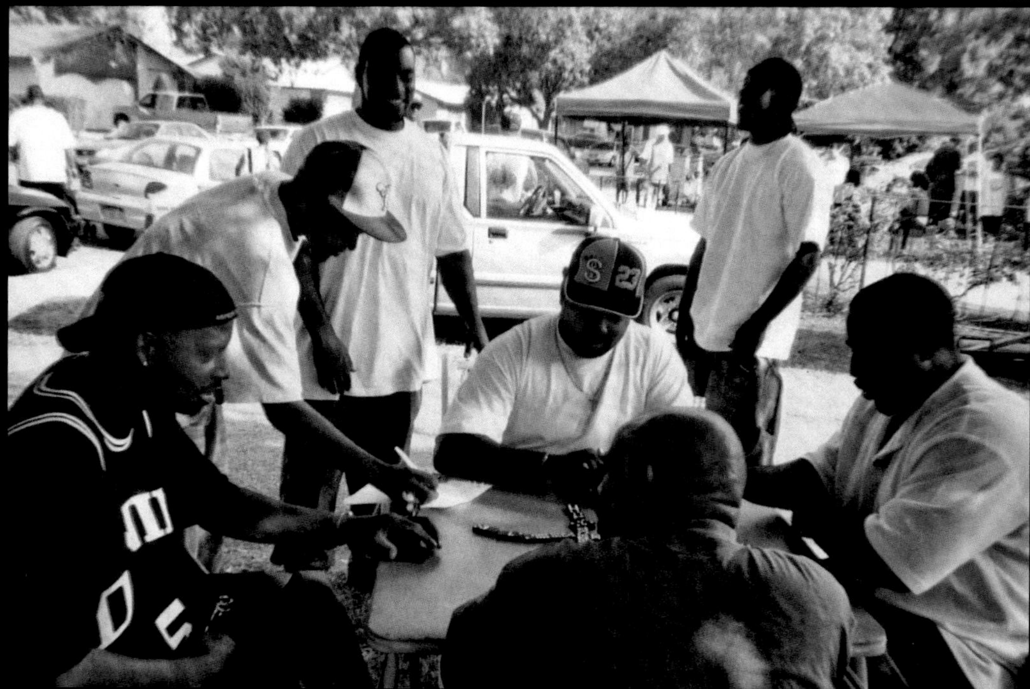

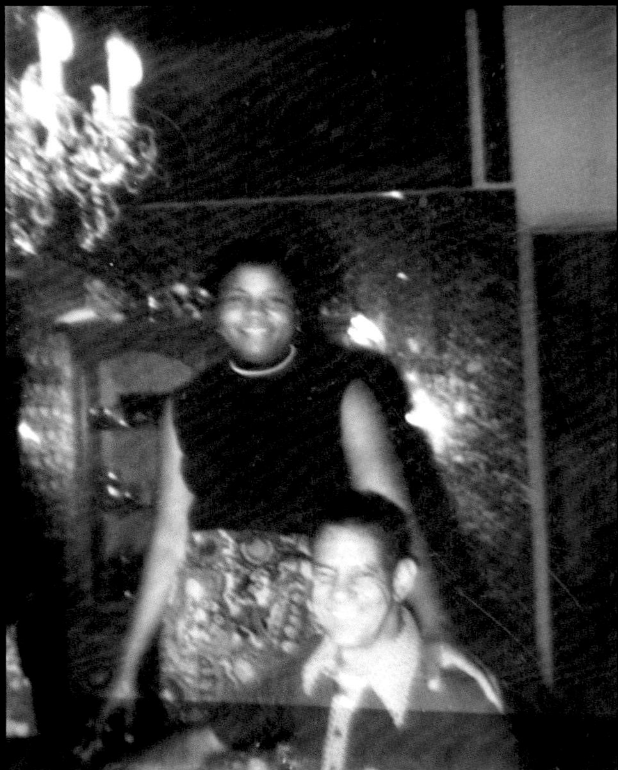

18.

Alberta's funeral was in 1995, and I helped my sisters-in-law clean the kitchen where she taught me to cook smothered steak in a cast-iron frying pan, the one she gave me, the one my daughter puts on our stove every day. That night, I began to cry near the sink and had to go out to the driveway and stand in the dark.

General's funeral was in 2008, and after his casket was carried down the steps of Allen Chapel, after the burial and the repast, we sat for two days in the driveway. How could it be any other way, for the man who dispensed history (Black cowboys, Oklahoma, Jesse James) and hilarity ("I don't know why those boys lost at North – I told the ball to fall every single time they hoisted it up in the air!") along with the songs of Earl Grant from a blonde-wood stereo console?

Barber chairs, couches, a black-leather bench seat from a truck, brown metal folding chairs and white plastic chairs. A barbecue and smoker so massive Trent Chatham has to tow it. Trent, Montrell Hamilton, Keith Harris and Derrick Sims got Doug McCulloh a plate the second time he was in the driveway. They had a hot link social that Friday afternoon. They gave a full plate to the mail carrier when she came by. That is how it works. Twenty strong each afternoon. More than a hundred on holidays like Super Bowl Sunday, when Ernest "Butch" Carter Jr. and his wife Hyacinth Valentine eat at a long table, or Memorial Day when General's surviving brothers Robert and John come. Friends and family range from 90-years-old to a few months young, all shades of face, all textures of hair. The driveway doesn't care.

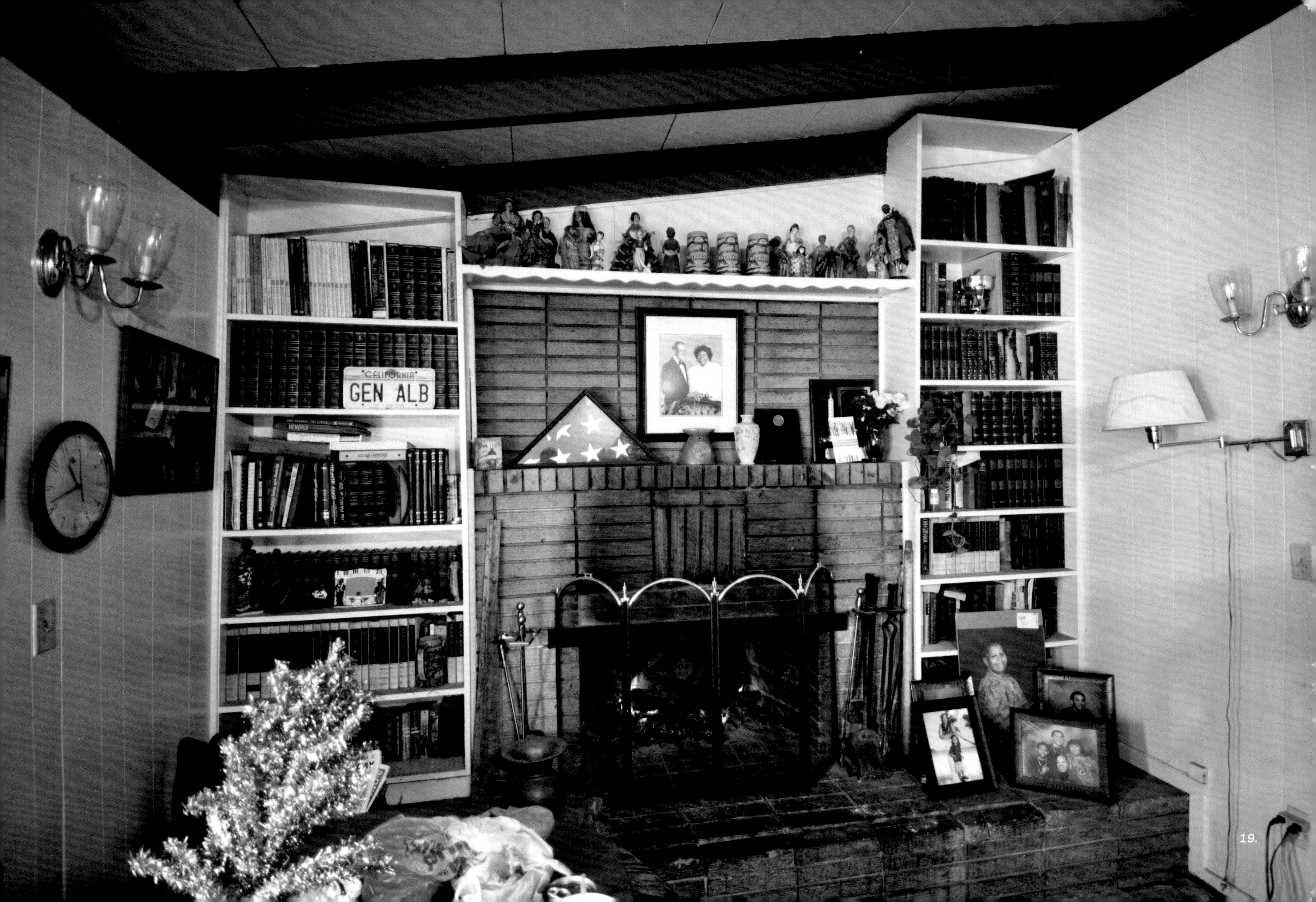
CALIFORNIA
GEN ALB

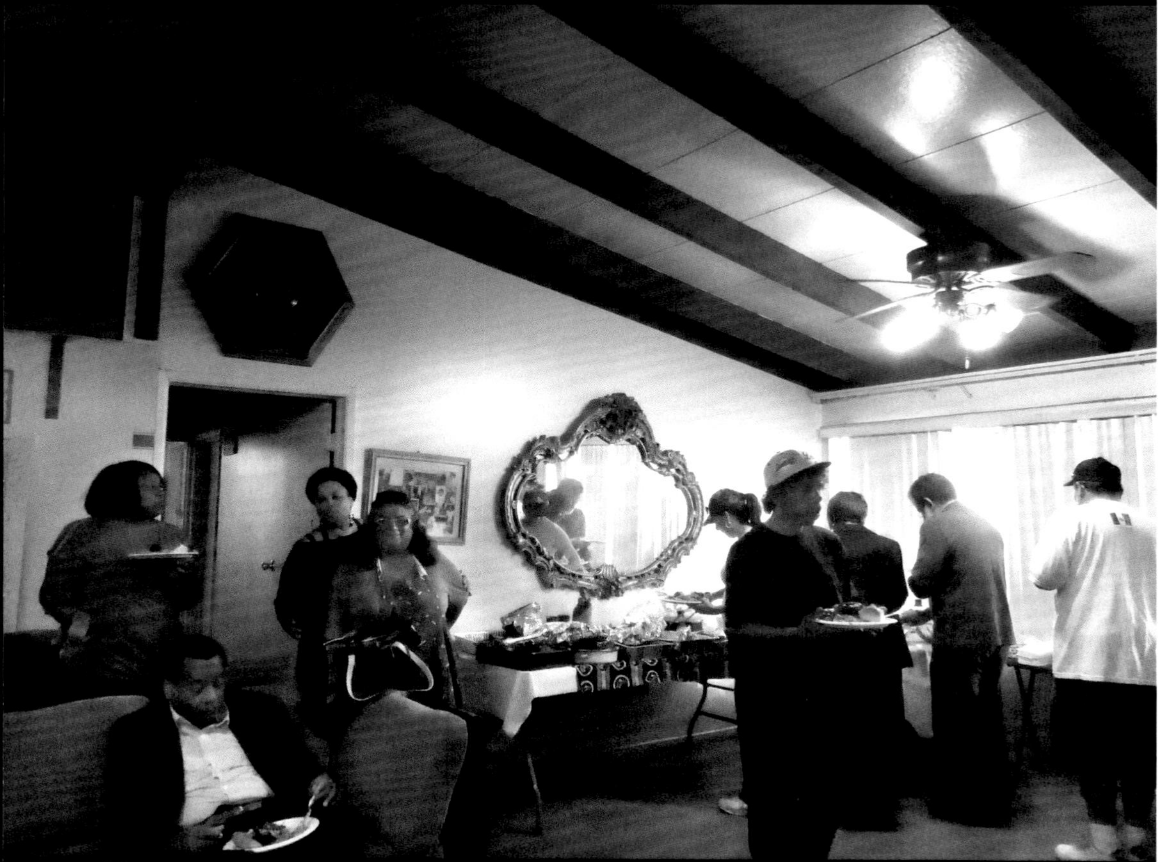

20.

Everything I needed to know about life, I learned in this driveway. Don't pretend to be someone you're not. Try to tell good stories – or no one will listen. Recycle the aluminum cans at the side of the house. Bring the dish you are known for (Doris Aubert's green beans, Shirley's macaroni and cheese, Carol Bagley's salsa) and bring enough for at least 50. Contribute to the 100 pounds of ribs and chicken and hotlinks being barbecued for hours by Eddie Chandler II and Carnell Sims near the wall built by Tony Chavarrias. Respect every single person sitting here in a folding chair (when I was 18, I sat in the truckbed, where the young ones sit now; then I became part of the women setting out the food).

Most important: Always be willing to make a plate for a stranger who might be hungry or a new member of the family who needs to talk. Watch the newest child learn to walk – last week, Dustin Ozzy Sims took his first steps across that cement, near the bonsai-sculpted olive tree planted by his great-grandfather General. Then listen to every story. Every word. ■

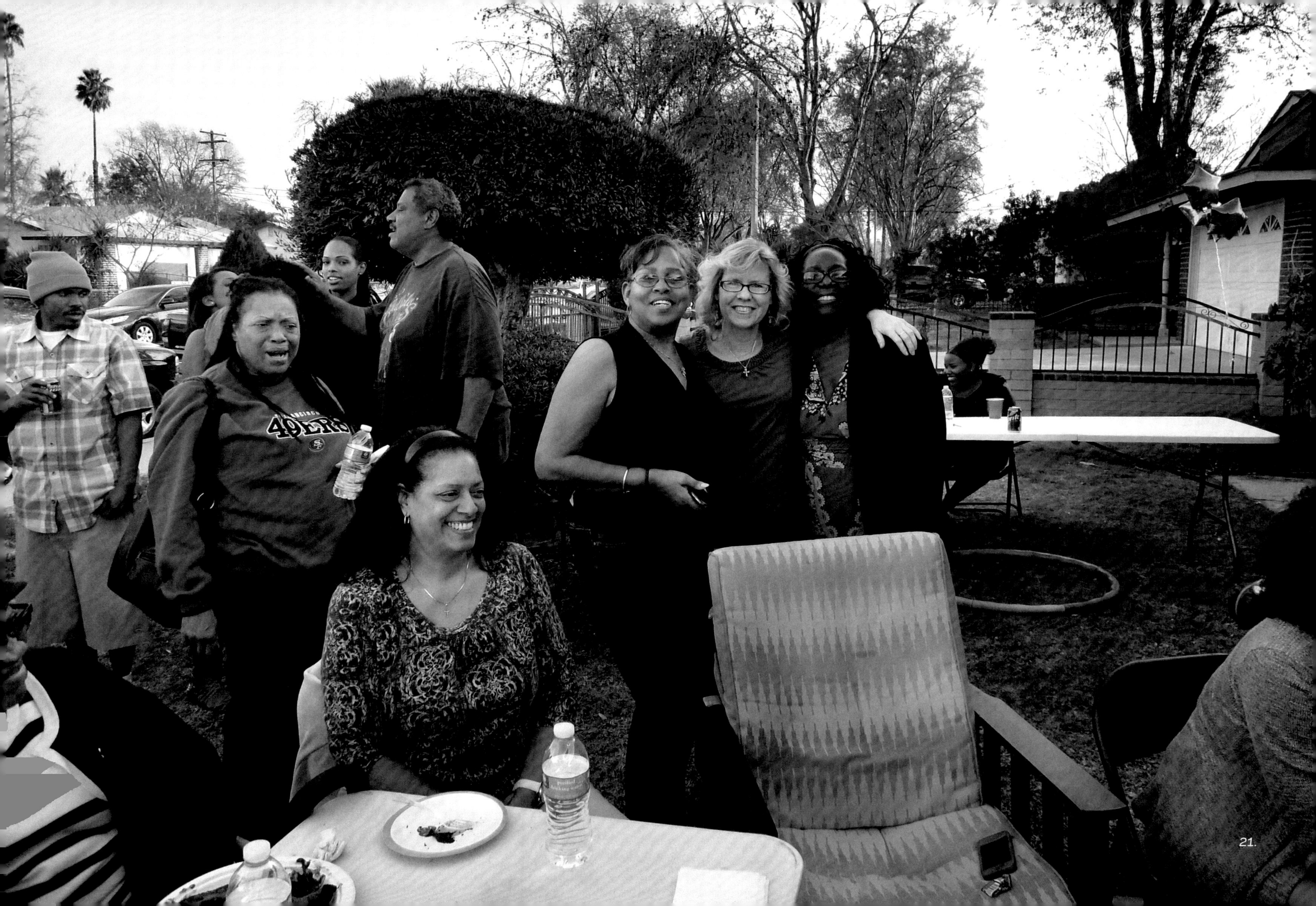
49ERS

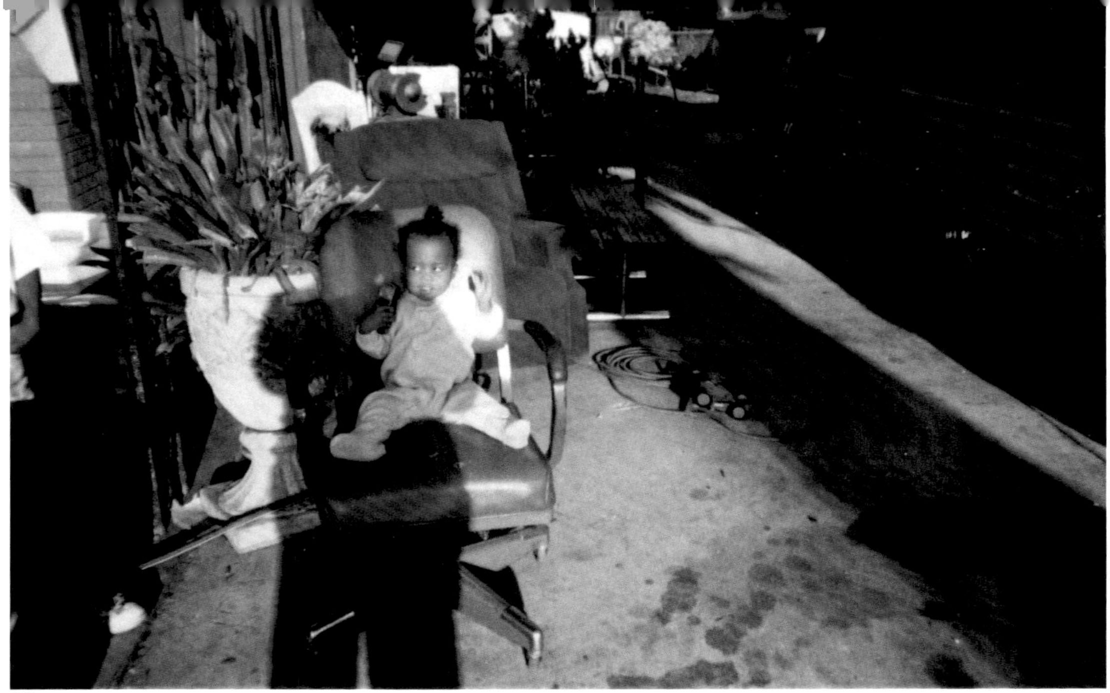

22.

11. *The driveway on Michael Street at night*
12. *General Sims and Jesse Lee Collins after work, 1980s*
13. *Alberta Sims in front of the fireplace built by General Sims and Tony Chavarrias, with her sons, General III, Carnell, Dwayne and Derrick, 1978*
14. *Dwayne Sims at Tony's Market*
15. *Late afternoon laughter in the driveway: Montrell Hamilton, Derrick Sims, Keith Harris, Trent Chatham, General Sims III, Susan Straight, Howard Fields*
16. *Catching up at Michael Street block party, summer 2005*
17. *Dominoes at Michael Street block party: Trent Chatham, Montrell Hamilton and players, summer 2005*
18. *General and Alberta Sims in the living room on Michael Street, date unknown*
19. *Forty years of family at the hearth, December, 2012*
20. *Memorial Day, 2013: Fatimah Sims, Ernest "Butch" Carter, Christine Sims Stuckey, Marcella Vargas, and more family on Michael Street*
21. *Gathering of extended kinship and barbecue in the driveway: Left to right: young man unidentified, Eunice Williamson, Sheryl Masters, Eddie Chandler III, Margaret Chandler Cain, Teri Andrews, Susan Straight, Pamela Larkins*
22. *The next generation, 1980s*
23. *The casket of General Sims borne down the steps of Allen Chapel AME, Riverside's oldest Black church, by his pallbearers: Derrick Sims, General Sims III, Dwayne Sims, Carnell Sims, Angela Sims, and Trent Chatham, 2008*

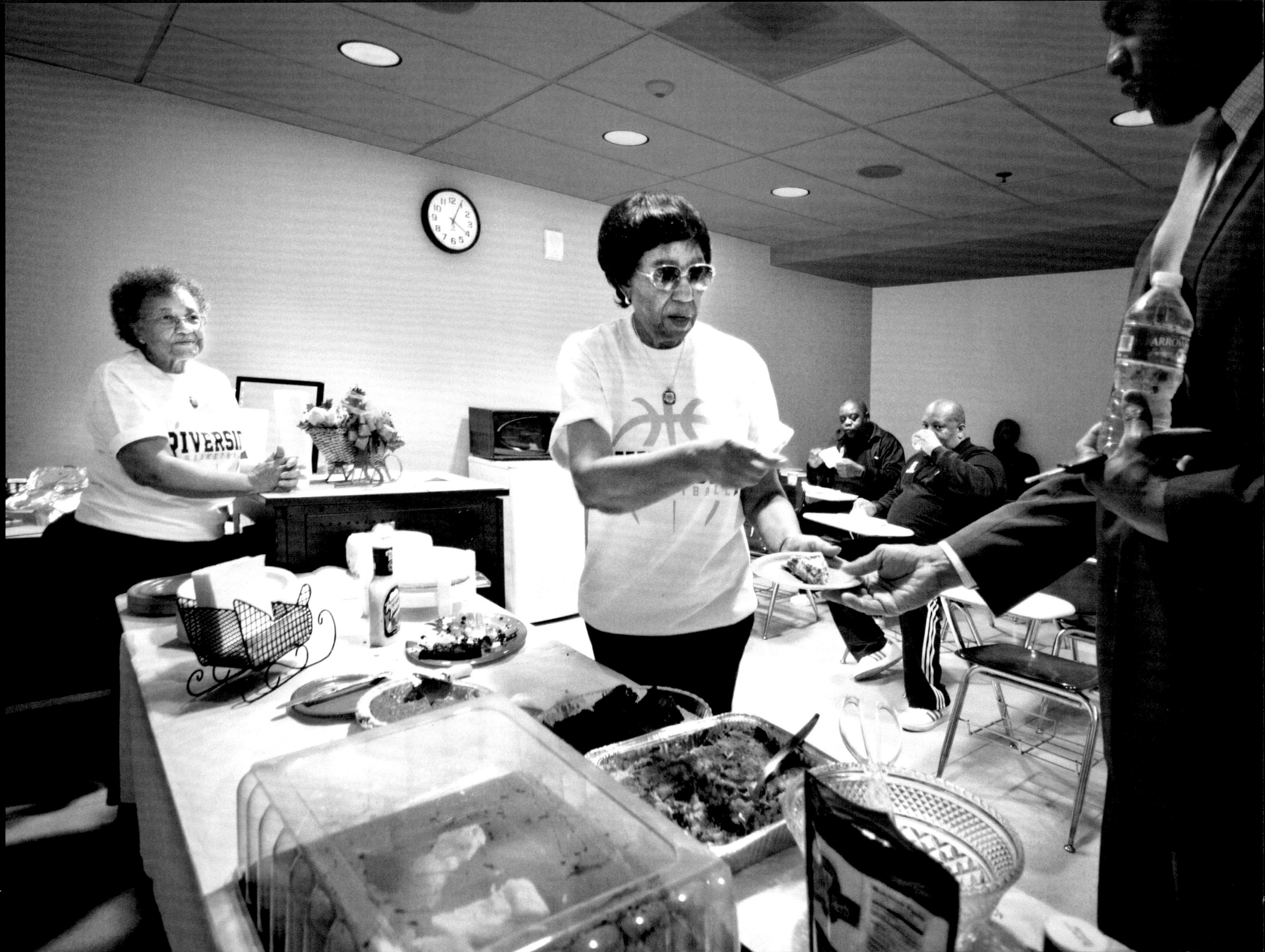

Build Me a School: The Queens of the Holiday Classic

They enter the Hospitality Room at Riverside Community College tentatively, these big men wearing sweats and ballcaps that identify them as coaches and scouts – UCLA, New Orleans Hornets, Antelope Valley College, and more – and say to Alicestyne Tyson Smith and her sister Roberta Tyson McClinton, "Is that sweet potato pie?"

Alicestyne says firmly, "Did you eat your dinner yet? If you haven't eaten your dinner yet, you shouldn't be taking pie."

The UCLA coach takes a piece anyway, and then huddles behind me to finish it quickly – because he can't resist. Alicestyne made it that morning, from a recipe given to her by her sister, who got it from their mother Isabella, who might have gotten it from her own mother, Joicie. And there is the lineage of these queens of higher education in the hands of two sisters handing out full meals to about sixty coaches and referees and scouts attending the 40th Annual Holiday Classic, where the head coach John Smith is Alicestyne's son.

There are six sisters in this story, and one brother, all educated in a one-room schoolhouse, ninety children and one teacher, and all of them went to college, and their kids went to college. In this family are Roberta's husband Charles, who was a CFO of NASA – yes, space NASA – Alicestyne's nephew Keith Jones, head trainer and operations manager of the Houston Rockets, and her cousin Leadell Lee and his son, both FBI agents.

This story, and the sweet potato pie, come from slavery, which Americans don't like to talk about any more. The Tyson sisters didn't hesitate to tell it. "Our grandmother, our father's mother, was a slave," Alicestyne said, sitting in the bleachers after feeding all those people. "Back in South Carolina. She was five years old when they were freed, and she had to walk to Mississippi. They had nowhere to go, and so they walked."

That woman's son, Ben Aaron, grew up in Mississippi, and went to Arkansas to sharecrop on the Coleman Plantation. Twelve miles down dirt roads from Osceola, Arkansas, about seventy miles from Memphis, Tennessee, the vast plantation grew cotton. There were about 250 sharecroppers living in tiny houses, and one long woodframe building. Ben Aaron met Isabella there. And as her daughters tell me, "They had to build that school for our mother and her brothers and sisters. Her father came up to Arkansas from Sunflower, Mississippi. They wanted him to work at Coleman, and he said his kids had to go to school or he wouldn't work there."

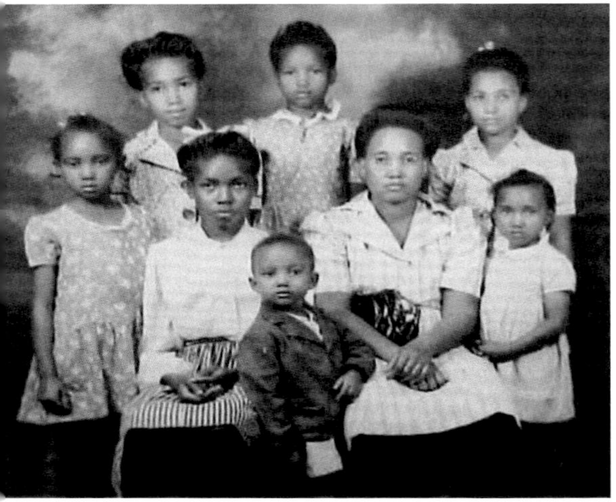

25.

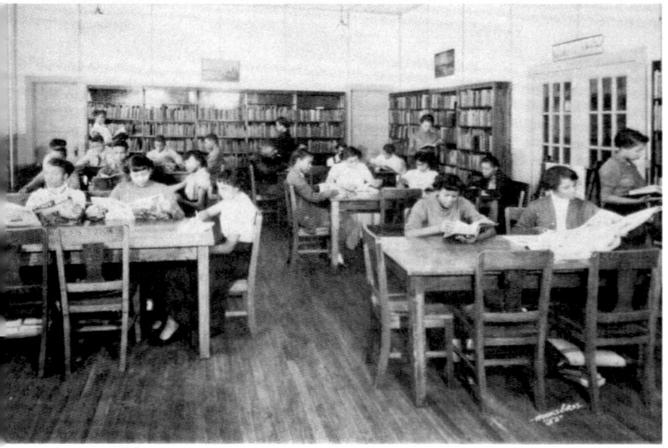

26.

There were 14 children in Isabella's family, and she was in the middle. When her mother died, Isabella was 13, and she carried her 3-year-old brother on her back to the old schoolhouse. Some years later, Isabella married Ben Aaron, and had six girls – Charlene, Rosa Lee, Eddie Mae, Roberta, Alicestyne, and Bennie Mae – and Ben Lewis Tyson. "She was Superwoman and Wonderwoman," Ben told me. "She upholstered furniture. She sewed drapes. She grew all our food and made all our clothes." Roberta added, "You should have seen the zippers and buttonholes on our pants. Our mother did everything."

Isabella ran the wood-frame bungalow for the entire plantation community. "That building was full to capacity every single day," Alicestyne said, while we packed sweet potato pies, cherry dump cake and chocolate cake into her car the next day. "We had church on Sunday, school every weekday, and movie night every Saturday." She imitated the hand-cranked projector. "A man came with the movie, and my mother put up her own white bedsheet on the wall, and everyone came. She sold popcorn for 5 cents a bag."

On weekdays, there were the ninety or so students, and the one teacher. Roberta said, "Our parents set the standard for education where we lived – my father would drive 18 miles to Blytheville to get a teacher when one left. When they couldn't make it back home on the weekend, they'd spend the night at our house." "Then he built an addition onto our house for the teacher to live in all the time," Alicestyne added. The Tyson girls were the first on Coleman to graduate from the 8th grade – but there were no high schools for Black students in the 1950s. "A big yellow school bus would pass right by every day, headed to Osceola."

So Isabella and Ben Aaron had to send their girls away, with the popcorn money and all their savings. "My mother told my older sister she would wear a boot and a shoe so we could go to school," Alicestyne said. Roberta and Eddie Mae went to Holly Springs, Mississippi, to boarding schools, and Alicestyne went to Lucy, Tennessee, outside of Memphis. "My father drove me 70 miles, and I was only 13 years old when he left me there. I cried and cried – I had never spent the night away from my mother and dad."

Her parents paid $16 a month, and she worked in the kitchens and grounds. There were 60 girls in the dorms, and Alicestyne went to summer school, as did most of the kids, because she had to return to Coleman for September and October to pick cotton.

But Ben Aaron died in 1956, when he was only 60. Isabella was 43. She and the girls couldn't survive sharecropping, and her son was still in school at 16. "I said I wasn't farming anymore," Ben Lewis told me. His sister Rosa Lee had joined the Air Force, serving as a WAF at March Air Base in Riverside, California, so Isabella headed out there, and eventually, the rest of the family followed.

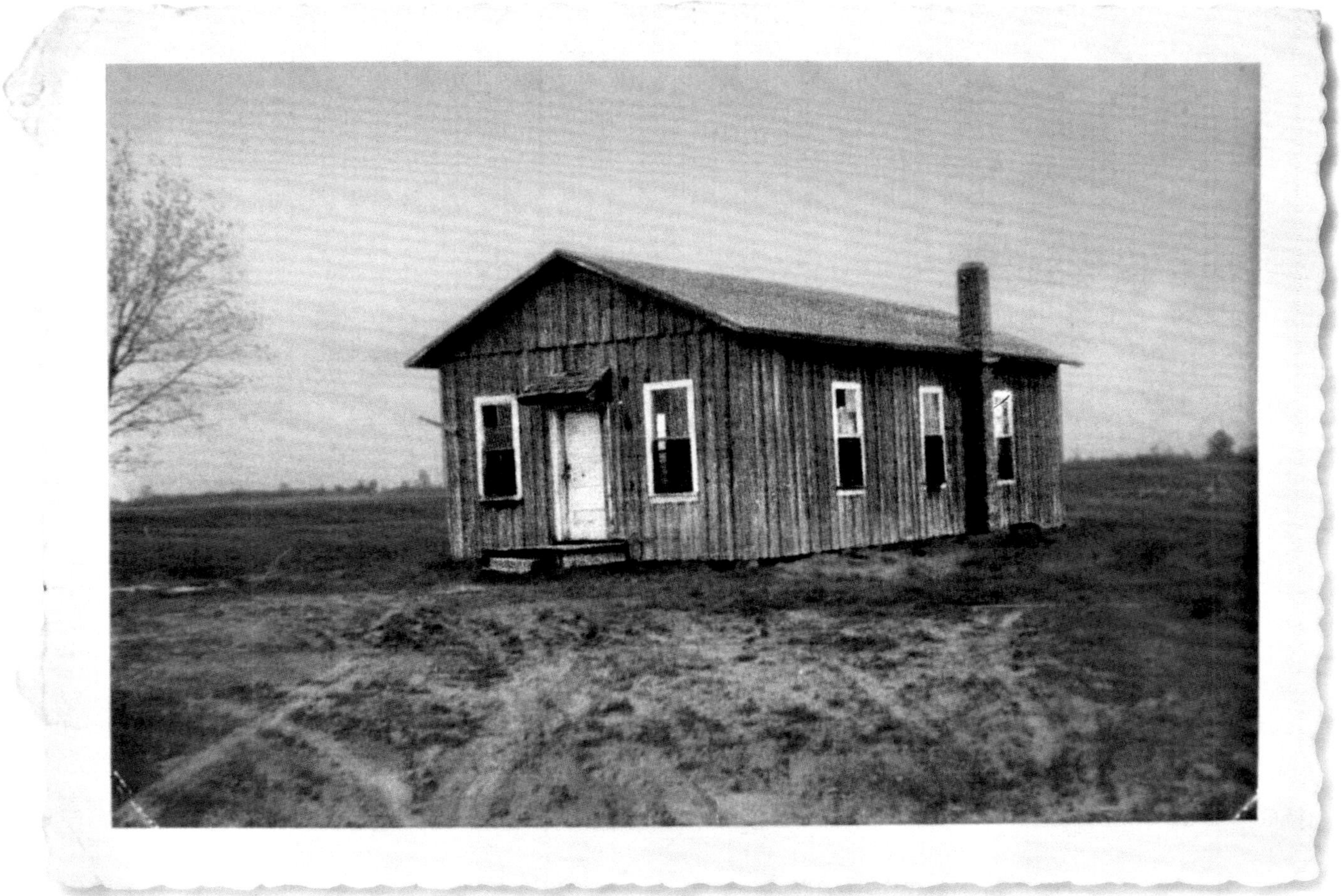

27.

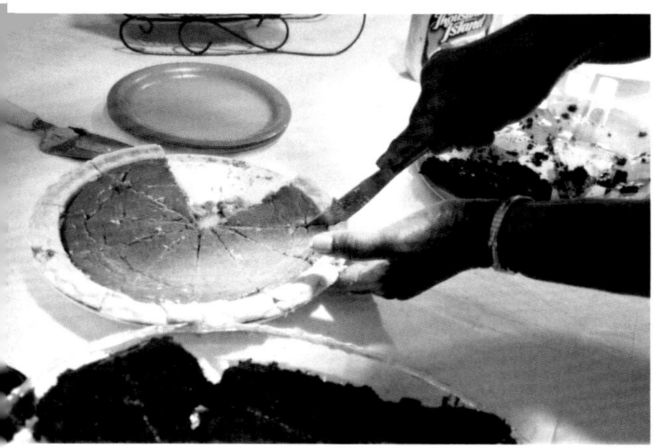

28.

Ben came in May 1957, he remembers. "I was 17, and I just graduated from high school. I was in the back of the bus, you know, because it was Arkansas. When we got to New Mexico, the driver turned around and told us, you can sit wherever you want now." Sitting in the bleachers, Roberta laughed and said, "Oh, we'd already refused to sit in the back of the bus before! You remember, Alicestyne?"

They'd gone from Osceola to Blytheville, after their father died, and they'd sat directly behind the driver. "He turned red, you know, and he said, You need to move back, and we told him, We'll be sitting here until the conclusion of our journey." They laughed again and she said, "He didn't know what to do. That was before Rosa Parks! And then we got to Blytheville, and our aunt who was picking us up saw where we'd been sitting, and she said, "Don't you know you could have been killed?"

Roberta came to Riverside with her husband Charles in 1957 as well. She added reflectively, "When we left Little Rock, we passed the troops on the highway. They were coming in, and we were going away." Those were the Federal troops coming to assist in the integration of Central High School.

Some things were not different in California then. Not yet. Charles had a degree in Business Administration from the University of Arkansas, but initially was only offered work as a sandblaster. Eventually, he was the first counter employee at the Downtown Riverside post office, where Ben Tyson later worked as well. Now, he is retired from NASA.

In 1957, Alicestyne was the first Black employee in the Circulation Department at The Riverside Press-Enterprise. But not without a pointed and queenlike exchange which her mother would have applauded. Young white applicants passed her by and were immediately hired, but she was told she had to take a spelling test. "A hundred words," she said, smiling. "Perfect. Then the supervisor carried it around the office –" she held her fingers up high, imitating his act – and said, "look at this, where'd you learn to spell like this?'" Her voice turned icy-cool. "In elementary school," I said.

Her demeanor remained royal and professional. "After two weeks, one white man said he'd rather quit than work with a nigger. So the next week, the supervisor called him into the office, and he thought they were going to tell him they were letting me go – they handed him his check."

We watched the game in a moment of quiet after that. Her son, John Smith, was born in Riverside in 1969. He played for North High in 1987, under Coach Mike Bartee, and then went to the University of Nevada, Las Vegas, to play for Jerry Tarkanian, who'd become famous for coaching in this very place, the historic Wheelock Gym built in 1915. Wheelock re-opened for this tournament after a two-year renovation. In the stands all around us were the loyal fans, like my ex-husband Dwayne, who played with many of these veteran ballers, and Dwight Tyler, who played for RCC, and John Bennett and Eddie Talbert Jr. We see the same faces every year, at the Holiday Classic.

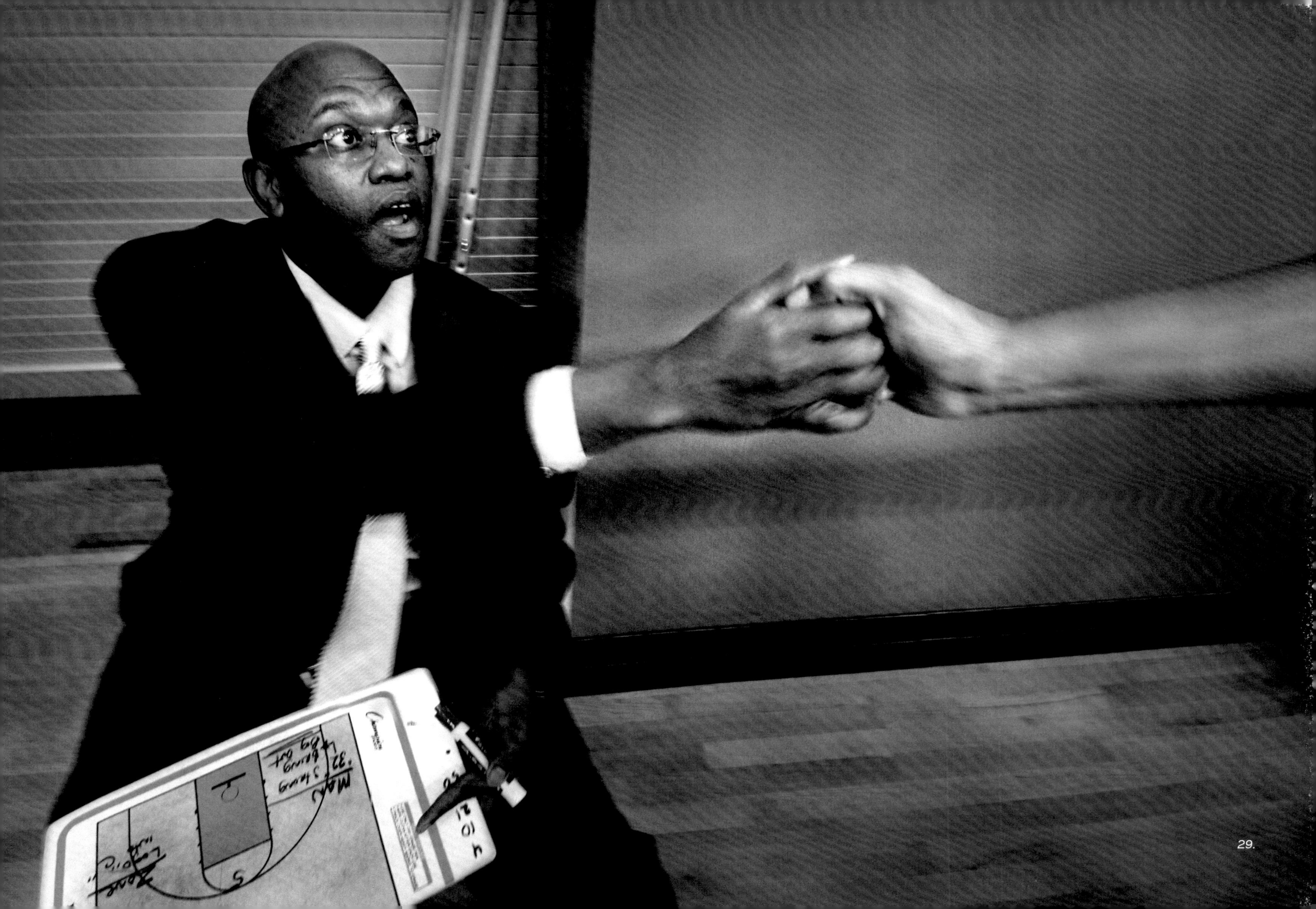

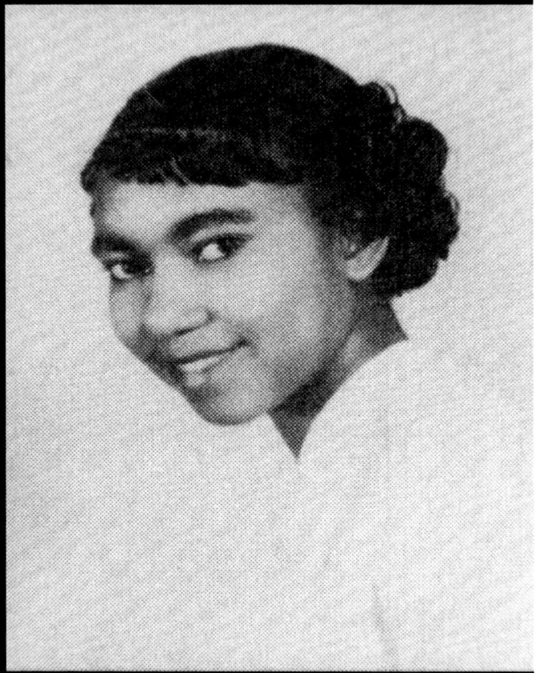

30.

Ben Tyson's son Anthony, known as Red, is one of John Smith's assistant coaches. During the second day of the tournament, he was in the Hospitality Room, where the feature was spaghetti and meatballs, salad and garlic bread, and more pie, along with Roberta's peach cobbler. Roberta lives in San Jose, where she works for a hunger project which fed 15,000 people last year, she told me. And for vacation, she comes to Riverside to feed hundreds of huge coaches and scouts.

"My aunts," Anthony Tyson said, holding his plate of food, getting ready for the game. "They told you some stories, right? About education and this family?" His aunts were wearing necklaces paved with diamonds, in honor of Coach John Smith's 2009 State Championship team. He bought them for the "Team Cooks," but really they are like crown jewels. Watching the college players hustle down the court an hour later, Roberta and Alicestyne and Ben looking at both coaches standing poised, waiting for the ball to float through the basket, it's easy to think of Isabella and Ben Aaron Tyson, and their own parents, walking and surviving, carrying each other on their backs, driving a teacher, or a daughter, miles down a dirt road toward a desk. ■

24. *Sisters Roberta Tyson McClinton and Alicestyne Tyson Smith wearing team T-shirts and championship necklaces, dispensing pie to coaches and scouts, RCC Holiday Classic*

25. *Isabella Tyson, born in 1914 in Swan Lake, Mississippi, surrounded by her children on Coleman Plantation, Arkansas: Charlene, Rosa Lee, Eddie Mae, Roberta, Alicestyne, Bennie Mae, and Ben – "We always got in this same order for our family pictures." 1940s*

26. *The library at the boarding school in Lucy, Tennessee, where Alicestyne Tyson was sent to high school, 1952*

27. *The one-room schoolhouse, movie theater, church at Coleman Plantation, Arkansas, 1940s*

28. *Sweet potato pie from Tyson grandmother Joicie's recipe, handed down from pre-Civil War South Carolina to Mississippi to Arkansas to Riverside, California*

29. *Coach John Smith before a game in historic Wheelock Gym*

30. *Alicestyne Tyson Smith, class picture, Lucy, Tennessee, 1953*

31. *Assistant Coach Joshua Thomas, Assistant Coach Anthony "Red" Tyson, Alicestyne Tyson Smith, Head Coach John Smith, Assistant Coach Joseph Huff, at center court, Wheelock Gym*

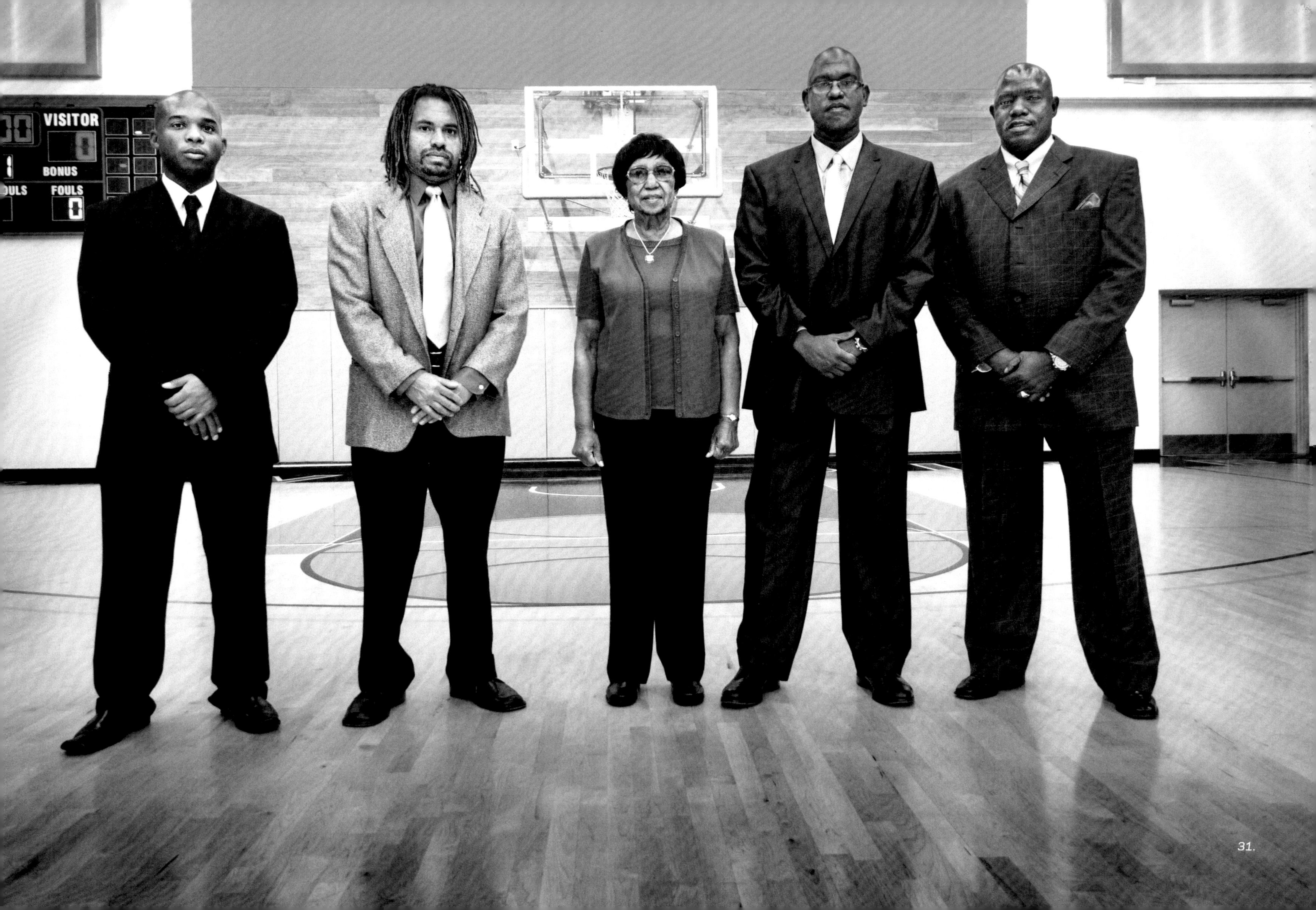
VISITOR
BONUS
FOULS

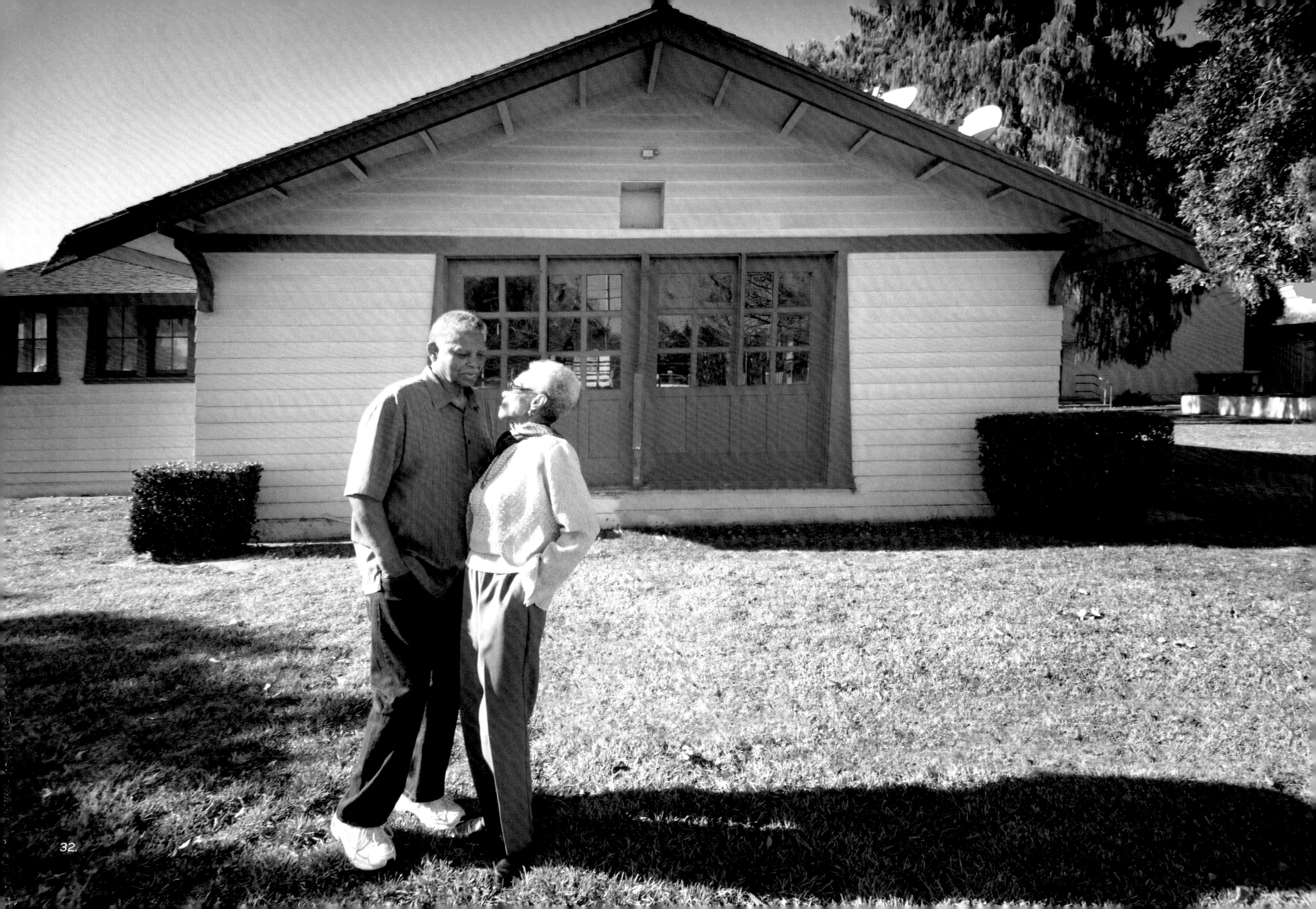

The Heroic Hours Are Not Always Measured by Drum or Trumpet

They are so young – Susan McCoy with her head tilted to the side and smile bright with confidence, Alberta Morris with braids and a shy grin. They are in first grade, in 1940. Oscar Medina at six years old, scowling as if he doesn't want to stand on the steps of Irving School with the other children. Tyree Ellison, Tony and Sarah Lopez. Generation after generation of people I knew as monumental – my mother-in-law Alberta working for the Heart Association, Susan Strickland teaching for 32 years, Dorella Anderson leading countless classes at the Community Settlement Association; Tyree Ellison a supervisor at Riverside's Juvenile Hall; Oscar Medina in charge of a bustling restaurant. They changed the city, but to see their faces here, row after row of children on the steps, makes me think of the valiant in everyday life.

The school is listed on the National Historic Register, and Susan Strickland, Dorella and Marshall Anderson, Tyree Ellison stand near the plaque they helped secure. Dorella and Marshall met here – "Well, he didn't come here until fifth grade," Dorella said, a little dismissive. Marshall grinned. "I started out at Longfellow," he said. "Then they told me I had to go to Irving – and look what I got!" He glanced at the woman he married in 1954 in her mother's house, only a few blocks away.

"Well, I wasn't gonna marry somebody I couldn't whup," Dorella said, cutting him a look. Then she grinned, too. "I lived across the street on Victoria. You know, I had perfect attendance one year but I'm not even in the school picture. Someone told me, Dorella, you know you were bad a lot – you were probably in the principal's office right then."

Linda Salinas arrived at Irving School as a nine-year-old in 1952, having been raised until then in Colton. On her first day of school, "My mother dropped me off and left. I had never seen Black people before – I'd lived in Colton in an all Hispanic neighborhood. And Jeri Lisby came up to me and we became best friends. She lived on 11th Street, and I lived on 10th Street. Every day we went to Tony's Market for our mothers."

Jeri Lisby's mother was born in a small village in the Philippines, where she met Alexander Lisby, a charismatic Black soldier originally born in Tallulah, Louisiana. Jeri has old photos of Linda Salinas and her brother Sammy, as well as Jeri's own husband, U.S. Ball. "Mary and her husband Tony Chavarrias were wonderful – after a swim at Lincoln Park pool, all the kids would go get a cool pop at their store."

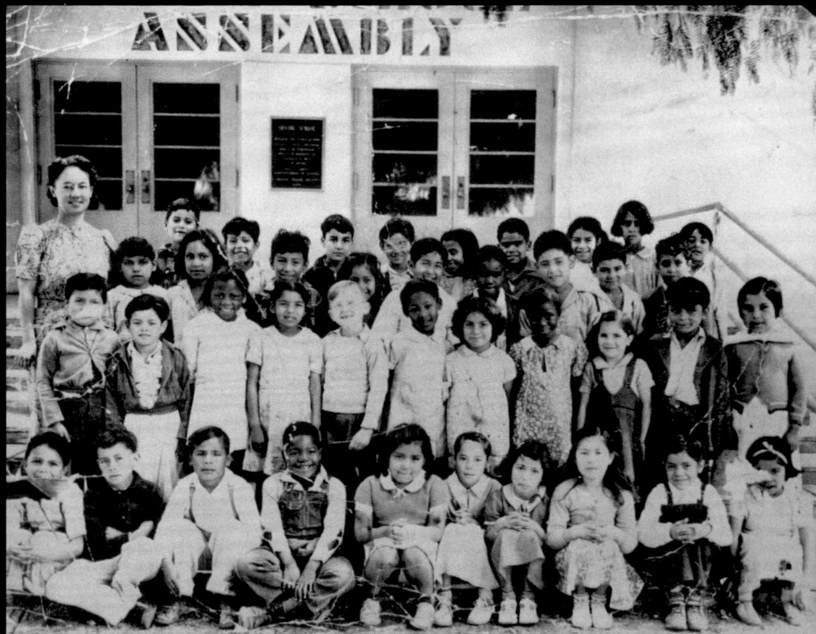

33.

34.

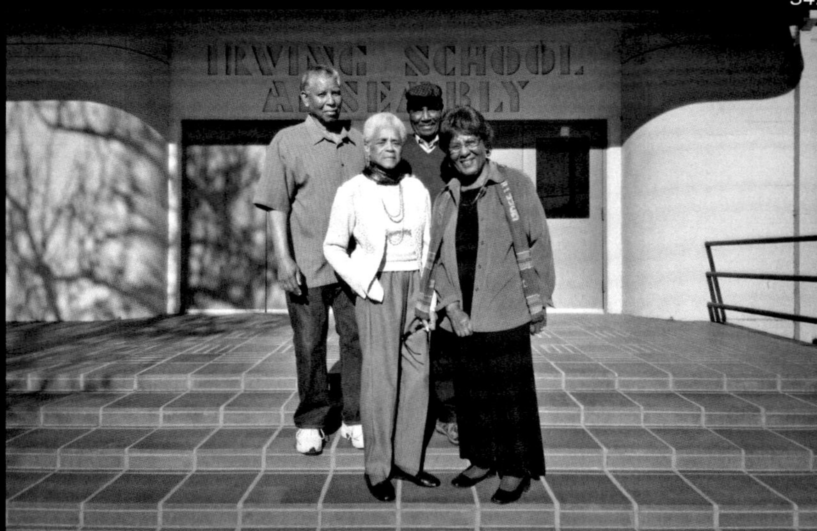

Linda Salinas remembers mornings before school, when Tony Hernandez, who lived on 11th Street, started the engine on his truck. "I was little, and I wondered why his truck was so big. Then I saw him picking up the people. Back then, Victoria Avenue and Highgrove were all orange groves. He drove up and down the streets all over the Eastside, picking up the people in the mornings, and then he came back with them at night."

Salinas' mother worked as a cleaning woman, and "most women we knew worked in the orange groves or the packinghouses." When Salinas saw Linda Viveros, the school secretary at Irving, she was changed. "I'd never seen a Hispanic woman in a position like that – and it inspired me to want to be someone." Now, Linda Salinas-Thompson is president of the Riverside County Mexican-American Historical Society.

Linda Martinez, who is a campus supervisor at Poly, laughed when she told me she went to Irving in the 1960s. "We called it Irving College. Our book company was Discard – that's what it said inside every one."

Within blocks of Irving School were Lincoln Park and the pool, the markets and barbershops and restaurants along Park Avenue. Dell Roberts was a lifeguard at Lincoln Park, and then decades later worked there for Parks & Recreation. But on some long nights in 1965, when he had just begun as football coach for Poly High, Roberts spent long nights inside the Irving School auditorium while school desegregation was argued.

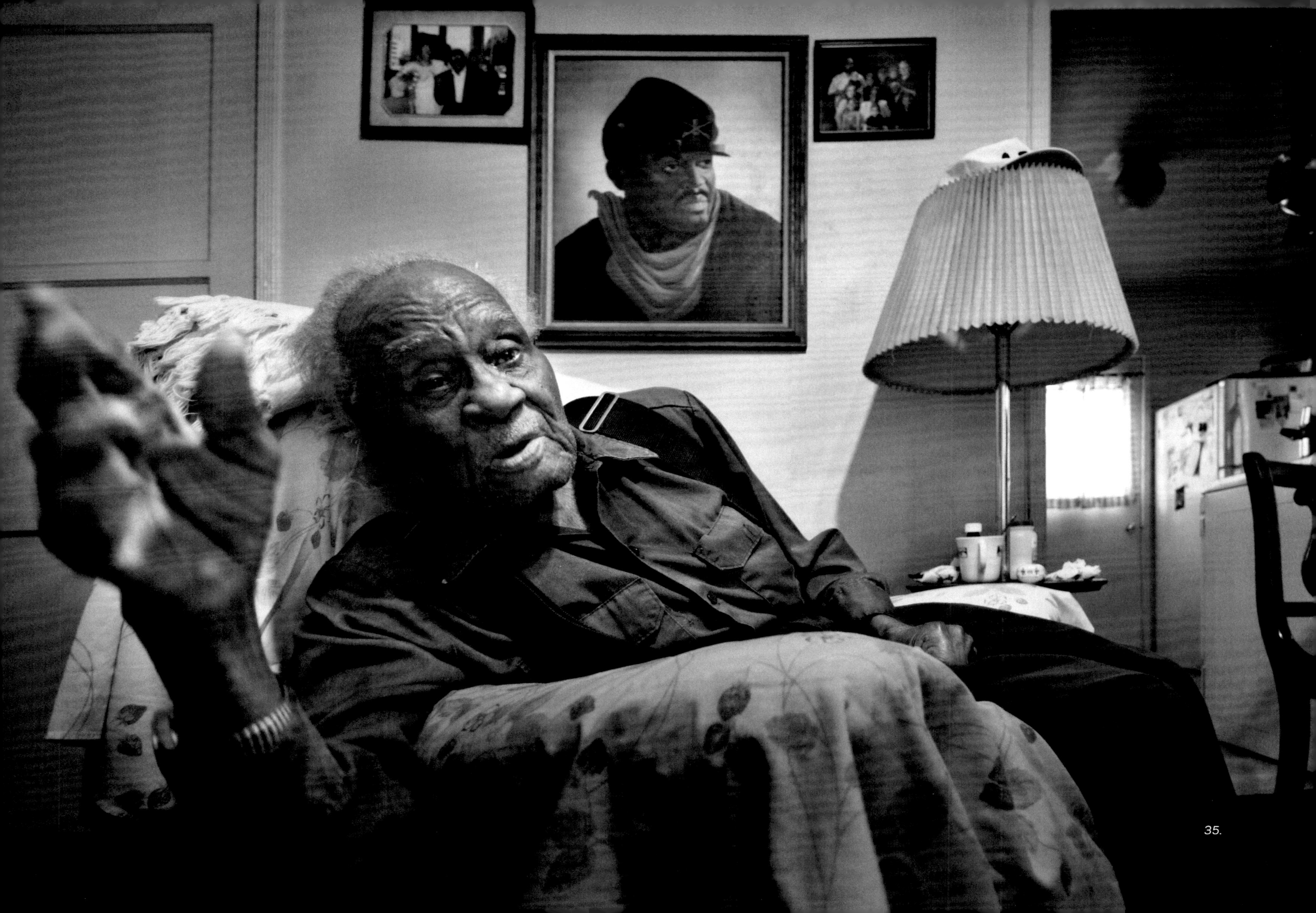

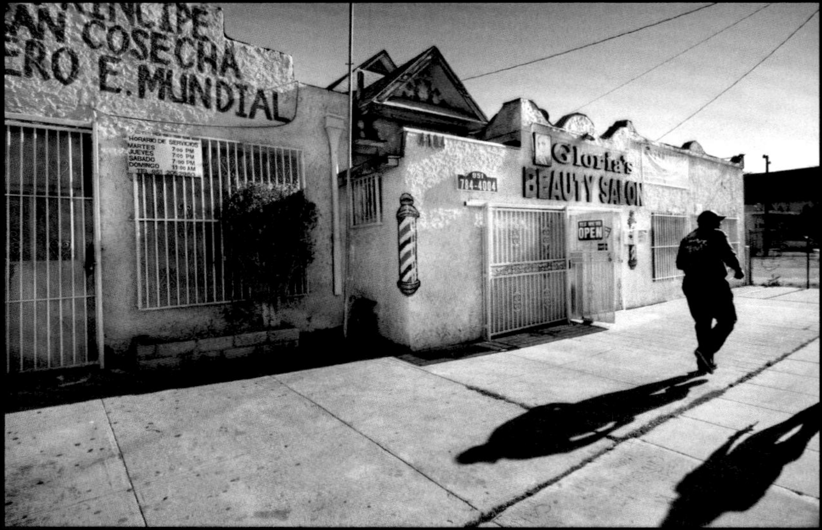

36.

37.

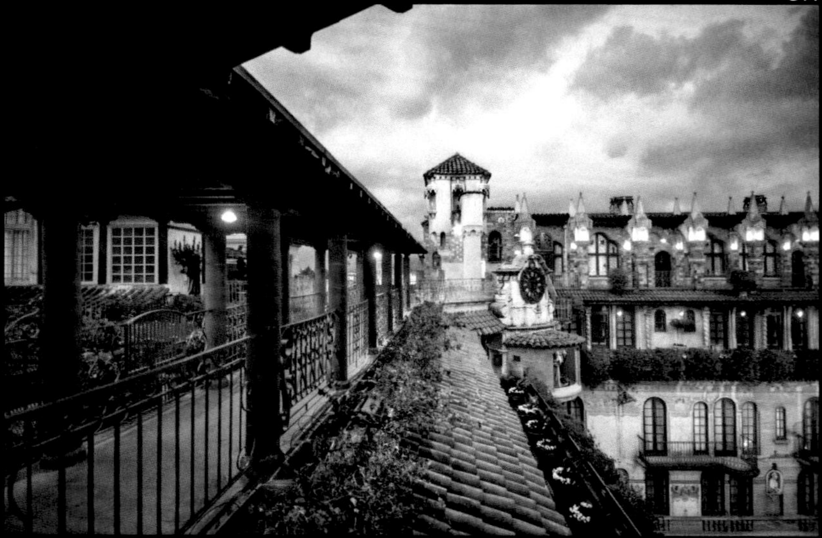

Roberts began working at Butcher Boy, not far from Lincoln Park, when he was in elementary school at Longfellow. "I was strong enough to work, so they hired me. I started doing clean-up, and then unloading the trucks that use to bring the meat three nights a week from LA. Harry Roberts had me hire crews to unload – I got all the guys from the football teams. Robert Bonds, Art Gilmore – they all worked with me. Eventually, I was in charge of operations for the trucks." Butcher Boy was supplying meat for the nation's first ever McDonald's, in San Bernardino. Dell Roberts was still in high school.

Susan Strickland remembered, "Mr. Harry Roberts at Butcher Boy – he was crazy about Dell, treated him like a son." She paused. "We all had swimming at Poly, and we swam at the YWCA pool downtown. Dell and Coy Williams, my cousin, they were on the Poly swim team, though. They had to dive, so they went to the Mission Inn pool. But they wouldn't let them swim there."

By 1965, Dell Roberts slept only a few hours a night. He worked at Butcher Boy from 4 am until noon, worked as a campus supervisor at Poly 12-3, then coached the football team, and then worked for Parks & Recreation until about 10. When Lowell School burned, Art Littleworth was taking heat for attempting voluntary desegregation. "I sat with Art many a night up there at Irving on the stage," Roberts said. "He was a brave man – people were really angry."

Now Roberts is on the board of the Mission Inn Foundation. (The hotel is now owned by Harry Robert's son Duane, who was on that swim team.) The heroic hours are often those spent awake every night in the dark, pulling out another box of beef, bending down to show someone how to tackle, and then facing a crowd of people who don't want their children to go to school with your own.

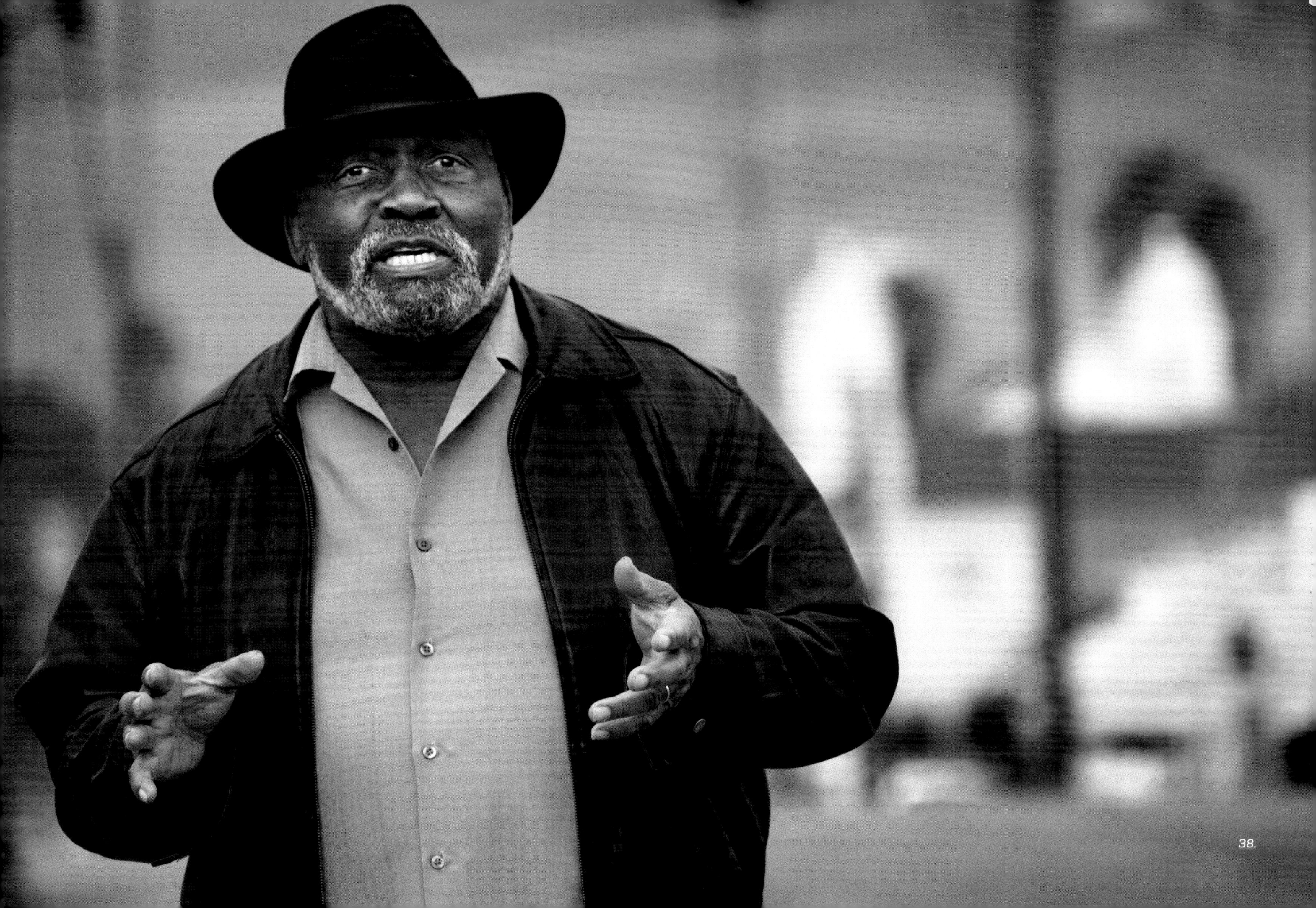

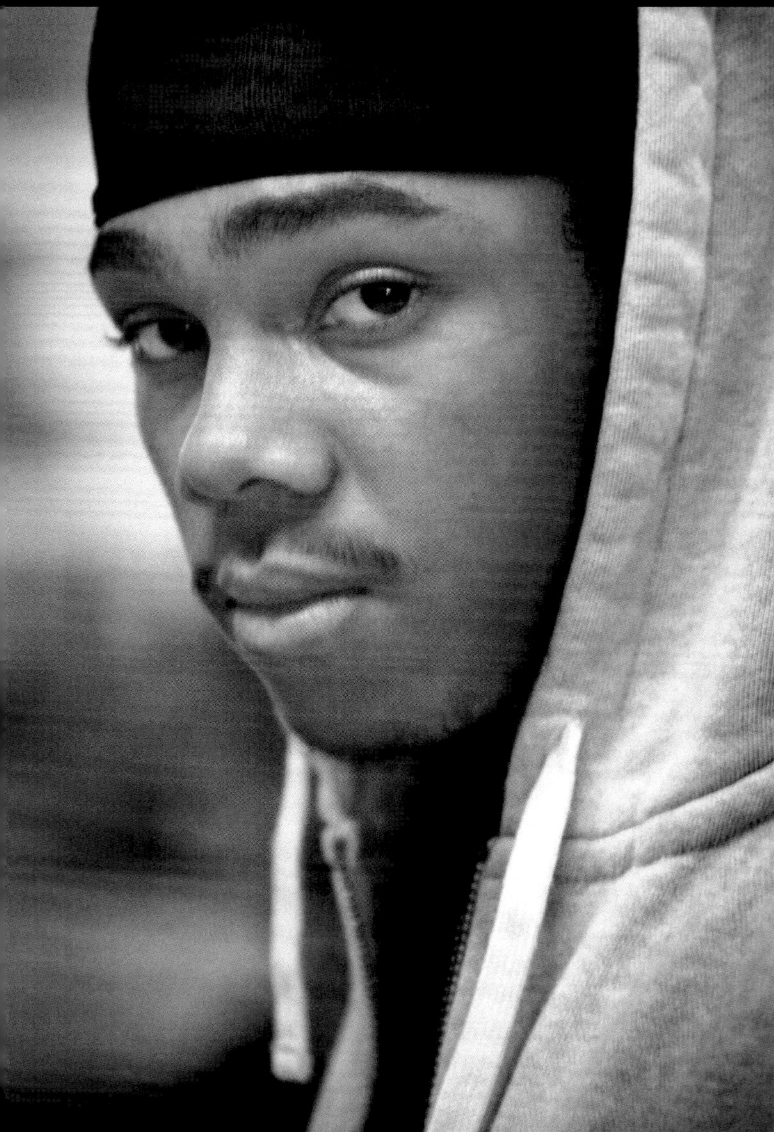

The old preschool is dark during the day. But every weeknight at 5 pm, without fail, for more than forty years, Larry Rios has turned on the lights, gotten ready his tape, and trained young boxers in the ring at the Lincoln Boxing Club. "I'm going for 90 in October," he said the other night. "But I'm not tired."

That evening, he presided over a gym full of faces and shouting and movement. Two girls prepared for a match. Five young men worked punching bags, shadow-boxed at the mirrors, or warmed up. In a strangely hushed island of calm, Rios sat in a tiny wooden chair, and the ritual began. Each boxer must sit across from him, formally shake his hand, and begin unwinding the white tape. Then Coach Rios tenderly wraps the hand and wrist, the webbing pleated delicately between the fingers, while speaking in a low murmur in English, then in Spanish. Soft questions, nods in reply. He worked on the long brown fingers of Fredrick Smith, who came from Jackson, Mississippi to Riverside only three months ago. He is 19. "My Uncle Dennis told me to come to the gym – to train," he whispered. Then Coach Rios instructed him to begin on the speed bag.

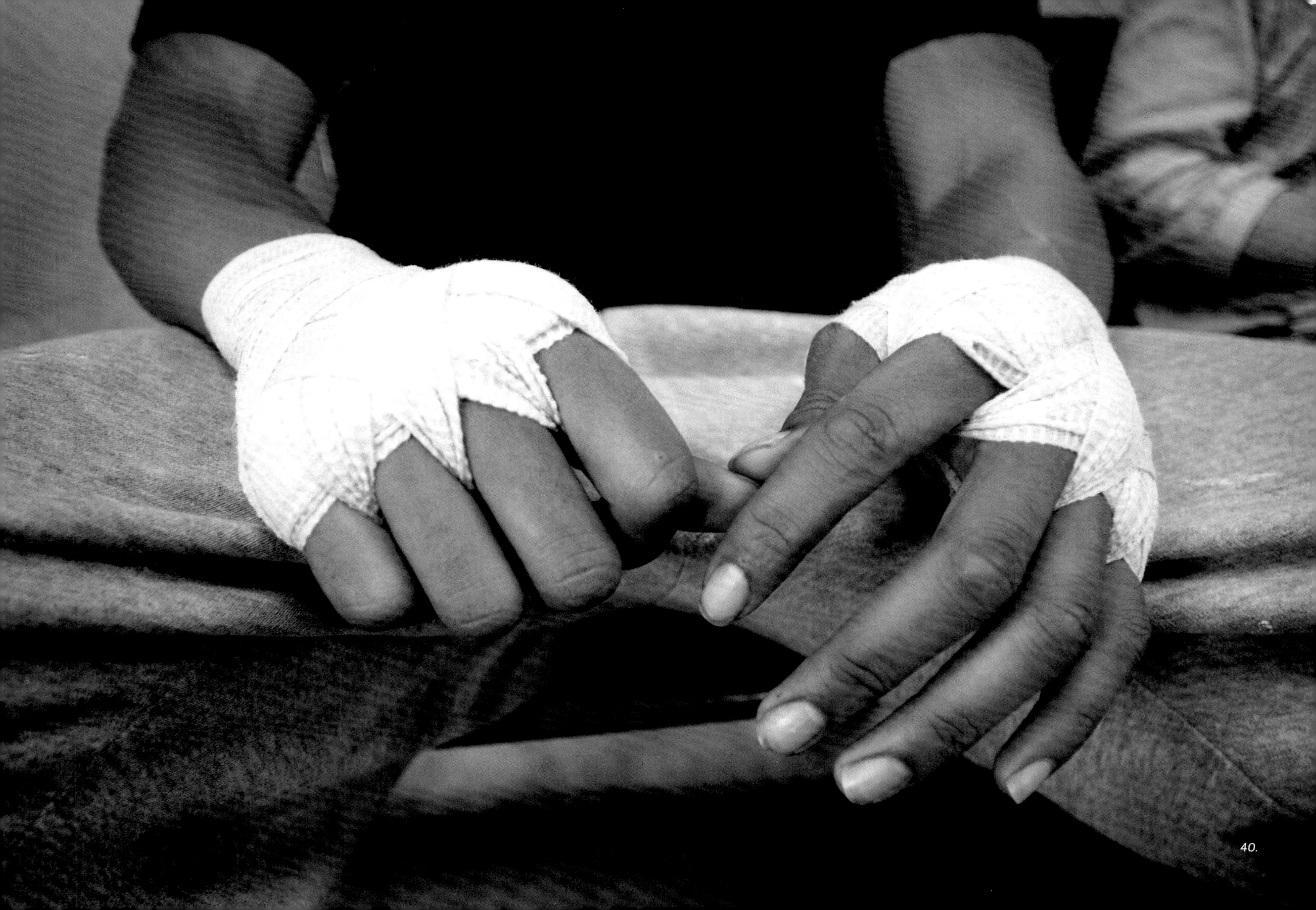

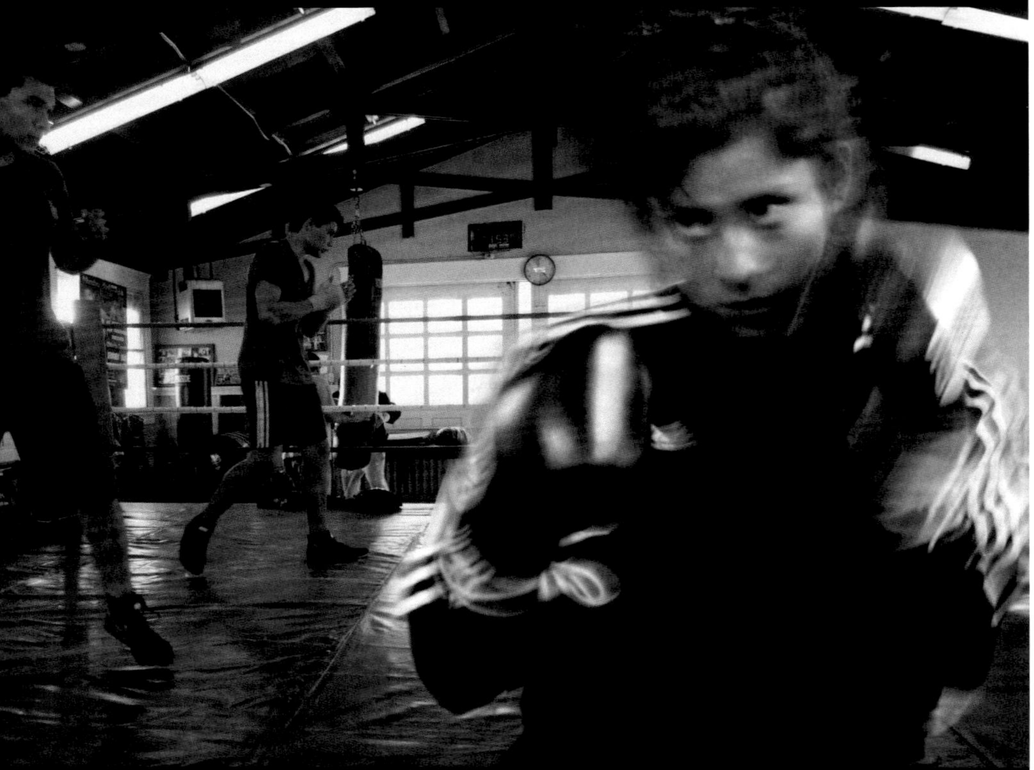

The two girls began sparring – three rounds of three minutes, one minute for water and rest. Nadia Morales is a junior at Norte Vista High, and trains with Henry Castaneda, who trained here himself decades ago. Genesis Flores graduated from Ramona High in 2012, and she's already had 13 fights under her trainer, Joe Escobar. This was Nadia's first match, and Castaneda called out, "Go forward! Go! Go! Don't quit! Now!" Nadia was aggressive in the first two rounds, while Genesis grinned behind her mouthguard, ducking and moving fast, crossing her feet. But in the third round, Genesis' entire face changed, and she landed blows while her feet danced below. Nadia was brave – at the end, taking her helmet off, her chin stayed high. Watching her was Noah Rodriguez, 12, who has been training since he was 5, his father bringing him from Perris. He wants to be a professional boxer like Richard Contreras, who's working out. Contreras went to King High, has a 9-1-1 record as a super bantamweight, and has fought in Las Vegas.

Larry Rios started the Police Boxing Club in the old YMCA building downtown in 1971, then moved it to Casa Blanca in 1972, but came here to Irving in 1972 to form the Lincoln Boxing Club. Now, he put on gloves and held out his hands so that Fredrick Smith could hit them. "Harder. Harder. Again. Again." Smith's gloves thud against Rios' – and Rios doesn't break a sweat as he moves back and forth.

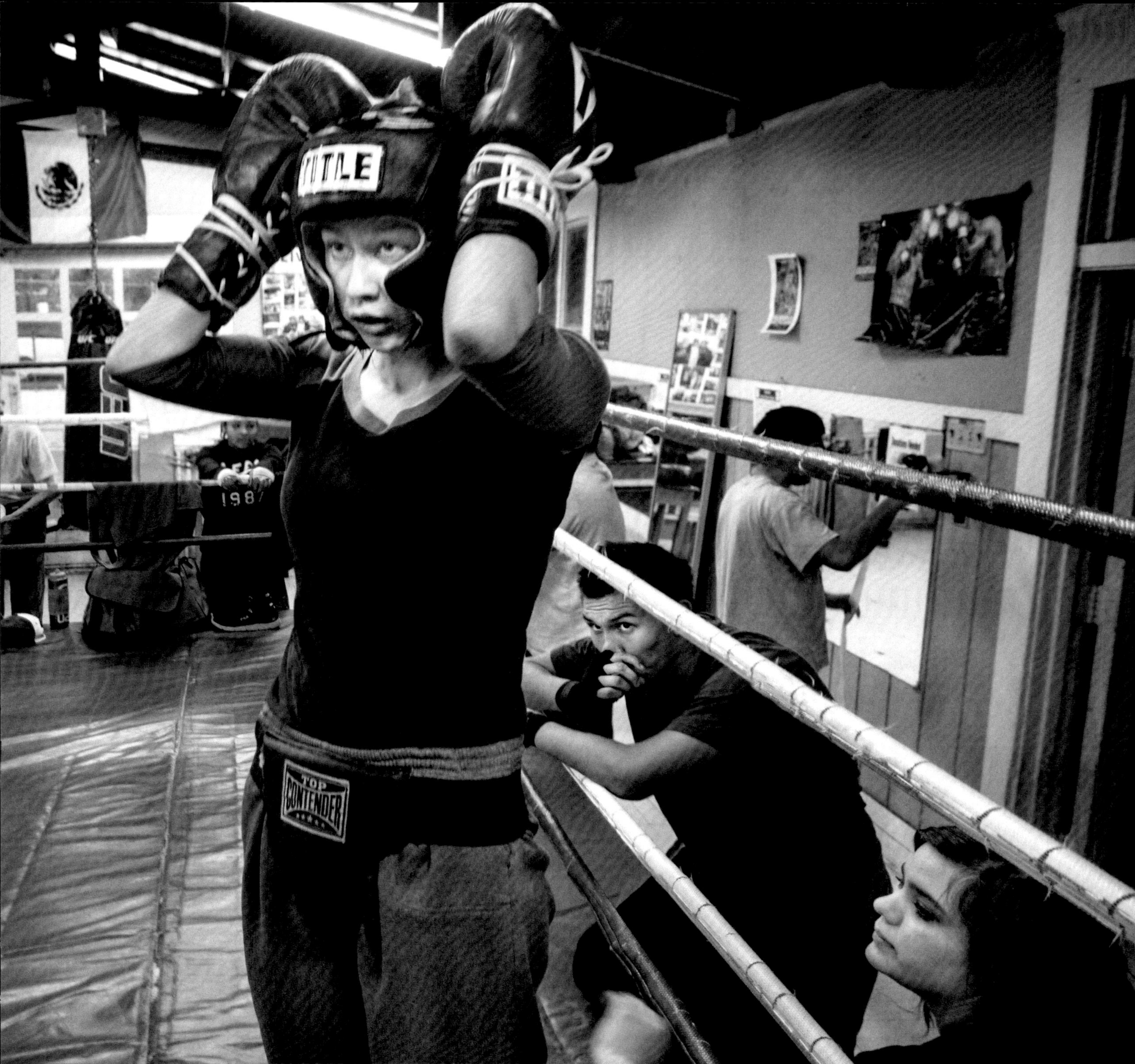
TOP
CONTENDER

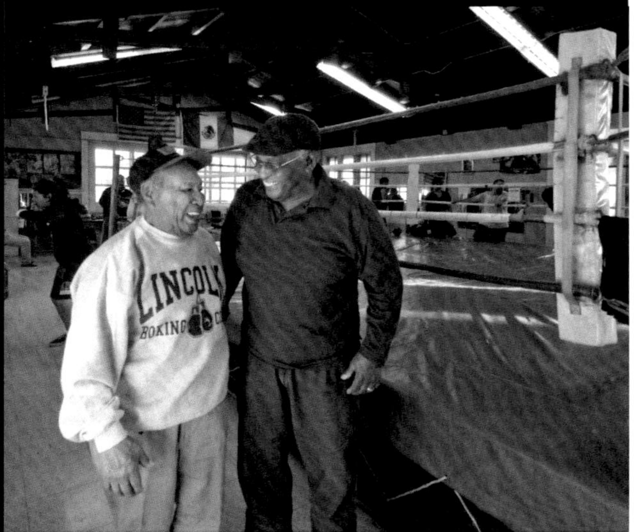

43.

"My parents raised me in Mexico City to respect everybody," he said when he was done. "One of my first coaches here was an African-American man, Floyd Mackie. 1946." Rios was a welterweight Golden Gloves Champion in 1948, and then he came to Riverside with his grandfather, who'd come to work for the Southern Pacific Railroad. Rios and his grandfather worked for Riverside Cement beginning in 1952. In fact, he fought two pro bouts in the old arena on Chicago Avenue, against Robert Anderson, who fought as an amateur. "I figured out by the second round I should just lay down and wait for my money!" Robert said when he came by to visit this night. The two men, their shoulders heavy and powerful even after all these years, hug each other near the ropes, their cheeks soft and brown.

Two years ago, the school board wanted to close the club because of liability issues, but Dell Roberts stepped in, working with Lincoln's principal, Elton Ross, and the school district. "I met Larry Rios at Lincoln Park," Roberts said, "back when I used to open the building for the Sociedad Progresista. I had his sons and daughter at Poly High. I told the school board this place had to stay open."

Those school steps where hundreds of children took their photos, just a few feet away from the door of this gym, propped open with a chair. The ancient timer above the ring, the squeak of shoes, the sound of leather hitting leather. Each young boxer who leaves saluting Coach Rios with respect. I sit across from him finally, in the tiny wooden chair. What does he say to each one who holds out his hands? "I start by teaching them to shadowbox. You have to use the whole body. And in the ring, you have to understand the ropes are for your defense. I show them how to tape the best way. I tell them how they have to train on a schedule every night and not take a shortcut." Then I had to rise from the chair, because Fredrick was done with the speed bag and gave me a look. Larry Rios got up, too, and said, "What's next, mijo? We have to keep to the schedule." ■

32. *Marshall and Dorella Anderson in front of the oldest building at Irving School*

33. *First grade class at Irving School – Alberta Morris, 2nd row, 3rd from left, and Susan McCoy, 6th from left – a lifelong friendship, 1940*

34. *On the Irving School steps, Marshall Anderson and Tyree Ellison, Dorella Anderson and Susan McCoy Strickland. Dorella met Marshall here, in the 5th grade; Susan and her future husband Reggie Strickland "had snack together in the 3rd grade – I remember they gave us cheese and apples, during the war."*

35. *Alexander Lisby, born in Tallulah, Louisiana, at his Riverside home at age 104*

36. *Eastside businesses, Park Avenue and 11th Street, one block north of Lincoln Park, Riverside*

37. *The Mission Inn, Spanish Courtyard and Author's Row*

38. *Dell Roberts, on Park Avenue and 10th Street, near Lincoln Park where he learned to swim, served as lifeguard, and later supervised buildings for Riverside Parks & Recreation while also working as Poly High football coach*

39. *Fredrick Smith, recently arrived to Riverside from Mississippi – "my uncle told me to come down here and work with Larry Rios."*

40. *Taped hands of Fredrick Smith, Lincoln Boxing Club inside the historic Irving School kindergarten building*

41. *Nadia Morales preparing to spar in the ring at Lincoln Boxing Club*

42. *Genesis Flores, veteran of 13 fights under trainer Joe Escobar*

43. *Decades after their professional bout, Larry Rios and Robert Anderson near the ring at Lincoln Boxing Club*

44. *Coach Larry Rios, 89, showing Fredrick Smith, 17, how to hit, after taping his hands – "Harder, mijo, harder."*

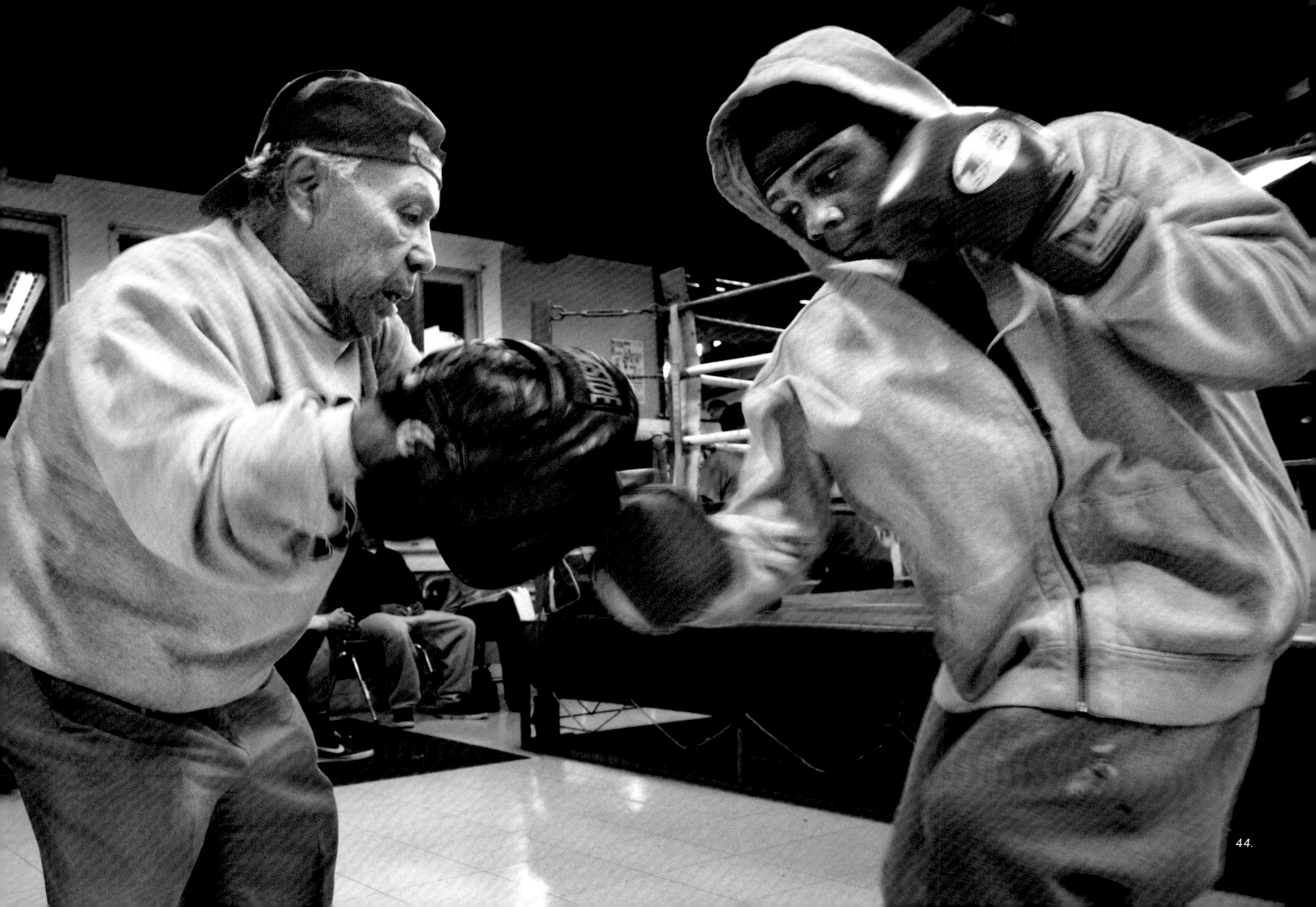

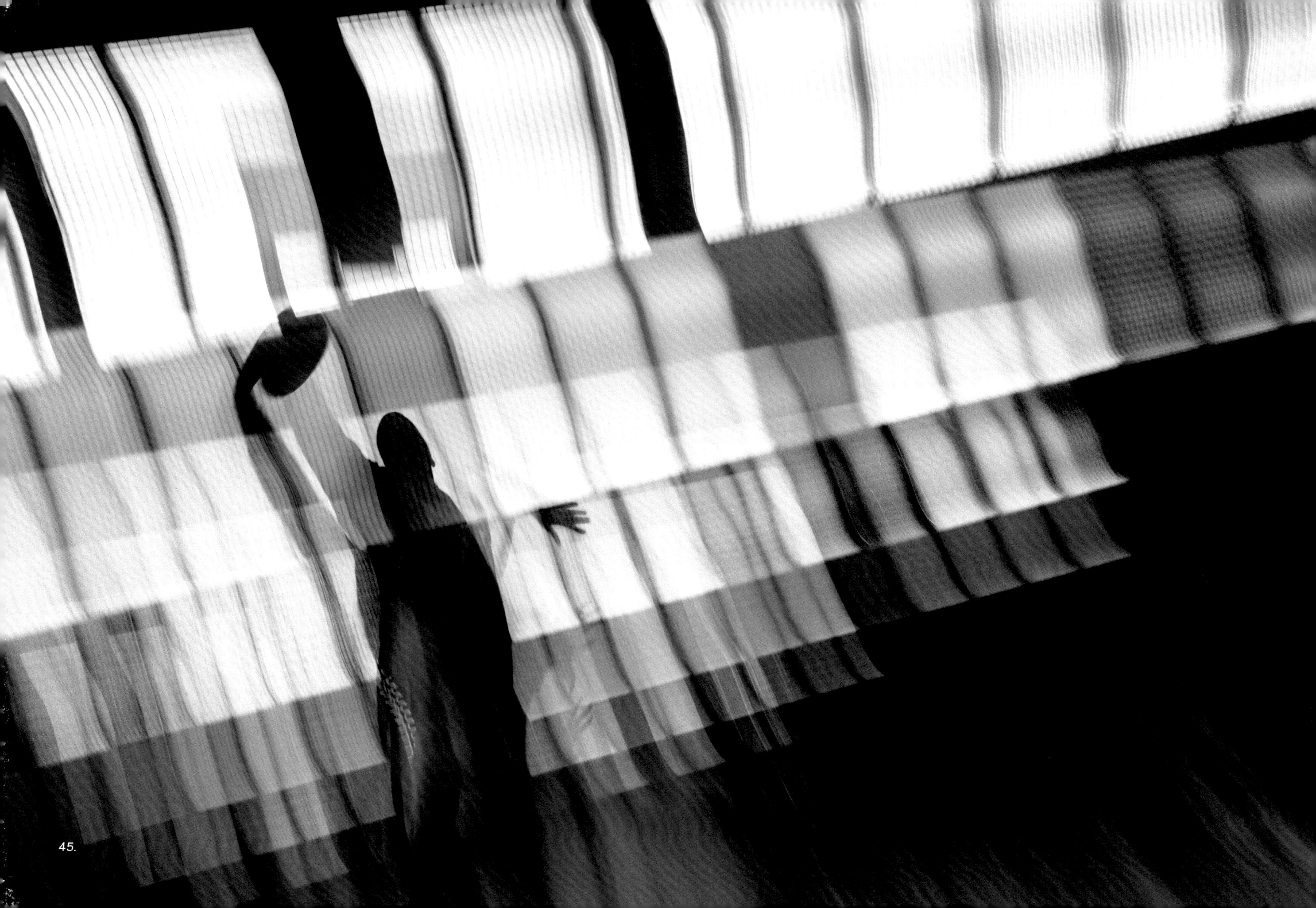

People Who Stay: Friday Night Lights and the Gym of American Dreams

The gym was rocking at J-Dub on a Tuesday night. That's the old-school basketball court at John W. North High School, my alma mater, and as my brother-in-law puts it, "Ain't no shame in our game."

Many Americans believe southern Californians all came from somewhere else. But I know people in Culver City and El Monte, in East LA and Crenshaw, in Pasadena and Anaheim, who live where they were born, and who still love their old high schools with a fierce and undying passion. Every game is like a family reunion – even if we see each other twice a week during basketball season, we wave, hug, and get ready to scream. North High, named for an early founder of Riverside, has that kind of legacy. Think football in small-town Texas, baseball for Boston guys who dream of playing for the Red Sox, and basketball in New York gyms.

That night, the Lady Huskies played Palisades High in the semifinals for the CIF Southern Section Regional title. It's a big deal. In 2010, North girls went 1-13 in league play, and morale was low. Then the school hired Leonard DeCoud, his first high-school head coaching job. His daughter, Simone, has played since she was four – I remember one of her first games, since she was playing against my own two daughters. She was an elf in knee pads, the youngest player in the league, stunning opponents with her fearlessness. Coach Leonard passed on confidence and humor and a work ethic like no other. Simone was now a junior guard, and at 5-5, not an elf unless the elf is Derrick Rose. That Tuesday night, she scored 31 points and got 11 rebounds against two "bigs," as she and her father called them – a Palisades forward and center who went 6-0 and 6-1, respectively.

It's fascinating to listen to visitor reactions to this gym. For thirty years, I've heard people say, "We're way out here in the country," if they were from LA, and others say, "Oh, my God, we're in the ghetto," if they were from more rural or suburban schools. We always thought it was funny – the way Riverside couldn't be categorized. In my yearbook photos of these bleachers, it's clear we have always been everything there is in America. There are Mexican-American families who've been in Riverside since 1900. Armenian families, and Japanese-American parents. Countless men and women who migrated from the South during the 1940s and 50s in that great journey taken by so many African-Americans who left behind segregation and violence and dead-end jobs, who wanted their kids to have a California chance.

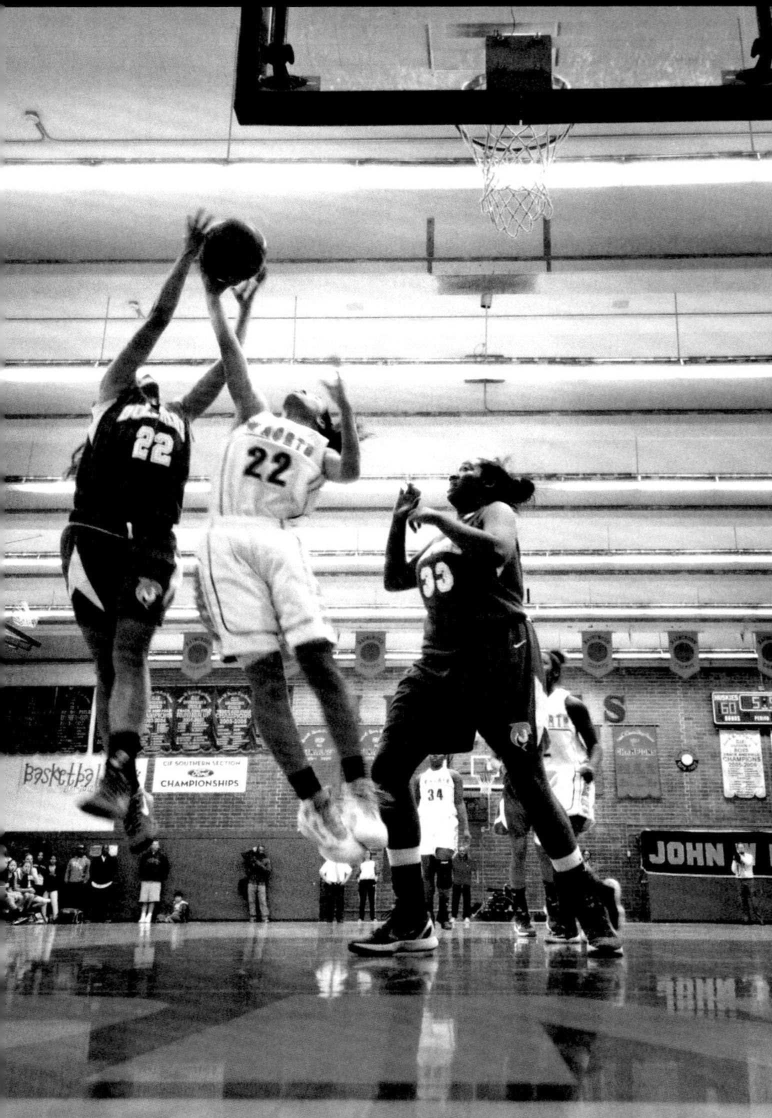

Leon Culpepper introduced senior guard Tatyana Calhoun as "one of the legendary Calhouns." He isn't kidding. There are Calhouns on many of the championship football and basketball banners in the gym. There are so many Calhouns in the bleachers I could never keep count. Rose Calhoun's husband was a legendary high school football player in Montgomery, Alabama before he joined the military, which brought them here – she is often in the bleachers, in her 80s.

There are Chathams, as in Trent, whose name is on the banners, too, along with his brother Brent. The Chathams' mother was born in Columbus, Georgia, their father in Gary, Texas. Also born in Texas was the legendary Mama Bonds, whose son was Bobby, whose grandson is Barry Bonds.

The Jones family came from Louisiana, and sometimes I'm lucky enough to sit with Mr. Jones, who still attends at 84, and his son Darryl. There are Joneses on the banners, too.

George Chiranian graduated in 1975, played on the soccer team, and managed the football team for years. (He has three huge CIF champ rings.) He's at every game, often with his granddaughter. Our community might not always have what is immediately measureable. But that's why we have each other.

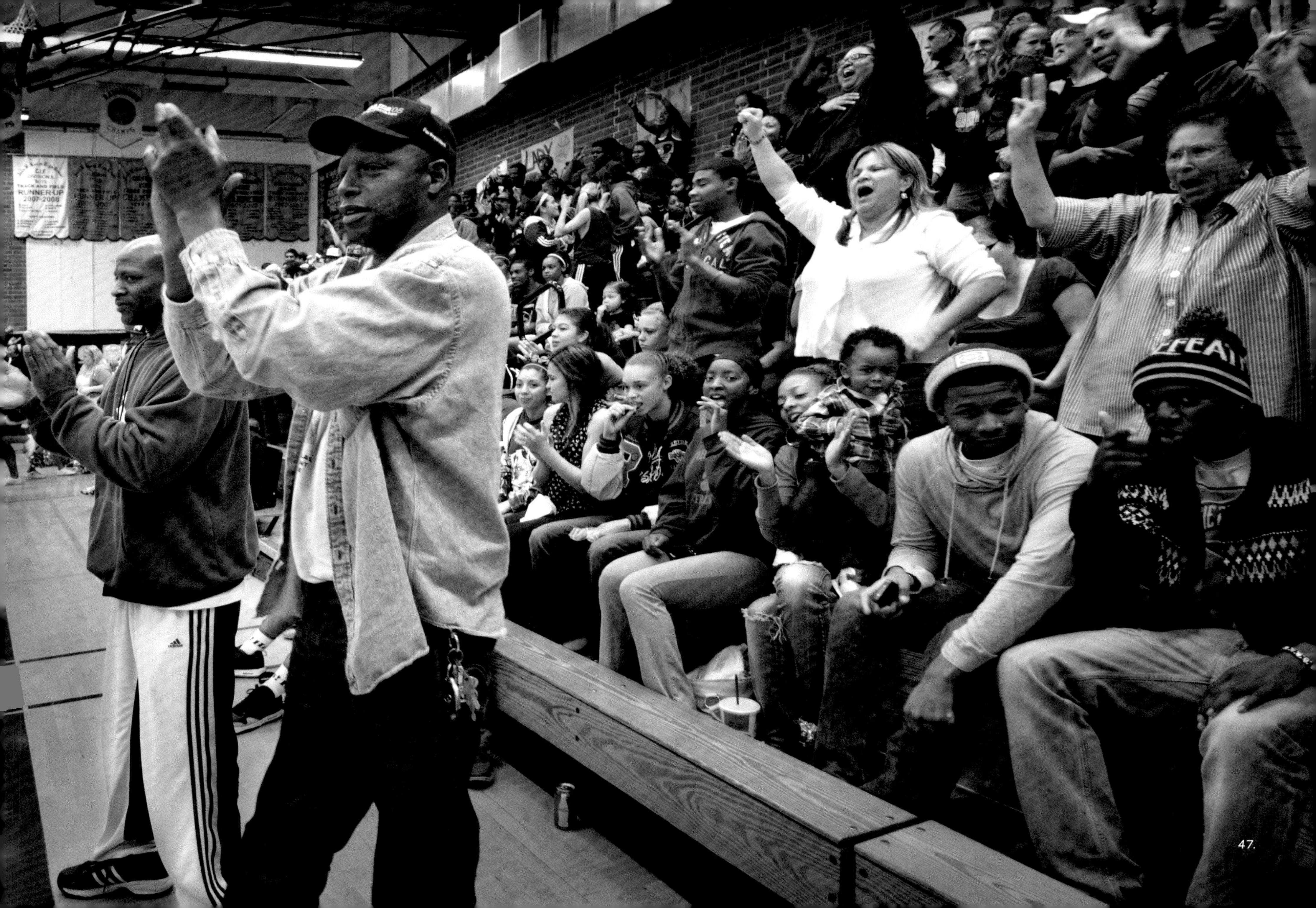
RUNNER-UP
2007-2008
CHAMPS

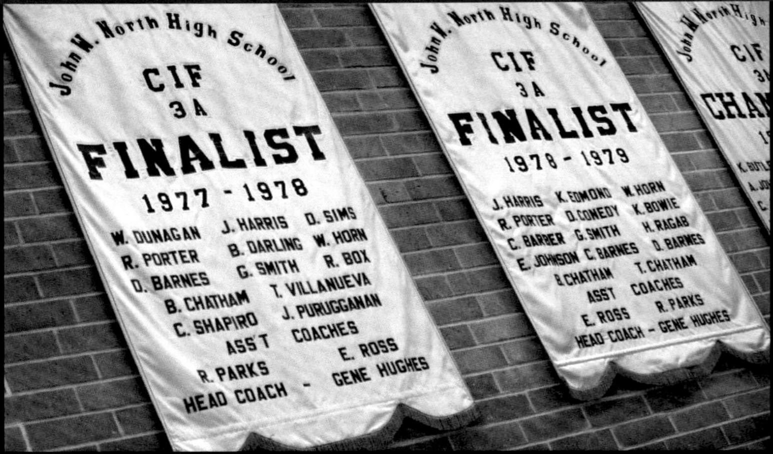

48.

49.

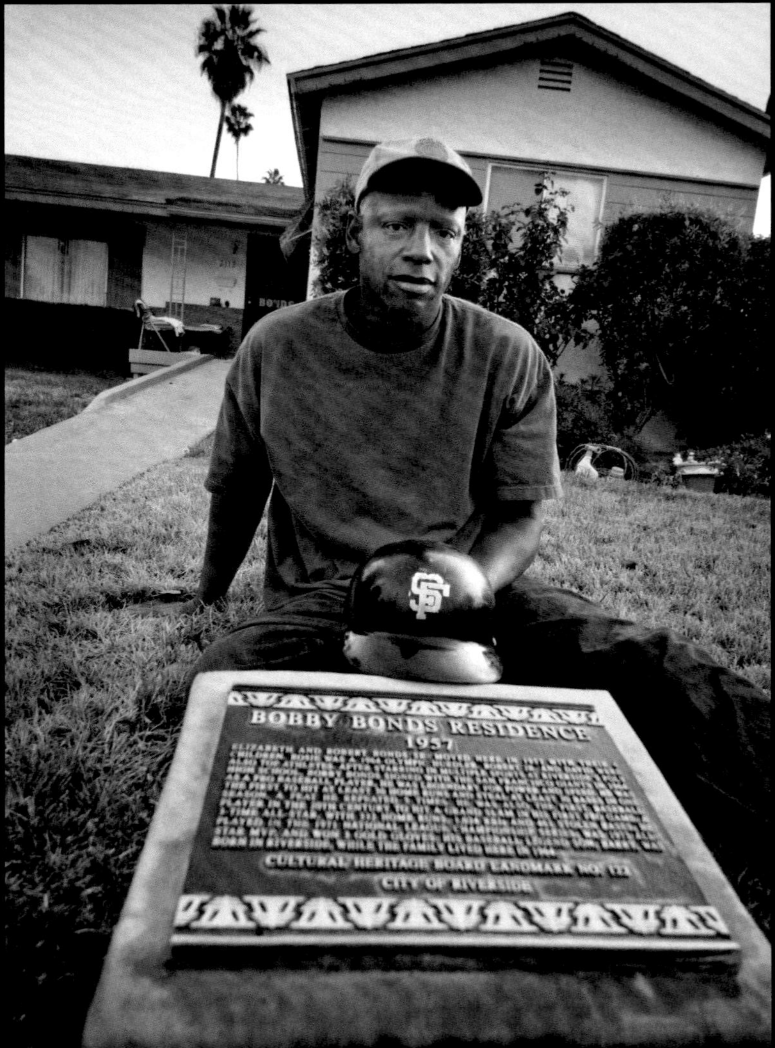

Back in 1978, when my future husband Dwayne Sims played forward, I worked the scorer's table. Our star guard, George Smith, had a Japanese mother and a Black military father. (At 5-7, he could dunk. Really.) Our star forward, Richard Box, was the son of a German mom and a Black military father, and other players were Mexican-Irish, Egyptian-Mexican, Alaskan Native-white. My mother, born in Switzerland, sat in these bleachers, knitting at times. My father-in-law, born in Oklahoma, sat on the opposite side, top corner, a spot everyone knew was his, where he sipped from a flask concealed inside his large coat and yelled "Fall, ball!" when the players took a shot.

Now D Sims and T Chatham – as they are named on CIF banners – are those men. D Sims shouts his mantras – "Look up! Get back!" Plenty of people in the bleachers have a particular way of talking to refs – "You're missing a great game, ref! She's camping in the key! They're putting up a tent!"

I can look up at his father's old haunt now. On the court, Simone DeCoud really does look like Derrick Rose, dishing out no-look passes, somehow getting another rebound. Tatyana Calhoun floats in a jumper, and the Calhoun crowd roars. Coach Leonard DeCoud holds palms up if someone misses a layup; his wife Nedra came straight from her veterinarian clinic, and her relatives are here, too. Her parents left New Orleans decades ago for opportunity in Los Angeles, and here they are, three generations in a Riverside gym, watching these girls win. As we stream onto the court, Coach Leonard eventually sits down on a bottom bleacher, eats a hamburger, and watches the swirl of fans around his daughter. He tells me, "I never came into a gym like this – on the first day, they told me I was family. And they weren't kidding."

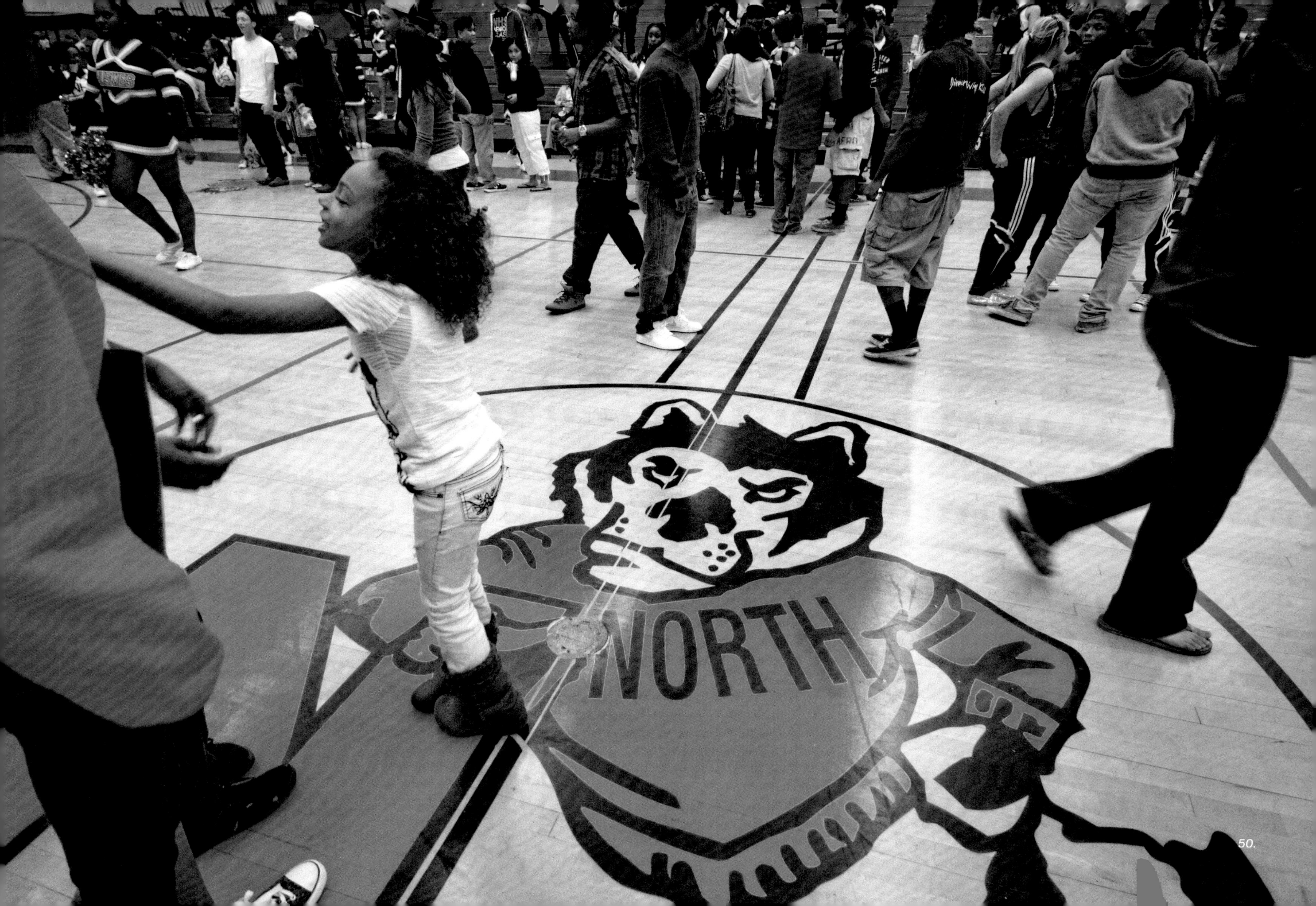
NORTH

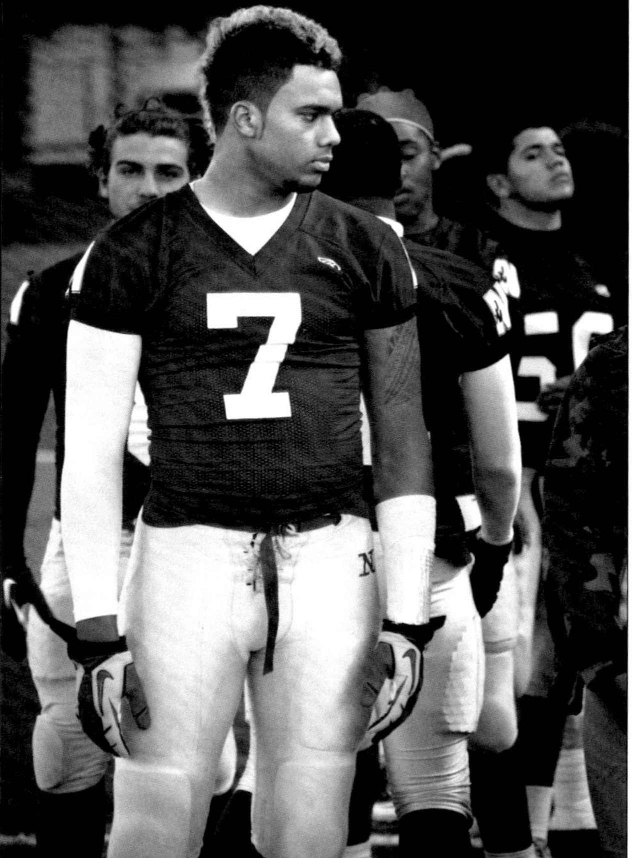

51.

The baby cheerleaders stood gazing up at the big cheerleaders who'd draped gleaming blue and gold beads around their necks, the girls who shepherded them around the infield. The senior football players burst through an arch of balloons with their parents. When my oldest daughter moved to Texas, she made us watch the TV series Friday Night Lights. "I realized you guys are exactly the same in Riverside. Everyone still goes to the football games, twenty years after they've graduated! It's crazy."

She was right. I sat in the stands with her father, and beside us Glenn King and Pete Anderson said, "We haven't missed a game in twenty years." King taught Dwayne and his brother Derrick in elementary school, and Pete Anderson was the assistant principal. "Well, I missed two," said Marshall Anderson, sitting beside us, ducking his head shyly. He was a track and football star at Poly High in the 1950s, and his sons played on that same field lit up below us.

This was the historic cross-town rivalry between JW North and Riverside Polytechnic, the kind of rivalry played out in every city and town in America during the fall. Neutral territory – the field at Riverside Community College, where the classic quad on the hill was built in 1924, when this was Riverside High School. My mother-in-law Alberta graduated from Riverside Poly in 1952, after walking these same steps and paths that led us here tonight.

It's a classic October night, the Santa Ana winds softened to breeze ruffling fronds of the century-old palms. The stadium is in Tequesquite Arroyo, a beautiful bowl of old buildings and bougainvillea spilling over walls and eucalyptus shivering like silver feathers in the night air.

Both schools have sent generations of athletes to college and professional sports. Bobby Bonds and Art Gilmore went to Poly, Alvin Davis and Adam Kennedy went to North. On the sidelines is James Calhoun, who played for North, then Riverside Community College, and now helps coach the freshman team. Down on the field, the Baugh family celebrates wide receiver Marcus, headed to Ohio State next fall on a full scholarship.

Football is the American tradition of spectacle and community. Also on the sidelines: Chuck Beaty, who was our principal, along with Dale Kinnear, former principal. Sue Rainey, former Superintendent of Schools. Coach Mike Bartee, and Rebecca Porter, who was a cheerleader in the class of 1977 and now Director of Student Activities.

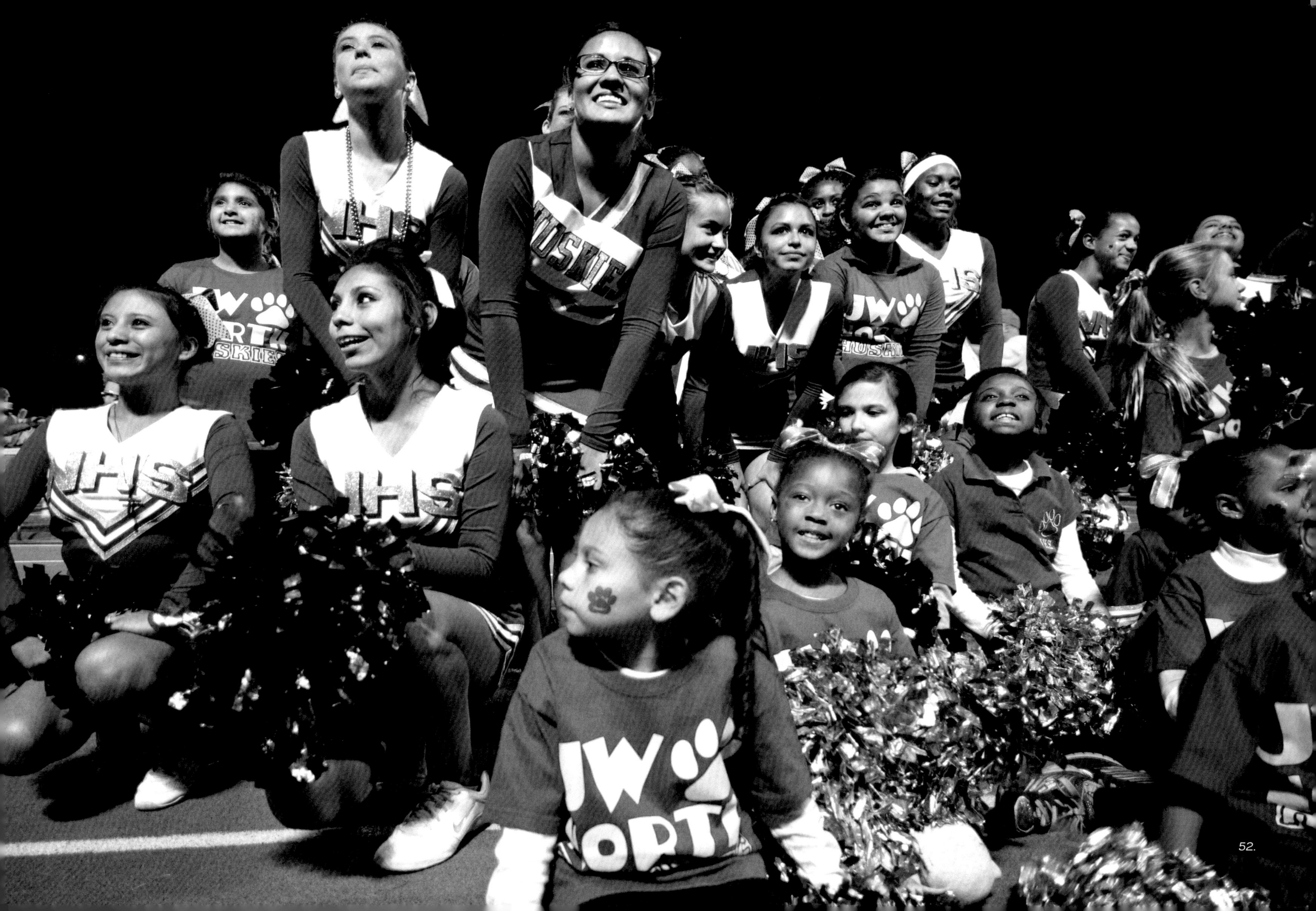
IHS

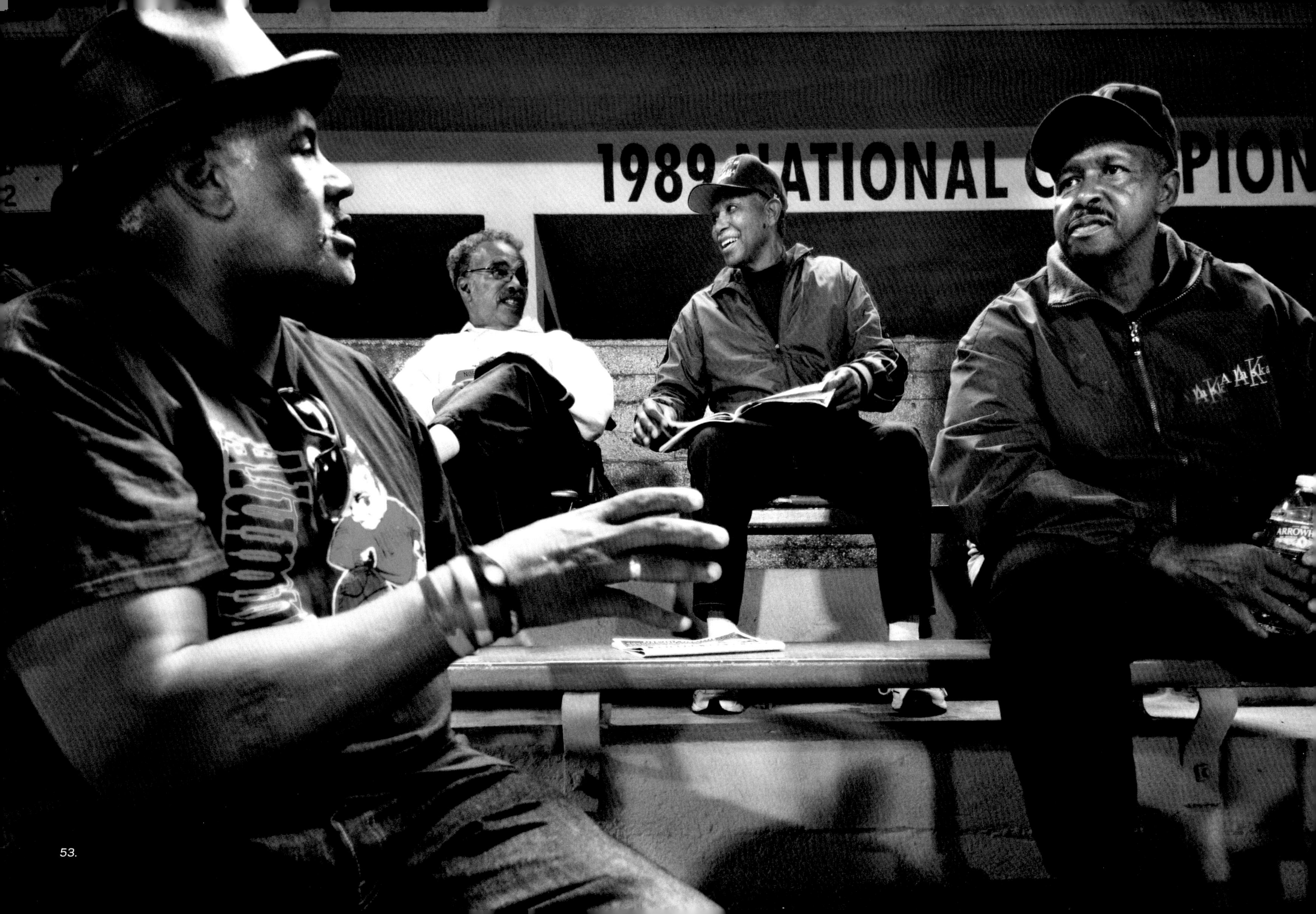
1989 NATIONAL C PION

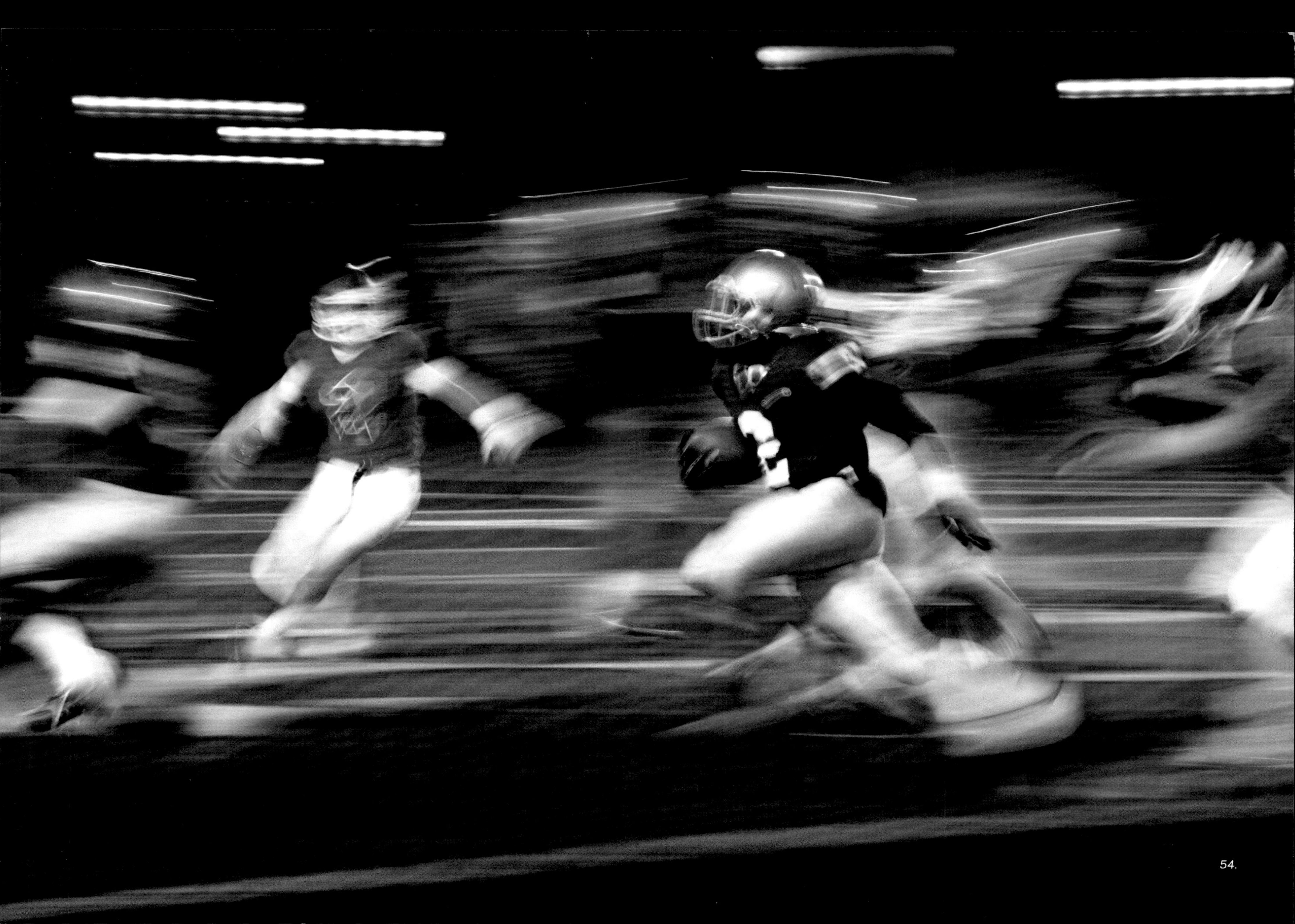

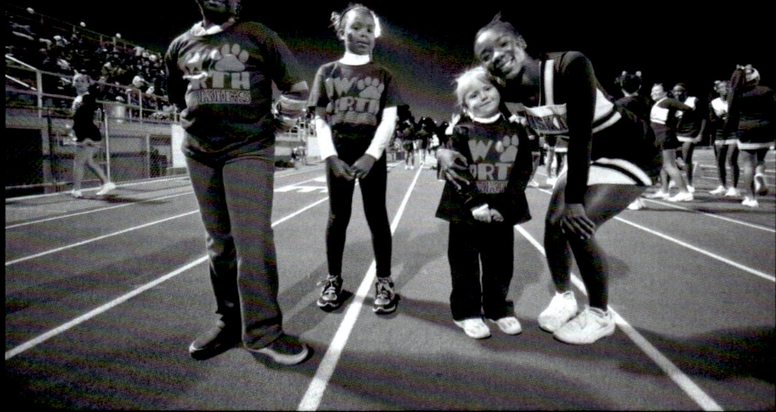

55.

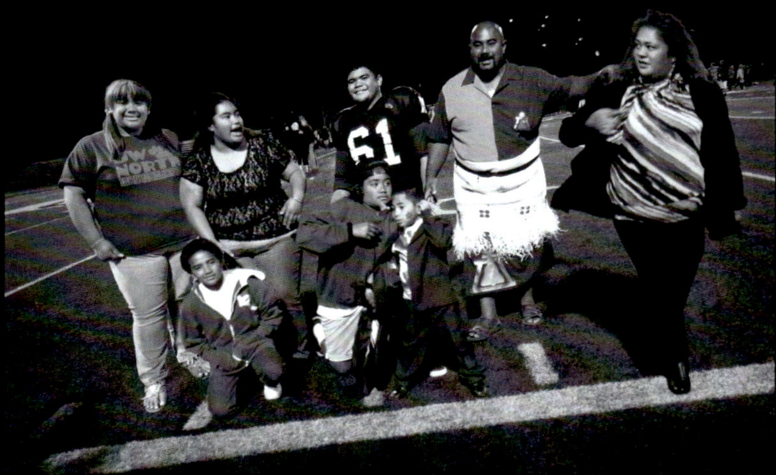

56.

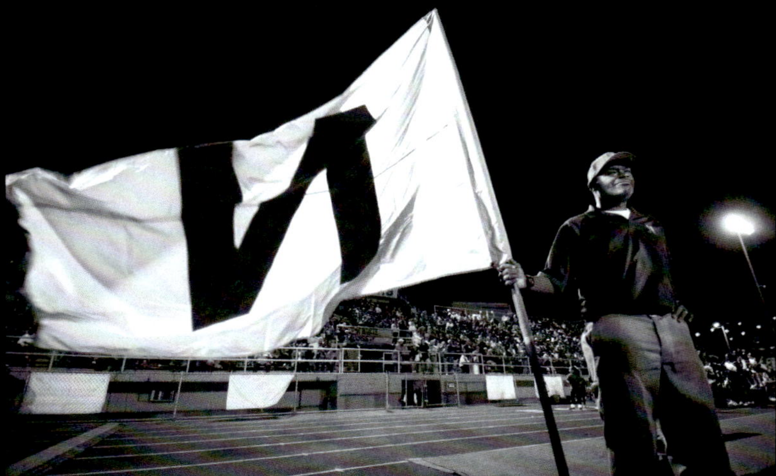

57.

Tonight Porter is everywhere, helping the mini-cheerleaders get ready for their half-time performance with the big cheerleaders. Running around the track whenever the Huskies score a touchdown, Bobby Magby (Class of '78) wields a huge flag and a CIF championship ring. Though his kids graduated, the same year as mine, he doesn't miss a game, either. He was in elementary school class with Mr. King, who laughs about that in the stands.

At game's end, everyone's still visiting. The Avatongo family gathers on the sidelines – their daughter Finau was 2012 Homecoming Queen, wearing traditional Tongan dress along with her father Uhila. Some places in America appear to be re-separating into distinct communities, dividing by race and religion and class, but that doesn't work in this arroyo. Where my mother-in-law Alberta, a Black woman with many white friends, walked on these cement paths, my own daughters have friends on both sides of the field – North and Poly. Pete Anderson recalls that when he first came from Richmond, Virginia to Riverside, after being stationed at March Air Force Base, he couldn't buy a house where he wanted to, back in 1953. The children of now laugh with each other, tackle each other, cheer with each other, and marry each other. We all sit in the autumn wind in this place carved out by rushing water over thousands of years. I can't help but miss Alberta, who walked up these stone steps with her friends in 1953, giggling, wearing a cinch-waisted dress and her bangs curled, and wish she were here to see the baby cheerleaders in their shiny beads.

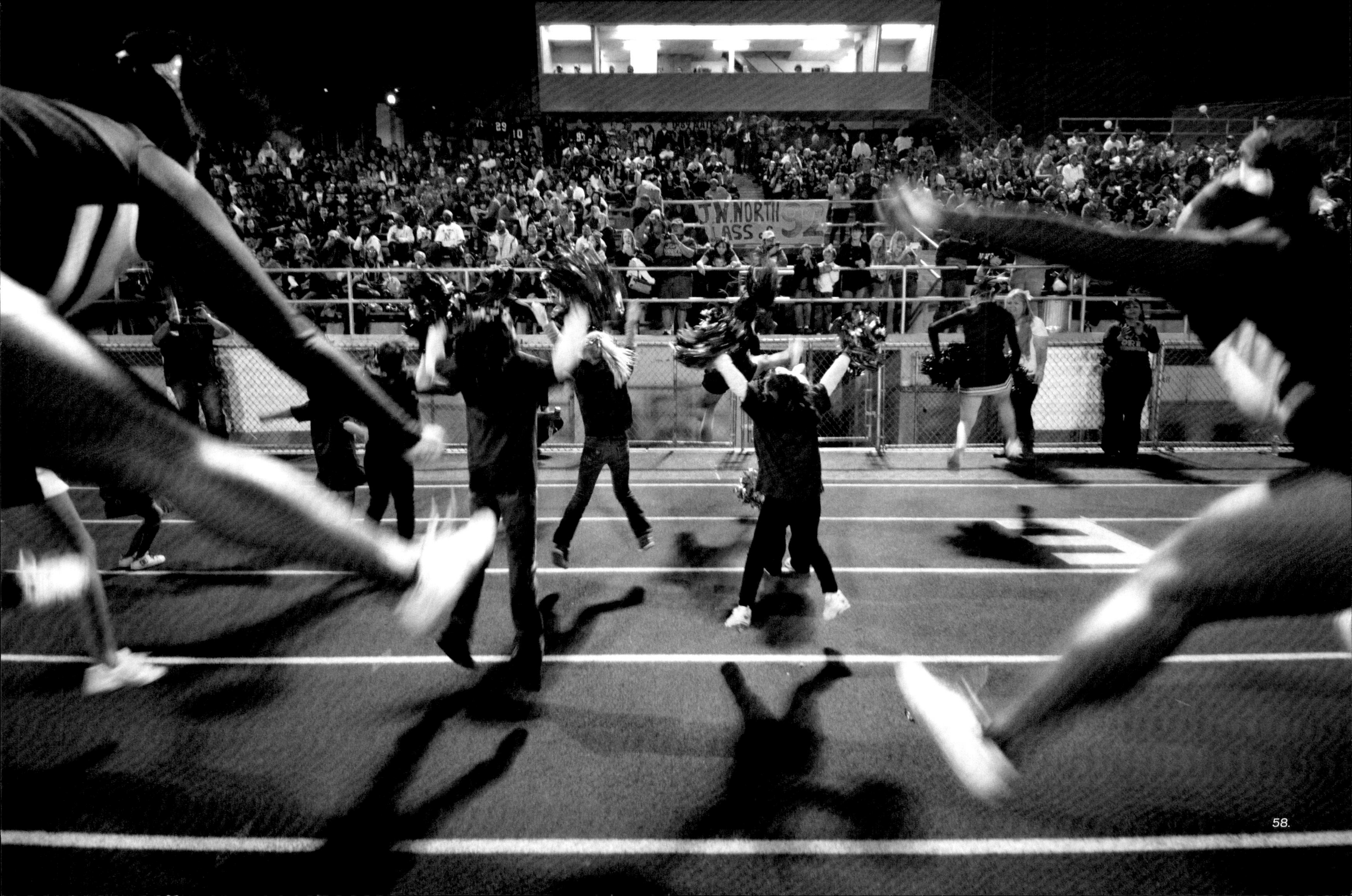
J.W. NORTH
LASS 92

Mike Bartee gathered his players around him – he had something to say about defense, and sharing the ball, and in the faces shining with sweat, in the circle so close to his words, every eye was trained on his hands and his mouth. They want to do what he asks – every single trip up and down the basketball court – because he would never spend his entire life here if it didn't mean the world to all of them.

He played his own basketball on this court, and his own coach, Gene Hughes, who spoke to him about defense back in 1967, was in the stands last week. Gene Hughes had driven many miles to watch Coach Bartee go for his 603rd win, in the third round of the CIF Southern Section Playoffs, against Lawndale High. When he won the 600th game, Bartee became one of only 26 coaches in California to mark that many victories – and his players gathered around and told reporters how they'd wanted to win it for him. Three of his players, Adrian Hughes, Dorian Butler, and Marcus Baugh, have fathers who played for Coach Bartee during their own careers at North High.

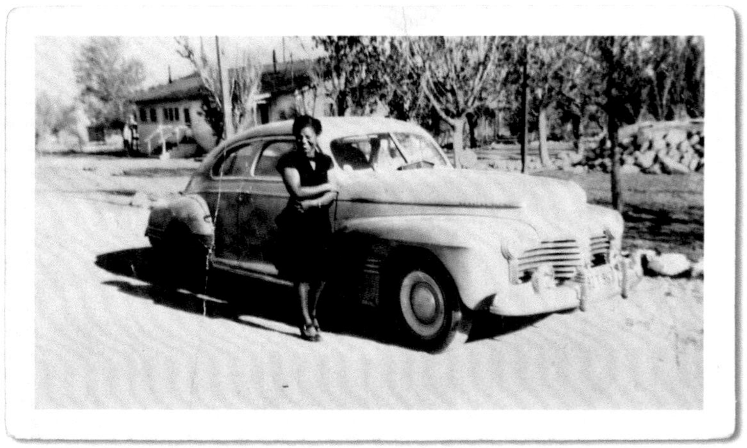

59.

What does it mean to spend your whole life in one place, on this wooden floor, running alongside young men where you ran yourself? Their shoe soles flashed past where I sat in the bleachers. Maybe there are only two kinds of us here on earth – people who stay and people who leave. Some left a continent for better work or to flee war, or left one city to live even thirty miles away.

Hillard and Mary Anderson left Willis, Texas in 1923 bound on a train for southern California, and after a short time in Los Angeles, they moved to Riverside in 1924, settling on 11th Street. Their daughter Inona Anderson was only five years old, born in Colmesneil, Texas. Nine more children were born in California, including Marshall and Robert Anderson.

Nona had six children, one of them Michael Bartee. Bartee graduated from North High in 1967, leading scorer on the basketball team. The day after Lawndale, he sat in the bleachers behind me and said, "I only left Riverside for six months, when I was in the military. I played here at North, I played at Riverside City College, at Cal Baptist. Then I got my education degree at UCR." He smiled at the court, where the girls' team was winning their own playoff game. "I love coaching these kids. Where else would I want to be?"

The thing he's most proud of is how many kids he's sent off to college, how many of them still come back and talk to him, and how many lives he's changed. He remembers every name – and when I spoke to Coach Gene Hughes in the bleachers, he asked about my brother John, whom he coached in tennis back in 1982. Coaches and fans remember every face, every kid, and they always ask, "What's he or she doing now?"

A few days later, they closed the gym doors five minutes after the start of the semifinal game against Mira Costa because the entire place was already full. But even from outside, everyone could hear the resonant bass voice of Leon Culpepper. "Three-Ball! Dikymbe Martin with the trey!" He sits ten feet behind Bartee, at the scorer's table. For decades, Culpepper has announced football and basketball games in that deep golden tone: "Too Many Steps – Traveling is the call!"

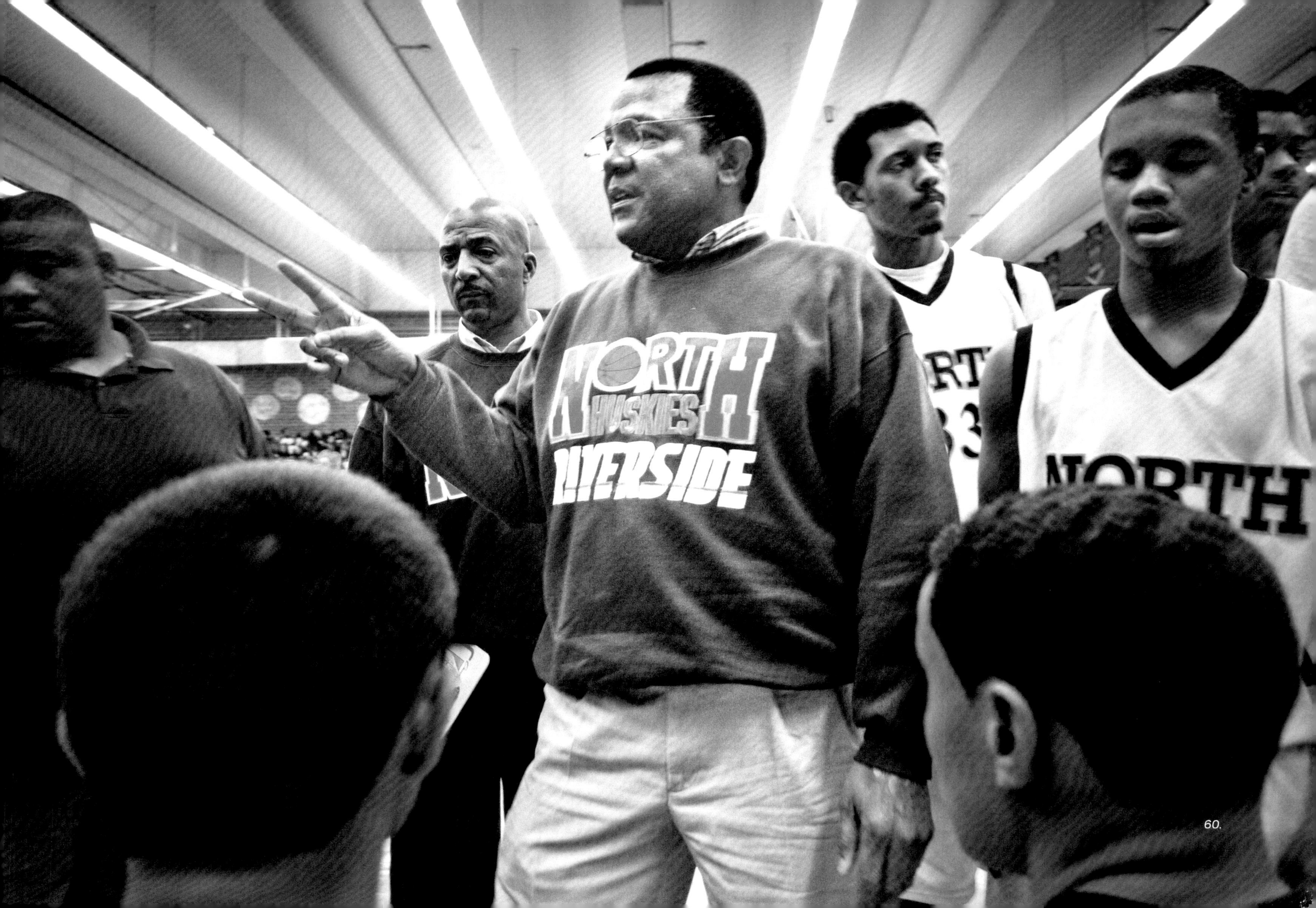
NORTH
HUSKIES
NORTH

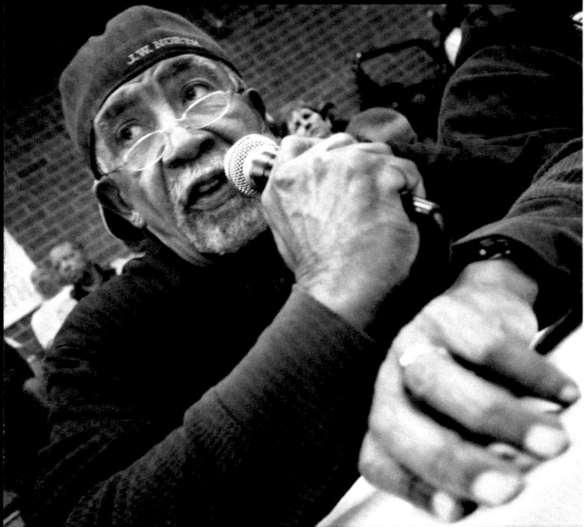

61.

His mother was born in Canada, and she arrived in Riverside in the early 1920s as well. The Culpeppers lived on 12th Street, in a Victorian house edged with gingerbread trim, where family still remains even now. Leon Culpepper went to Poly High with Bobby Bonds, the Baseball Hall of Famer. "Bobby and I used to caddy with Cliff Strickland," he told me. "Cliff Strickland was a legend – he set the course record at Victoria Club, shot a 65 and that record held for years. But he had to play on Caddy Day – that's when Black men could play back then."

After a drink from the snack bar at halftime, he gets back up behind his microphone to call another ten baskets, another twenty. "Three-Ball! DeShon Taylor with the trey," he says. In the bleachers, Marshall and Dorella Anderson watch their nephew coach, and Kelvin Butler watches his son Dorian score 21 points. Kelvin played for Bartee on the 1984 team that won the CIF Championship, and he is faithfully entrusting his son to the same man, who calls plays in the semi-circle of fierce concentration. Tonight, the Huskies win 80-55. They won the CIF Southern Section Championship game for Coach Bartee days later – Game 605. Dorian Butler was named Division 2A Player of the Year – his father Kelvin had that title in 1984. Mike Bartee was chosen Coach of the Year for 2013.

And I realize there is another category of people – the ones who leave for a time, and then come back, to stay. Some of these teenagers in the gym, the same one where I used to sit at the scorer's table a few elbows down from where Leon Culpepper sits now, will be back. Some will not. But we send them into the world with cheers lingering in their ears. ■

45. *J-Dub on a Tuesday night: "Ain't no shame in our game."*

46. *Simone DeCoud stealing a rebound from "the bigs" in the North High gym*

47. *The multitudes of faithful in the J-Dub gym, cheering a basket by Tatyana Calhoun*

48. *D Sims, T Chatham, and teammates immortalized on CIF banners*

49. *Trent Chatham with Bobby Bonds' batting helmet from his time with the San Francisco Giants, in front of Mama Bonds' house on Kansas Avenue*

50. *The swirl of fans after a game*

51. *Marcus Baugh, headed for the Ohio State Buckeyes*

52. *Big and baby cheerleaders on the infield at Riverside Community College ahead of the game, JW North versus Riverside Poly*

53. *In the stands: Dwayne Sims, Glenn King, Pete Anderson, and Marshall Anderson*

54. *Denzil Foster, JW North running back, moving the ball downfield*

55. *The next generation of Husky cheerleaders on a fall night in Riverside*

56. *The Avatongo family, including Finau, JW North Homecoming Queen, her father Uhila, and her brother Mafileo, on the varsity football team, 2012*

57. *Bobby Magby, class of '78, wields his flag*

58. *The big cheerleaders showing the baby cheerleaders how it's done, Husky style*

59. *Inona Anderson Bartee with a friend's car, 1950s*

60. *Coach Mike Bartee talking defense during a timeout*

61. *Leon Culpepper, the golden voice of announcing for Riverside sports*

62. *North High Husky dunking in the gym before a big game*

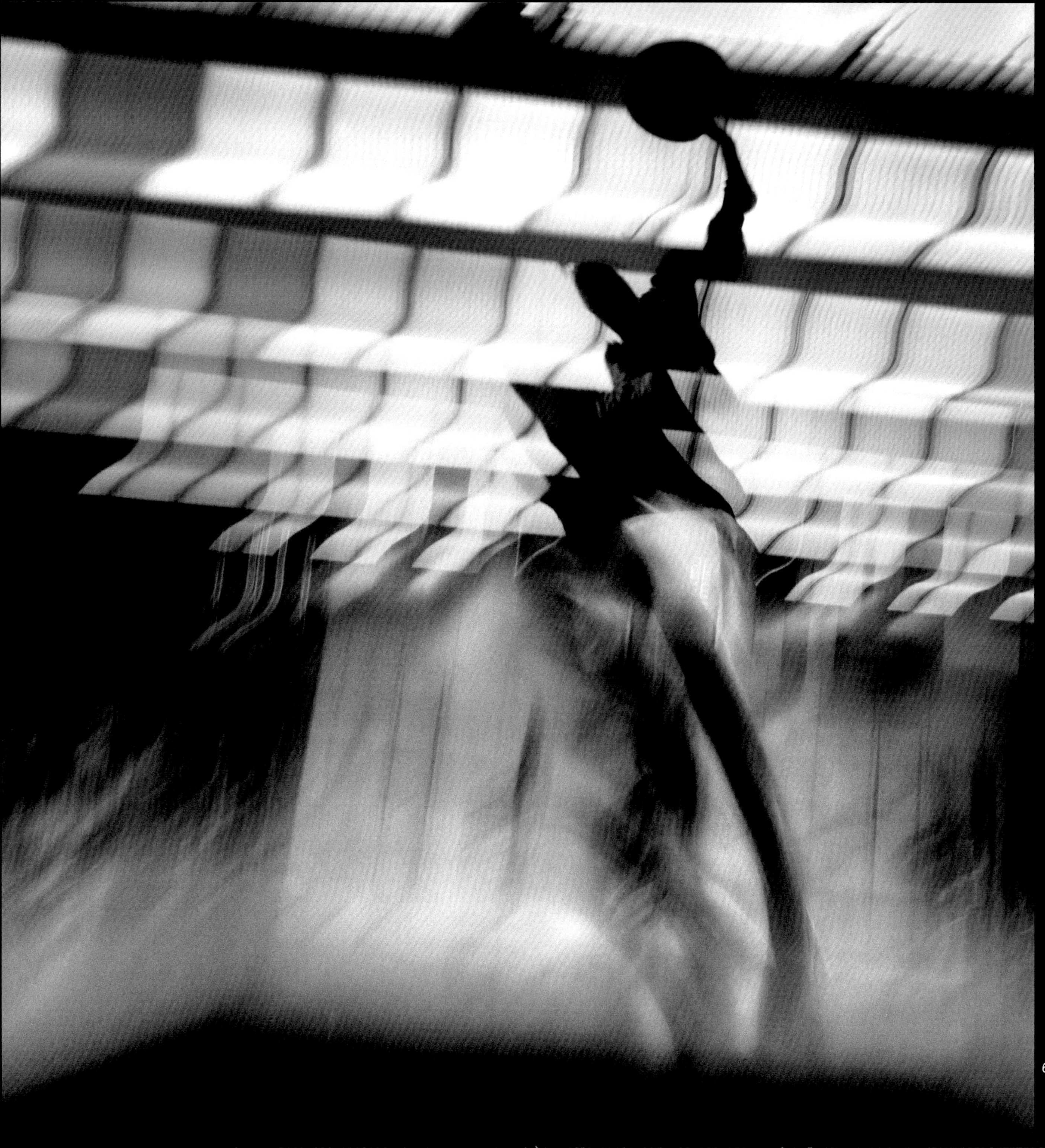

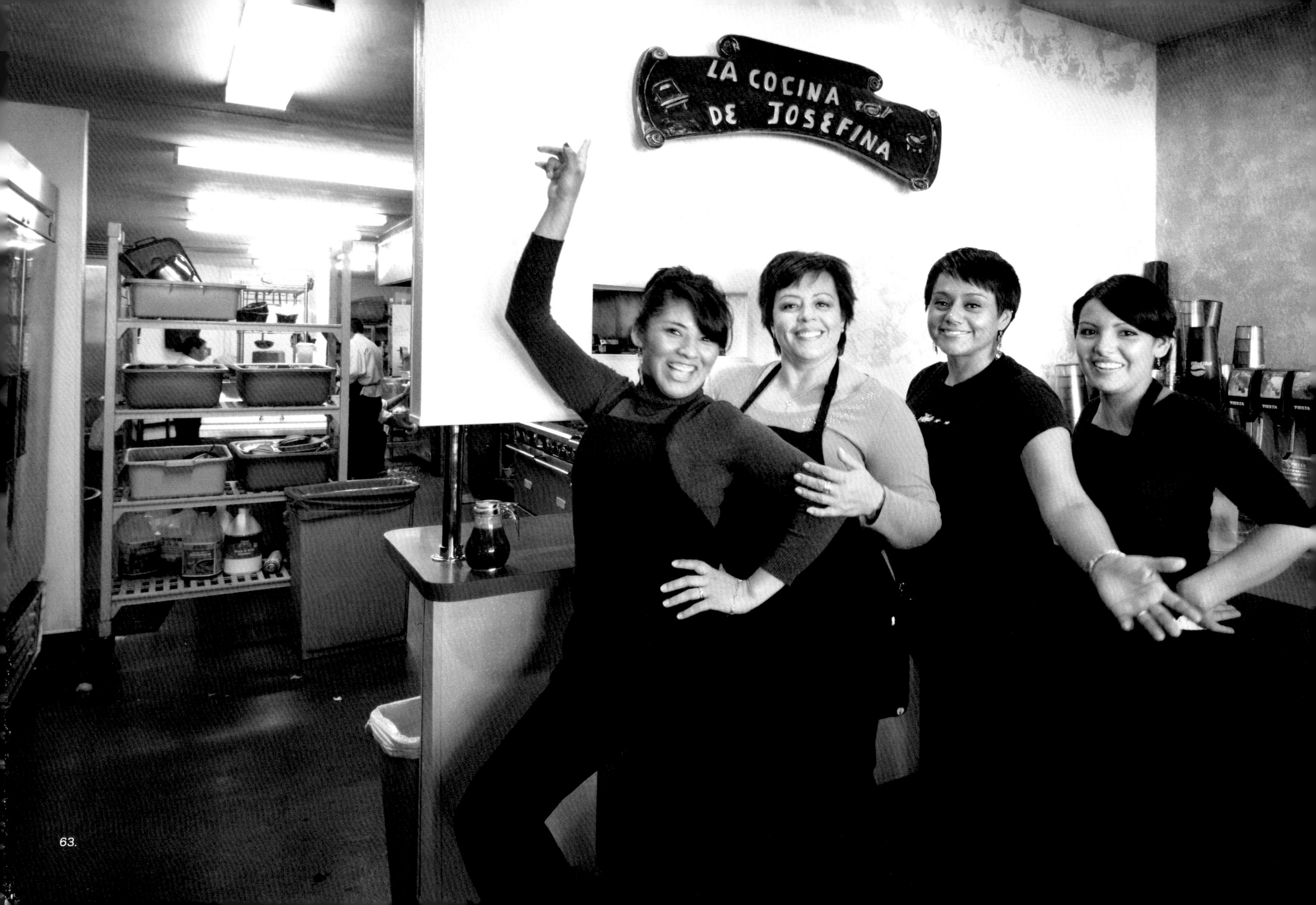
LA COCINA
DE JOSEFINA

The Red Sauce Equals Love at Zacatecas Café

Vicky Medina delivered tortillas one morning in 1989 from La Fiesta Tortilleria in Riverside's Casa Blanca neighborhood to the kitchen at Zacatecas Café, on University Avenue in the Eastside. Love? In a stack of tortillas? She was 16 years old. Jon Medina was 23 then, working there in his parents' restaurant. They got married a year later – now the tortillas are piled high in the refrigerator behind her, jaunty as layer cakes.

Oscar and Josefina Medina started Zacatecas in the fall of 1963, in a storefront space with stools and a counter. Josefina cooked mostly American food for the men who came for lunch while working at the railroad yards and offices, or the courthouse downtown. They moved behind the counter in a complicated dance, Oscar wide-chested, Josie diminutive, but both stirring their singular red sauce and ladling it over the food they served to their friends.

Zacatecas is the kind of place every American city needs – not just for the food, but for the daily contact of grins and handshakes and leaning over a table that makes us human. Watching the cooks move around in the kitchen, stirring pots of beans, pots of rice – millions of hard seeds plumped in boiling water and sauce to make the basis for all meals. "You have to have good rice," Vicky said. "Everyone loves our rice. And the beans!"

Robert Anderson made the smartest decision of his life in 1969, when he brought Mariko, the woman he wanted to marry, to one of these tables. He had known her for one day – the previous night he'd taken her to the Fox Theater to see Bonnie & Clyde. "He took me to Zacatecas for our second date!" Mariko said. "I had never eaten Mexican food." Her mother was from Yokohama, Japan, her father from Dangerfield, Texas, and they were on their way to Alaska to another military base. Mariko was 21 years old, Robert a Korean War veteran who was recently divorced, and friends had set them up. "I met Oscar, met all the Medinas that night, kids and everyone. Oscar made a special burrito for me, with red sauce on top. He couldn't believe I ate the whole burrito!" She laughs, and shows with her hands something the size of a small log.

Two days after that, Robert proposed. And two days later, Mariko wrote a Dear John letter to a lieutenant serving in Vietnam, to whom she was engaged. (Good thing, since it turned out he was already married.) One more day and she said yes to Robert.

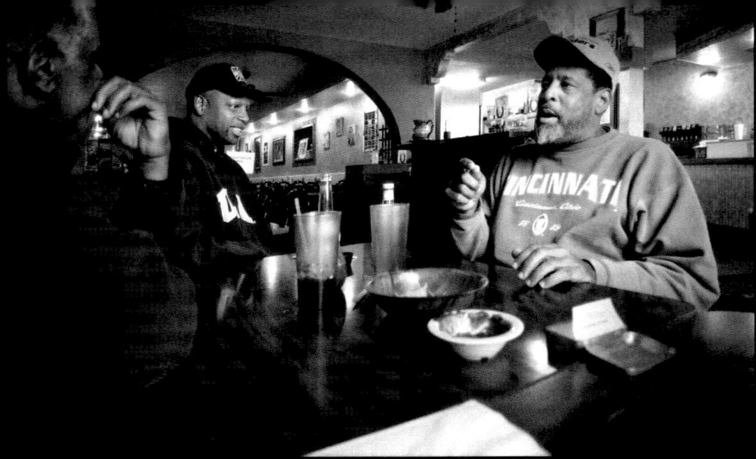

64.

65.

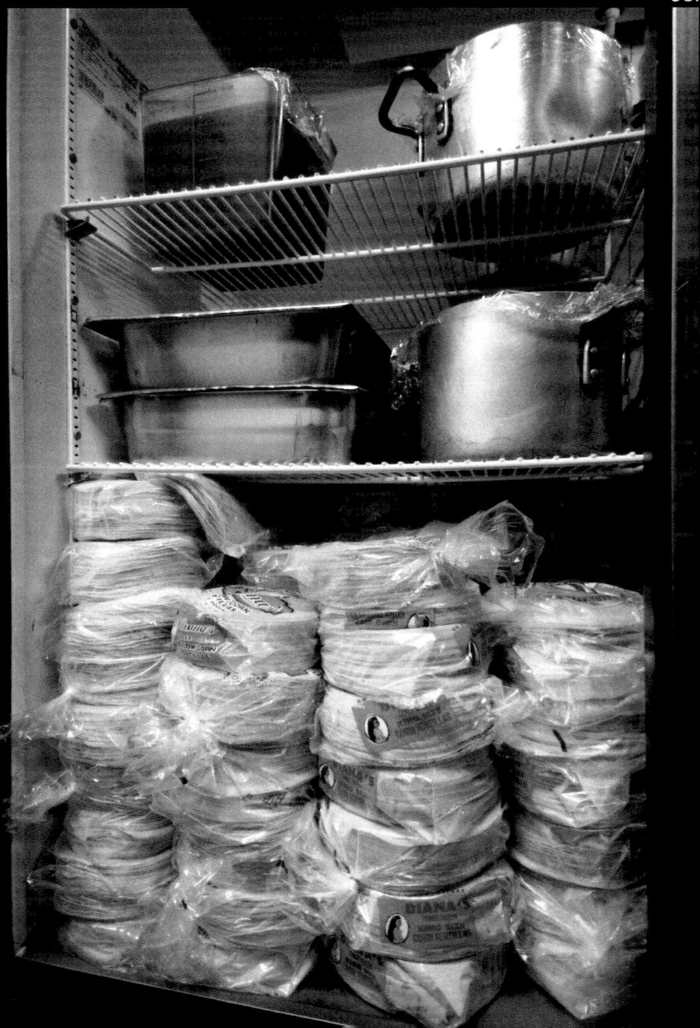

His parents came to Riverside from Texas, and Robert was born in 1930, in the house at 9th Street and Eucalyptus next door to Oscar Medina's parents. "We traded biscuits for tacos all the time, when I was a kid," Robert said. "That's how it was."

Oscar Medina is a shy, scowling child in the Irving School class picture where Vicky estimates that he's only six years old. He married Josefina, who was born in Zacatecas, Mexico, and her sign, La Cocina de Josefina, still hangs on the new wall in the kitchen the Medinas just renovated. Fifty years this fall, and her memory is still in the food.

But it is the people at the tables, too, who make Zacatecas Café the "Grand Central Station of the Eastside," according to Linda Salinas-Thompson. "You go to Zacatecas and you'll see someone you haven't seen for years. It's not just the food, which is great – it's the place."

On any weekday at lunchtime, you'll see the city at work. Councilman Andy Melendrez, reporters from The Press-Enterprise, elderly couples celebrating anniversaries, school board members eating with friends. It is not by design, but I've seen elderly Japanese-American women at one table, white contractors in dust-covered Dickies at the next, and at my own table, my brothers-in-law whose father, General, worked on the plumbing here decades ago for his close friend Oscar. General Sims and Jesse Lee Collins went by Oscar's house to pick him up, when they all worked night shift at Norton Air Force Base servicing aircraft; sometimes, Jesse Lee said, they napped in the cockpits after they finished maintenance. Oscar slept a little in the morning, and came to the restaurant.

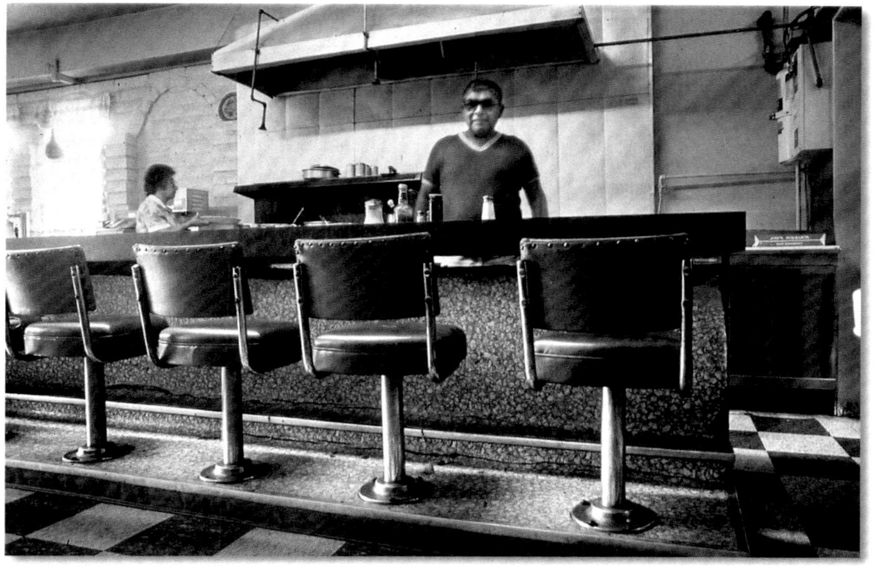

66.

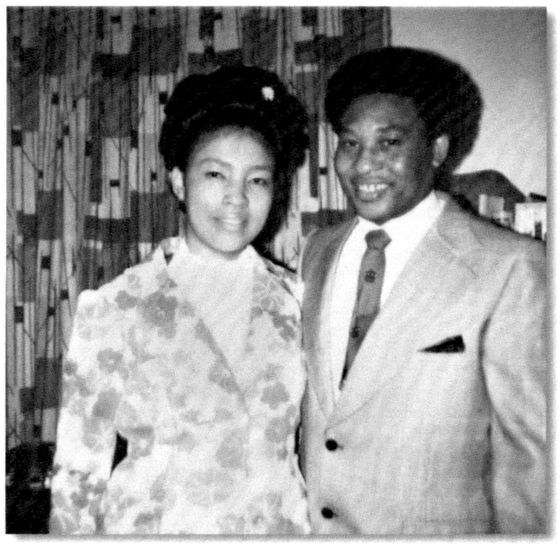

67.

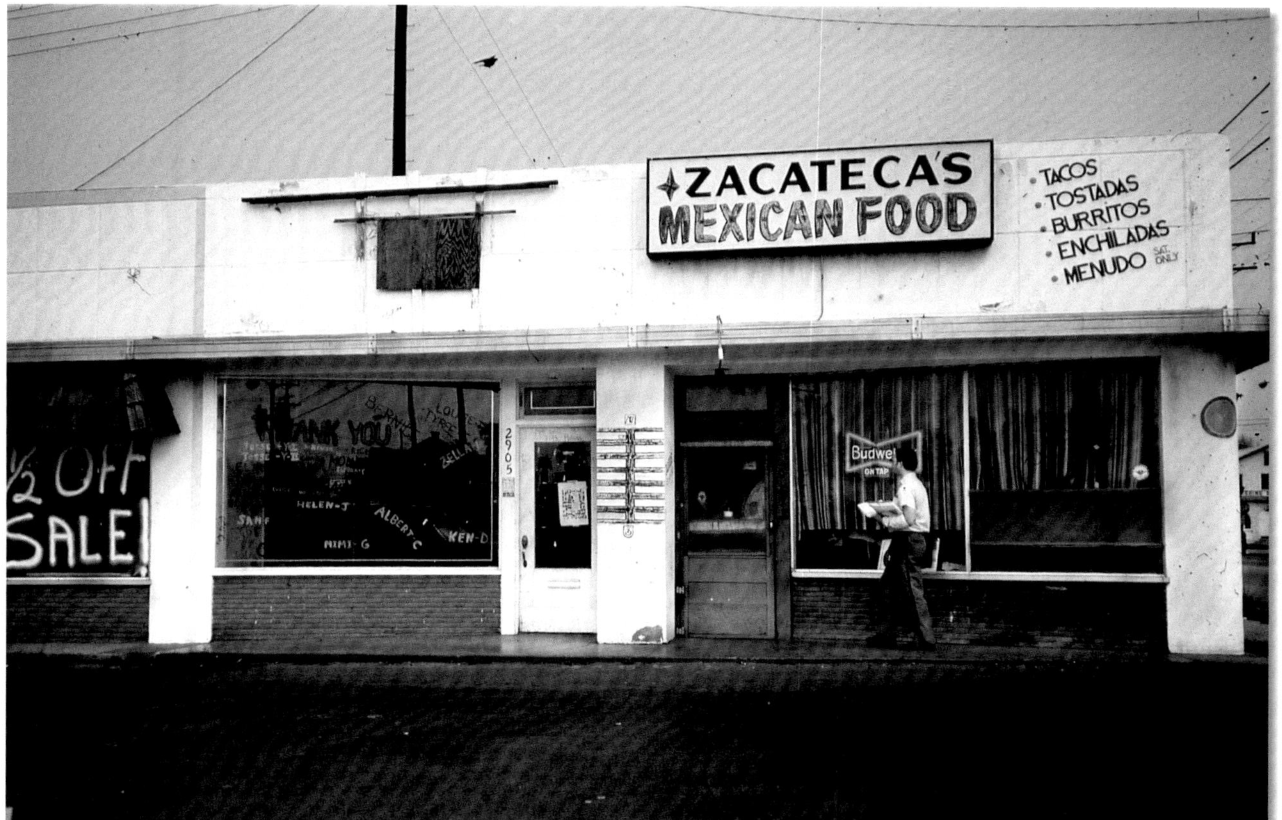
ZACATECA'S
MEXICAN FOOD
TACOS
TOSTADAS
BURRITOS
ENCHILADAS
MENUDO SAT. ONLY
2905

68.

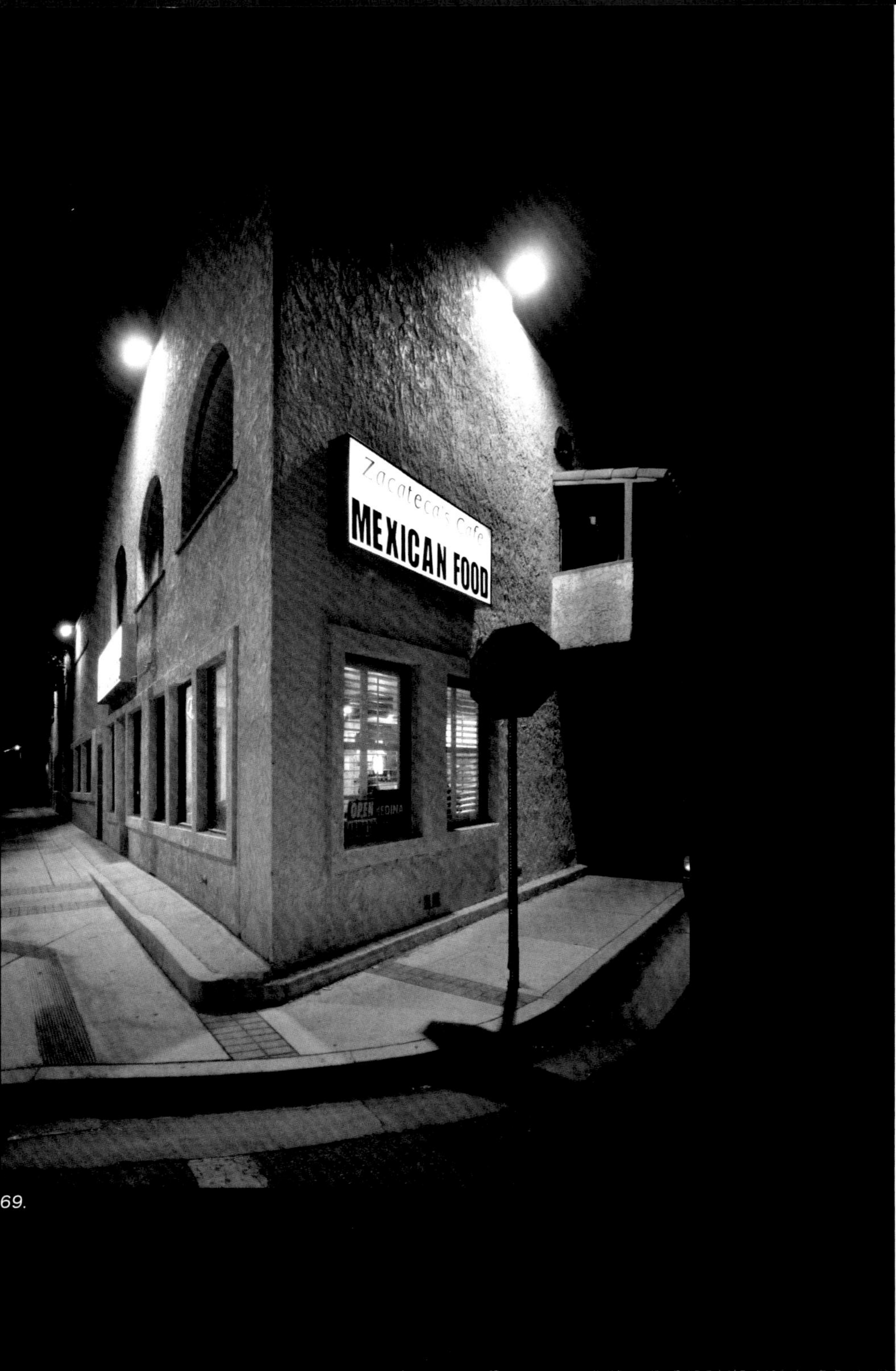

That is a different kind of love. It takes a loyalty involving a lifetime of long hours and work. It takes working nights at the banquet room here, where hundreds of people turned out to celebrate longtime Riverside educator Jose Medina's victory in November's historic California State Assembly race. Jon's brother Bill Medina, who was the best man at Jose's wedding to Linda, was greeting everyone with a smile. "We're extended family," Bill said. He now teaches history at RCC. "I was born here, in the kitchen, it feels like. My parents bought the restaurant in 1963, when it was a doughnut shop. Back then, the customers were all 'gringos' who used to work at the railroads or downtown, and they came here for lunch." Bill pointed to the parking lot. "Remember when General's big old truck would get four flat tires and he'd leave it over there in the corner for a month?"

Everyone was eating, drinking, and visiting while Jose Medina shook hundreds of hands. The Mad Marionettes, young musicians paying homage to accordion and violin as well as contemporary music, played. Then longtime Mexican-American activists had glimmers of tears when Jose Medina began his speech, mentioning his parents, and saying, "I will go to Sacramento to keep education within reach of the middle class – a community college education, a UC education. For my father, education was the key to success. It still is."

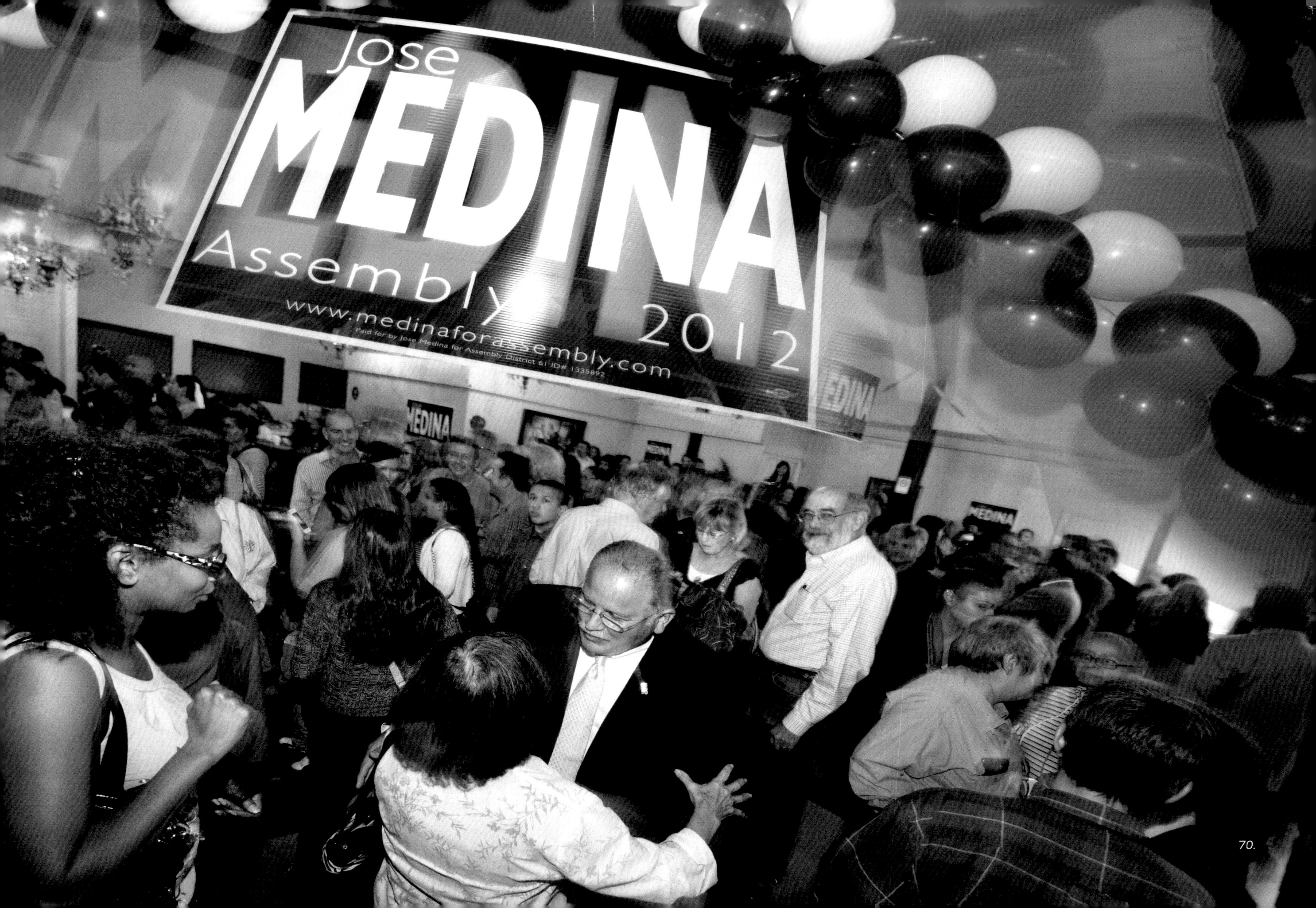
Jose
MEDINA
Assembly
2012
www.medinaforassembly.com
Paid for by Jose Medina for Assembly District 61 ID# 1335892
MEDINA

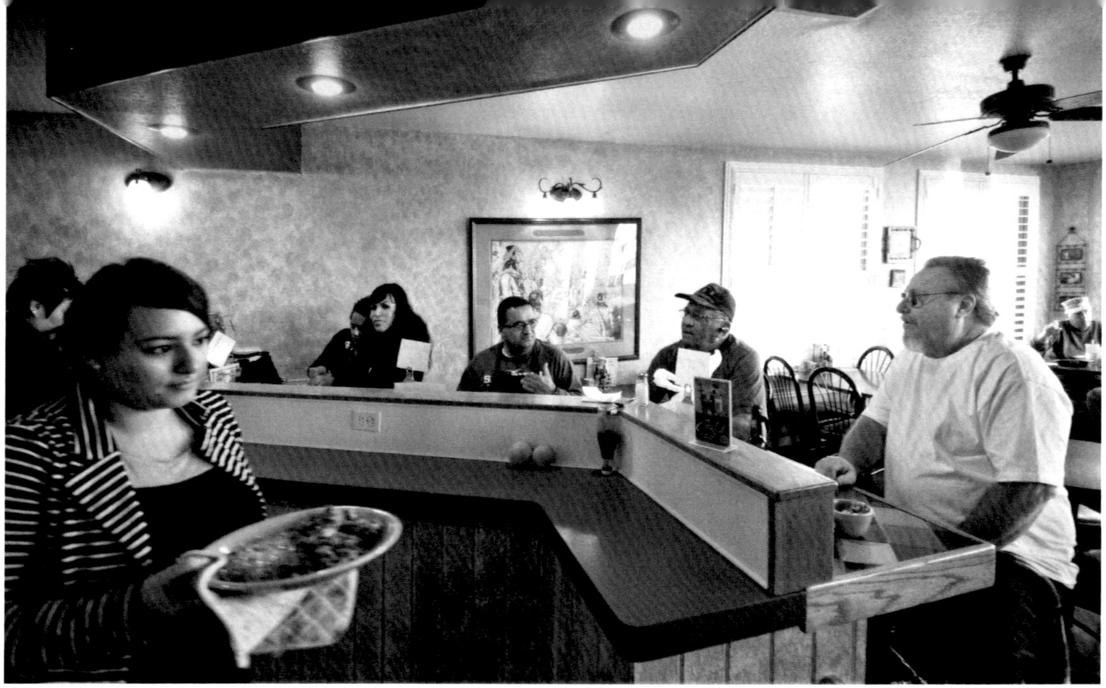

71.

Sabrina Perez, Vicky's sister, has worked seven years here. Vicky's daughters, Ashley, 22, and Elizabeth, 28, carry plates to the tables and lean down to hear a story from an abuela whose hair is covered by a chiffon scarf. They move effortlessly around the long dining room, pouring the red sauce from glass pitchers into the small bowls placed on each table like a benediction, with the fresh tortilla chips. Those tortillas in curls now, to hold the smoky thick sauce that makes people fall in love. Maybe a million tortillas, ground seeds of corn, hands rolling burritos so everyone can stay in love and go back to work after sharing their words – while Vicky arranges one more plate and places it before us. If Jon was born in the kitchen, as his brother says, he lives there now – he eats breakfast at the counter, surrounded by customers and family, then goes back under his mother's sign to work. ■

63. *Carina Morales, Vicky Medina, Sabrina Perez, and Gabby Garcia on a two-minute break, with the red sauce in pitcher*

64. *Dwayne Sims, Trent Chatham, and General Sims III eating lunch at Zacatecas Café*

65. *Stacks of tortillas awaiting their fate*

66. *Oscar and Josie Medina, working behind the counter in tandem, 1970s*

67. *Robert and Mariko Anderson's wedding – after she fell in love with him while eating a special burrito made by Oscar Medina, 1969*

68. *Zacatecas original building, 1970s*

69. *Zacatecas Café beckons at evening on University and Sedgwick Avenues*

70. *Hundreds of well-wishers at Jose Medina's election night party, banquet room, Zacatecas Café*

71. *Ashley Medina serving another plate, Jon Medina at center eating his breakfast with customers before heading into the kitchen*

72. *Weekday lunchtime at Zacatecas Café*

Not Facebook— Face + Chair: Orange Valley Lodge #13

“You know who was the first face I saw when I came to Riverside?” Oliver Winston said. “Him right there – and I see him almost every day now.” Henry Glover laughed, since he was the one sitting in the chair nearby. “I got off the bus, and he was there at the station. I said, Is March Air Force Base an easy ride? and he told me exactly which bus to take. Then I came back here a few days later, and I met this girl. I came to Riverside after that to see her, and we were on her porch talking, and I knew I had to get that bus, but it was after midnight. I walked all the way to March – that was miles!”

“But she was worth it, right?” Glover said in his soft, Cheshire-cat-grinning voice.

“Hell, yeah!” Winston said. By chance, he was not sent to Vietnam, and when the war ended, he stayed here. This is the sidewalk in front of Orange Valley Lodge #13, on 12th Street near Park Avenue, a social network of the highest order. The line of men in folding chairs is a changing cast, but some faces are semi-permanent. Glover came to Riverside in 1953 from Albany, Georgia, when he was 14; McCloud came in 1954 from Enterprise, Alabama, and he was 14, too. Now they sit with their legs out before them, comfortable, companionable, greeting everyone who slows and leans out a car window. “We start out here, in the summer, and then around four when it gets hot, we move across the street under the trees,” McCloud said.

My daughter told me this fall that a college athlete friend began a Twitter account, and within twenty minutes, he had 4,000 followers. If Twitter is “the water cooler of the internet, a place to make friends and network socially,” and Facebook users are advised to “be genuine and honest on your page if you want real friendships and more likes,” none of that would work in front of Orange Valley Lodge. You need more than 140 characters to tell a story right, and you can’t post digitally-altered Instagram photos of yourself.

The building has its own epic history. It was the Stokes & Wiley Grocery Store and Mercantile Hall, built in 1912 as a building used for many purposes by the Eastside’s African-American and Mexican-American community, housing businesses, an adjoining meat market now gone, and the order of Black Masons. Robert Stokes is called the patriarch of Riverside’s Black community, as he arrived here in the 1870s with a family from Georgia, taking their last name as his own. According to the historic accounts by his family, “He was a big heavy-set man, weighed more than 200 pounds and was over six feet tall.” In the Riverside City Directory, he is listed as a Special Policeman in 1889. He and his wife Mary owned a hog ranch at Seventh and Market – where the Fox Theater now stands. His nephew David Stokes came to Riverside in the early 1880s, and Mary Stokes helped him with the financing to build the Mercantile Hall.

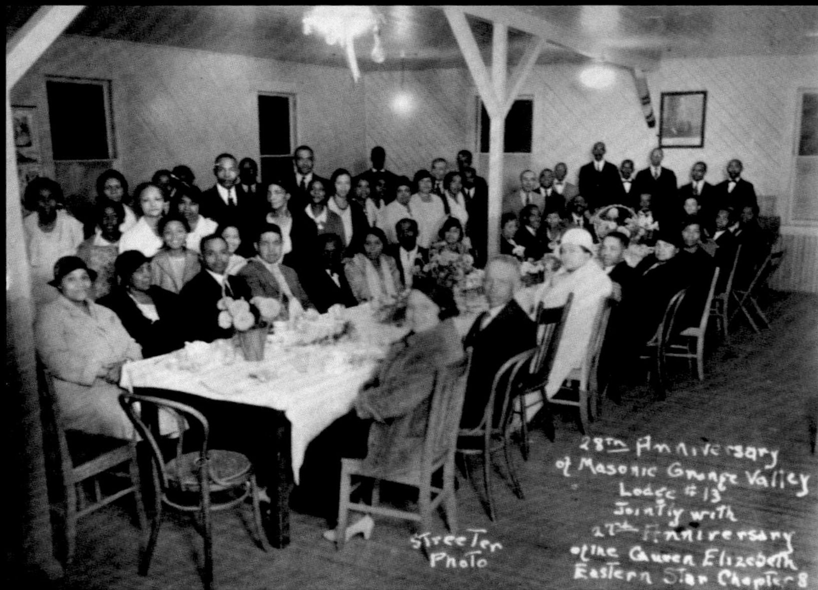

74.

75.

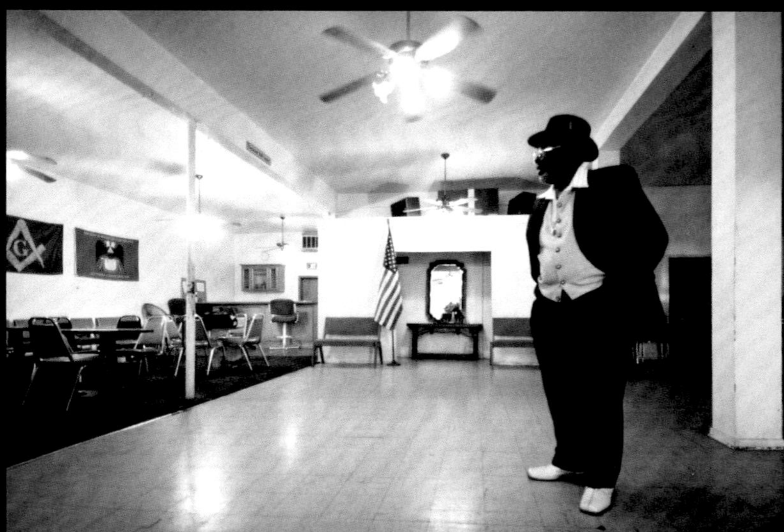

The document which created one brotherhood reads, in flowing script: *The Original Dispensation Formulating Orange Valley Lodge, by the Free Masons, Lodge Instituted October Fifth, Year One Thousand Nine Hundred and Five.* The men whose oval portraits look out somberly from upstairs are among the most influential Riverside pioneers: Goodwin, Beverly, three generations of Carters, Oscar Harris, who owned the city's sanitation contract for years.

In 1965, after Lowell School burned, a temporary Freedom School was set up on the second floor. One afternoon, John Bennett stood on the sidewalk looking up. "An older white man helped me with my homework," he said. "They had the picture in the newspaper." Then he turned to see the place where Lincoln Pool used to be. "I almost drowned in there!" he said, laughing, and the assembly of folding chairs began to recall dates at Sweet Shop, dances and socials in the clubhouse, and baseball games in the park. It is as if the grassy expanse where the wooden buildings and the pool once stood are an Impressionist painting – crowds of people caught in the retelling, their faces and clothes blurred in movement.

Many afternoons, a burnt-orange Hummer with starry silver rims and Bobby "Blue" Bland playing on the speakers is parked at the Lodge. "We'll go our separate ways," Bland sings, but sitting in a folding chair near the other men is LeRoy Barber, who's often dressed in immaculate pinstripes, vest, and fedora with a feather, his jewelry gleaming. Now that would be worth Instagram, but LeRoy dresses to impress himself – and his friends right here. A Master Mason at 81, Barber's name is inscribed on an elegant black table inside with other members. He joined the Air Force in 1952 out of Florida, became a Mason in 1962 while serving in Germany, and came to Riverside in 1975, stationed at March. "I have a key!" he said, and opened the door to the banquet room that has seen so many events. "I'm a midwife baby," he said, sitting at that table, gesturing with a pinky ring flashing in the light. "I was born in Florida or Georgia, and I've written to every place in both states to get records. But it doesn't matter – I have a passport now! I went everywhere in the service."

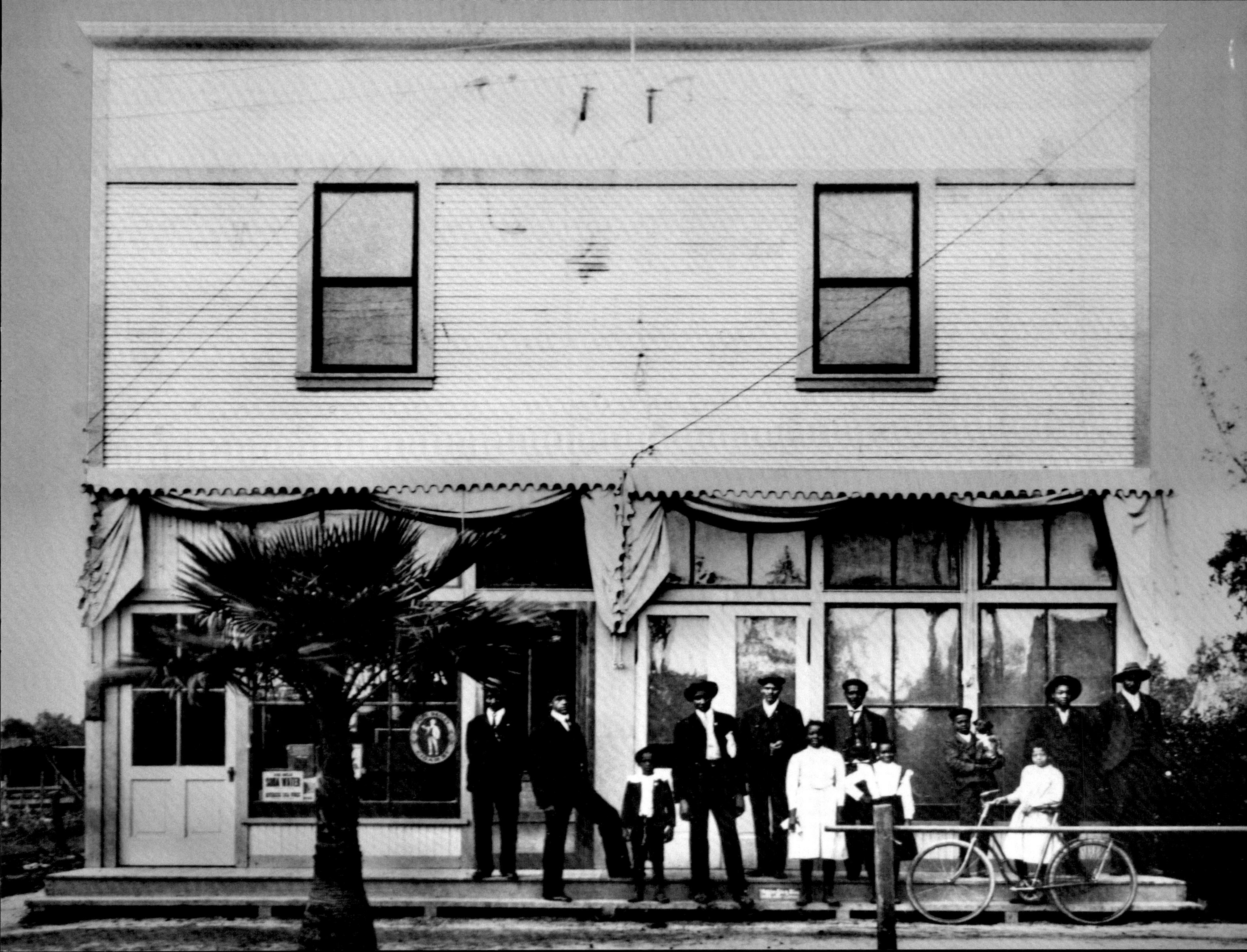
SODA WATER

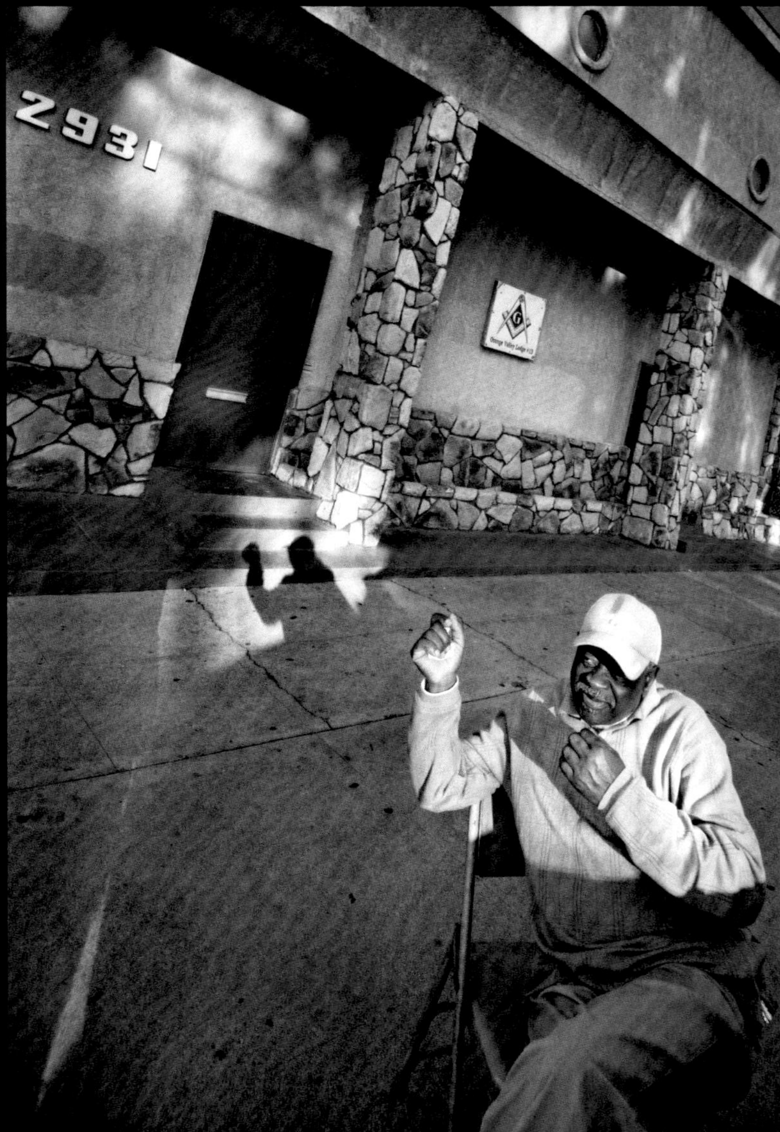

Barber wants Orange Valley to be open regularly, for cards and music and meals – he wants to run the bar and play his extensive collection of blues. "They used to play Bingo and Pinochle and Bid Whist," he said. "But we do good things – on Sundays, from 12-4, we feed 250 plus homeless people out here. We even take meals to the parks – Fairmount and other places."

Outside, the folding chairs have been rearranged again, as others arrive - McCloud, Glover, Dean Newton and others trade stories – some brand new, some everyday. Travis Coleman is here today – he came at 17 from Idabel, Oklahoma with his mother, in 1945. "We lived in Red Hollow, right there on 14th Street," he says, pointing across the old Lincoln Park. "I remember Daisy Carter, and the four sisters – they all worked at the Turkey House. Oh, yes, I remember those girls."

Gonzalo Gomez is here most days, too – he came in 1966 from Juarez, Texas. He sits next to Joe D. Hunter, who came in 1955 from North Carolina, and Robert Wood, who came in 1950 from Little Rock, Arkansas. "I was stationed at Camp Pendleton," he said. "Retired in 1962 as E-7 from the Marine Corps."

It is as if an older time is preserved here in the amber evening light, thick with remembrance but also shot through with frequent laughter. What does it mean, in 2013, when Facebook measures the social worth of one billion people, to park a truck or car at the same place most sunny days, even cloudy ones, and pull out your folding chair and set it on the same cement where you will see your ten friends, and the countless others who park for a few minutes to share news of a death, or a party, or a glimpse of someone they knew forty years ago? What does it mean that you talk today's politics or sports, but also tell the same story about walking ten miles to see a girl, or the story about the woman you met in Germany when you were a young soldier? What does it mean to carry Georgia or Alabama or Juarez in you, but to live your permanent days here in the place you chose, or the place that chose you?

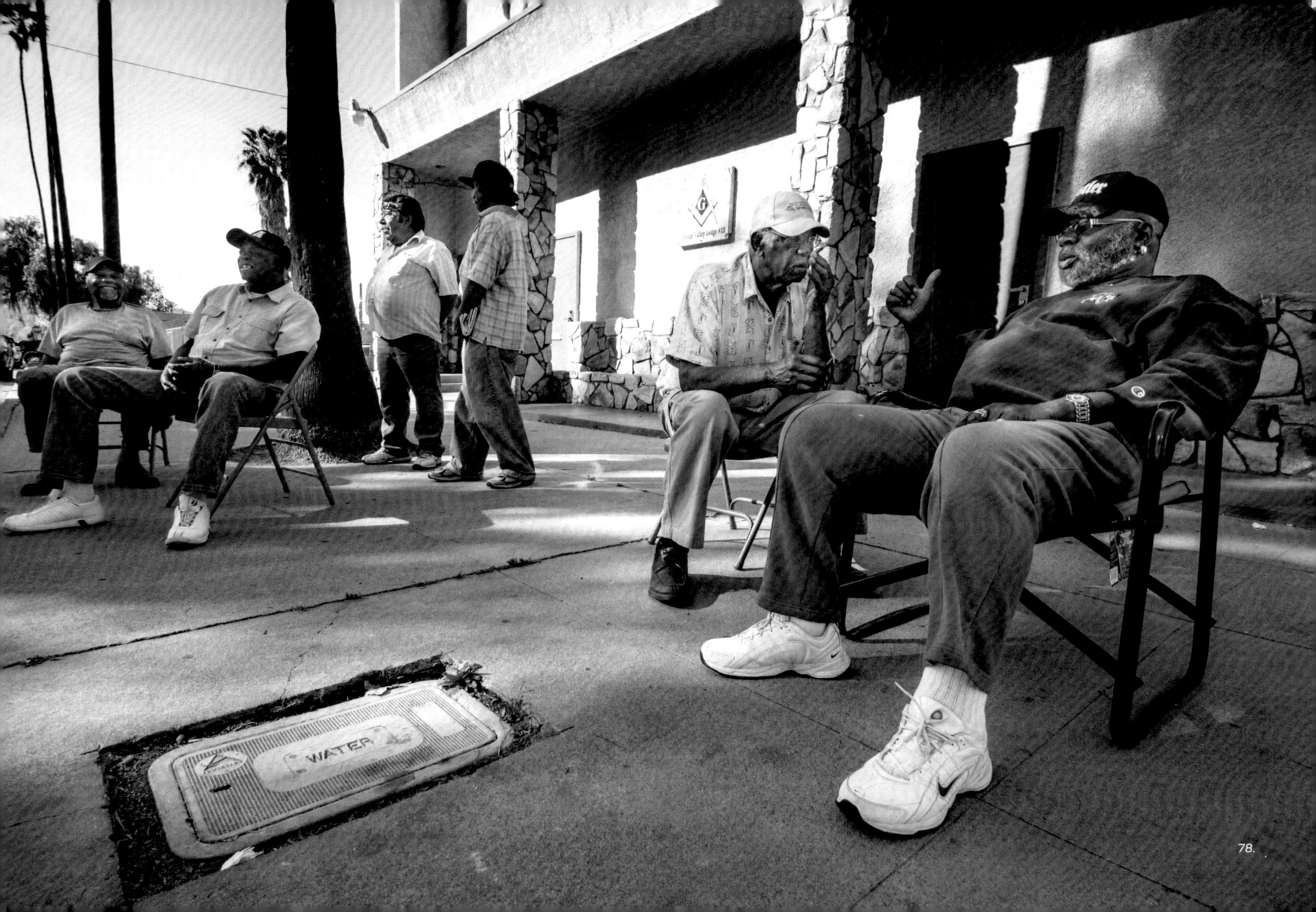
WATER

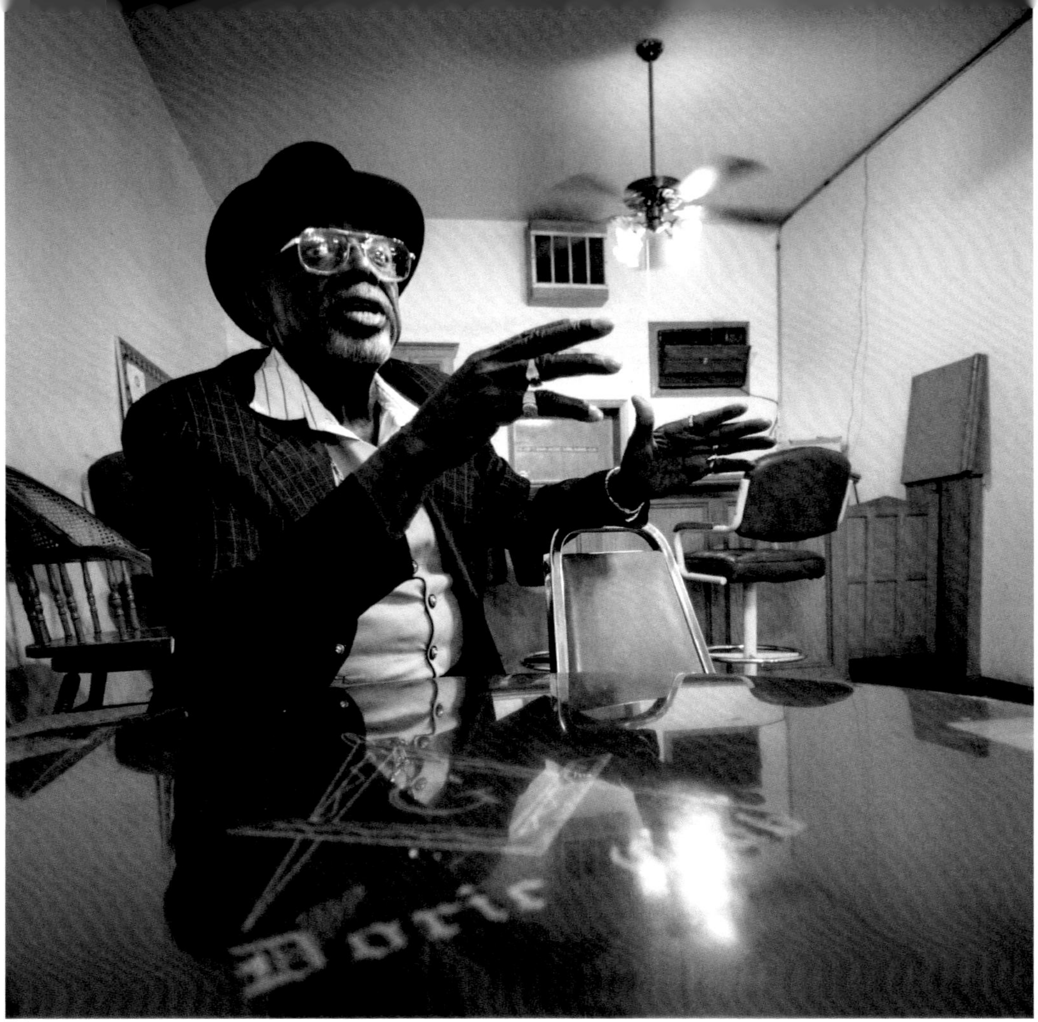

79.

"Going into the military, that was our way out of the south," Billy McCloud mused one afternoon, his sunglasses reflecting the palm tree nearby. That palm was only three feet tall back when the Mercantile Hall was built; it towers now into the sky. McCloud, whom passersby jokingly call "The Mayor of Riverside," adjusted his diamond ring and said, "I would have made a slave ten minutes. I would have told them to find a tree – not for me, but for them."

Coleman nodded and looked across the park. Gomez' dog lay at his feet, and Henry Glover said, "I heard *that*." ■

73. *Sharing afternoon stories in front of Orange Valley Lodge #13, LeRoy Barber, Billy McCloud, and Henry Glover*

74. *Dinner for the 28th Anniversary of Orange Valley Lodge #13, with the Eastern Star Chapter 8, 1933*

75. *LeRoy Barber, Master Mason, dressed for a Friday evening inside Orange Valley Lodge #13, in the same room 80 years later, March, 2013*

76. *Mercantile Hall at 2931 Twelfth Street built by David Stokes, which became home for Orange Valley Lodge #13, and also Stokes & Wiley Grocery store; palm tree approximately 12 feet tall, 1912*

77. *Holding court at Orange Valley Lodge*

78. *The chorus of story at Orange Valley Lodge*

79. *LeRoy Barber, inside Orange Valley Lodge #13 at the table where his name is inscribed*

80. *Gonzalo Gomez, Henry Glover, Dean Newton, Travis Coleman, and Billy McCloud – almost every day, catching up on past and present – palm tree 101 years old*

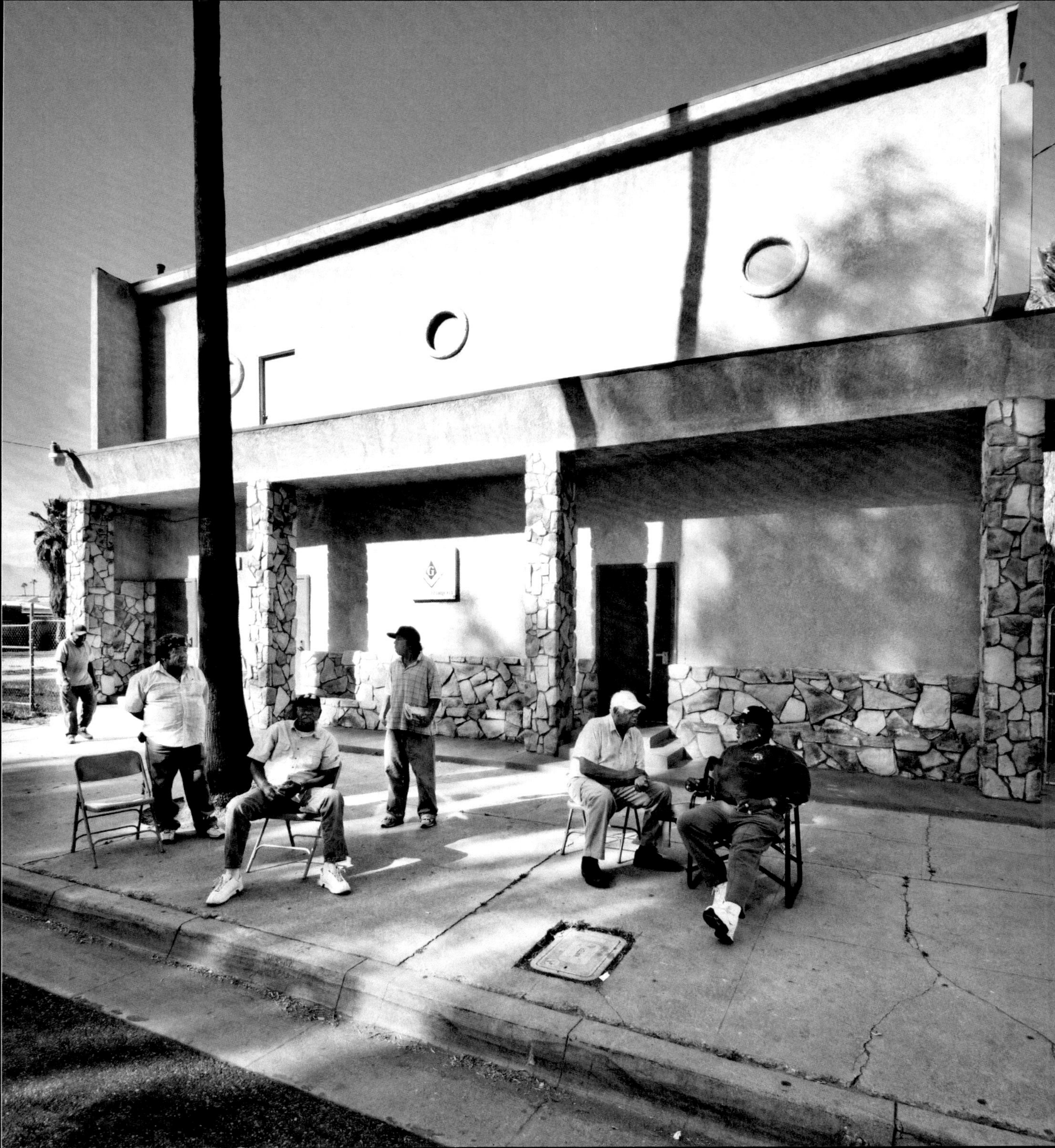

80.

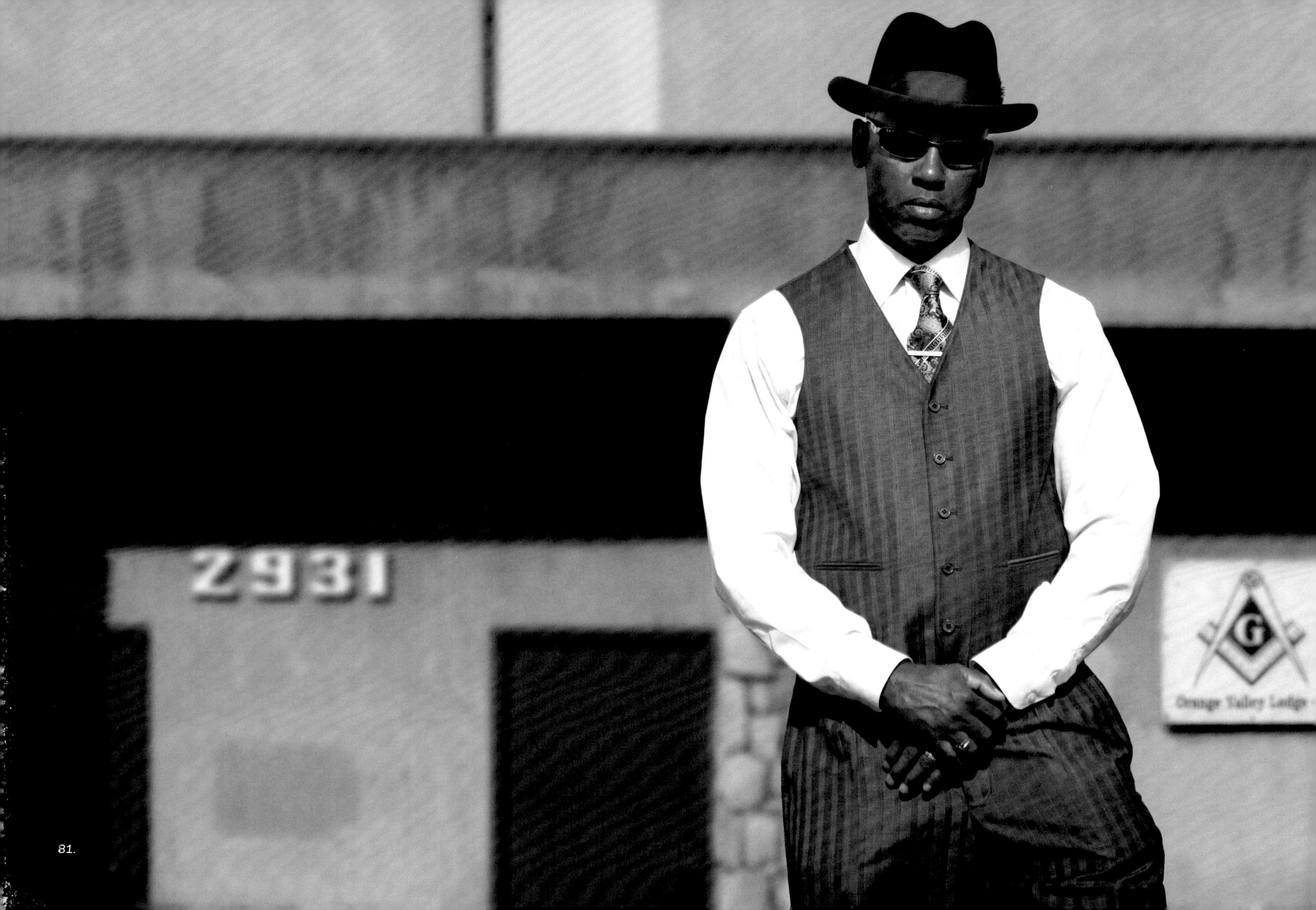
2931

Sacred Ground and Resolution on Victoria Avenue

“I could feel the heat, see the flames from my bedroom window – it was on the second floor,” Mike Bartee said. “We lived on Denton. It was Lowell School burning.”

It was a Sunday night, in the fall of 1965, just before the school year was to begin. Lowell School, where once only “a few high-performing Black or Mexican-American kids went,” according to Dorella Anderson, “like my uncle,” had changed dramatically when Alcott School was built on the other side of Victoria Country Club. Suddenly, almost every white child went to Alcott – and Lowell was falling apart.

It was a time of unrest – Eastside parents were angry about the inequities. Organizers had prepared to speak about substandard books, little food at the cafeteria, neglect at the building, and demand desegregation, to the school board. But that Sunday night, the school was aflame by some means, and to this day, no one knows how the fire was set, or who set it.

John Bennett was supposed to begin first grade at Lowell, and instead, he did his first day of lessons in a room on the second floor of the Orange Valley Lodge, under the direction of an older white man who had arrived to teach him. “A Freedom School,” it was called – just like the ones in the South, where civil rights battles were fierce. A photo published in The Press-Enterprise showed the man leaning over Bennett to help – a scene that could have been out of Mississippi.

Arthur Littleworth was already thinking about what to do. “It was a time of anger,” he said softly. His father had been born in England, a man in charge of hunting dogs on a huge estate; Littleworth was born in northern California, but had seen segregation during the war, and then in the city where he’d moved. While most of the Lowell buildings were smoldering rubble, the debates began. Should Riverside’s schools integrate? Art Littleworth was president of the Riverside School Board. “I thought we should be one city,” he said simply the other day, at his house in a hundred-year-old orange grove – on Victoria Avenue, only a few miles from where Lowell had burned. “One city.”

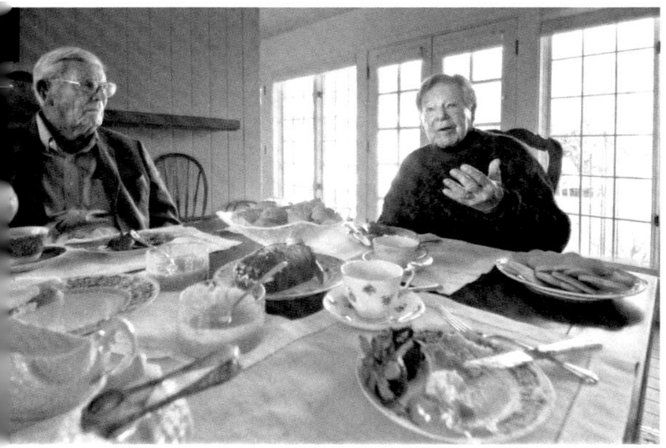

82.

Littleworth drew up a plan to bus Black and Mexican-American students from Irving and Lowell Schools, as well as Casa Blanca School, which were nearly all minority enrollment, to Highland and Hyatt Schools. This wasn't an easy decision – he sat on a stage at Irving School, Dell Roberts beside him, while invective and questions were hurled with equal force. As Judge John Gabbert recalled at Littleworth's house, sitting beside his friend, "Riverside had plenty of people who never wanted their children to mix. There was a strong Ku Klux Klan presence here in the 1920s – that's sometimes forgotten, but there was animus and distrust." Art Littleworth's stance was brave – he actually slept at the houses of various friends, for protection from possible retribution.

But Riverside became the first school district in America to voluntarily desegregate, without a court order forcing it to do so. Not easy for many of the children, or their teachers, who were bused away from the Eastside – Susan Strickland said, "I was teaching at Emerson then, and they took two of us teachers out of Emerson and had us ride the bus with the kids. I went to Highland. I had second grade. Lydia Wilson was probably in sixth grade, and one day early on, her teacher used the n-word. Oh, Marcille Wilson was upset. She called me right away and said, I'm headed up there to that principal in the morning." Marcille Wilson's family lived on Michael Street; she ran a successful hair salon. She spoke her mind, strongly, at Highland. "And Darryl Jones – he was the smartest kid I'd ever had at math – his teacher put him down from third grade to first because she said his math wasn't good. He lasted one day there – that teacher sent him right back up. You know Darryl graduated from college as a math major!" Her laughter pealed out, but she shook her head.

I was there, in kindergarten at Highland Elementary. My mother walked me the first day, and I walked the one block alone after that. I saw the big yellow buses, and wished for seven years that I could ride a bus with my face pressed to the window, as I'd seen on television. But because of Lowell School and desegregation, I never knew classrooms were not mixed almost equally with white, Black and Mexican-American students. For all those years, we were together on playground swings and sports teams, in the auditorium at Highland where I was the only white girl on my sixth grade dance team (I was so clumsy that Janet Aubert, Tyra Tatum, and Toni Winston had me in charge of the record player while they did a routine to "ABC" by the Jackson Five, but we did have matching dance outfits).

We all went to the new University Junior High, built in the orange groves equidistant from several neighborhoods. (I continued in my literal bookishness – when someone wrote lovely scripted words in marker on bulletin boards in my classroom – Eastside Rules – I waited for weeks for the actual rules to appear below.) We began to fall in love. I met my future husband there. And that is what Lowell's legacy, through Littleworth and Roberts and Strickland, accomplished. Dennis and Virginia Saucedo – whose father went to Irving School – married people of other races. Robert Magby married Jaime Troup, my kindergarten friend at Highland. Our children all went to school together – their skins and hair and voices the mélange of the future before the rest of America had figured it out.

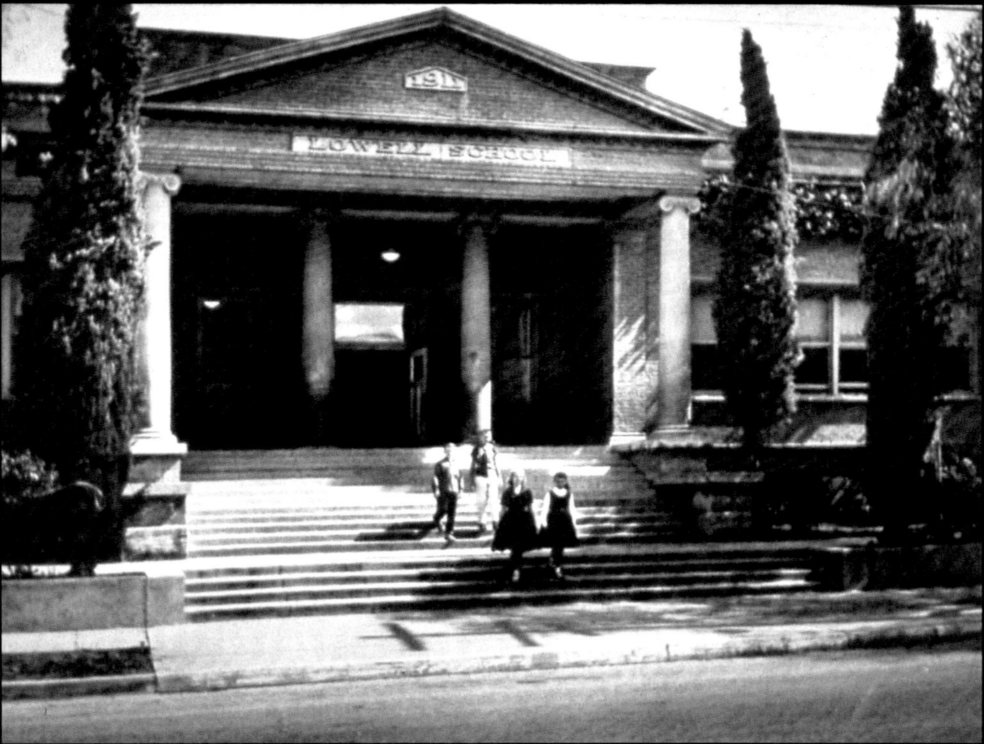

83.

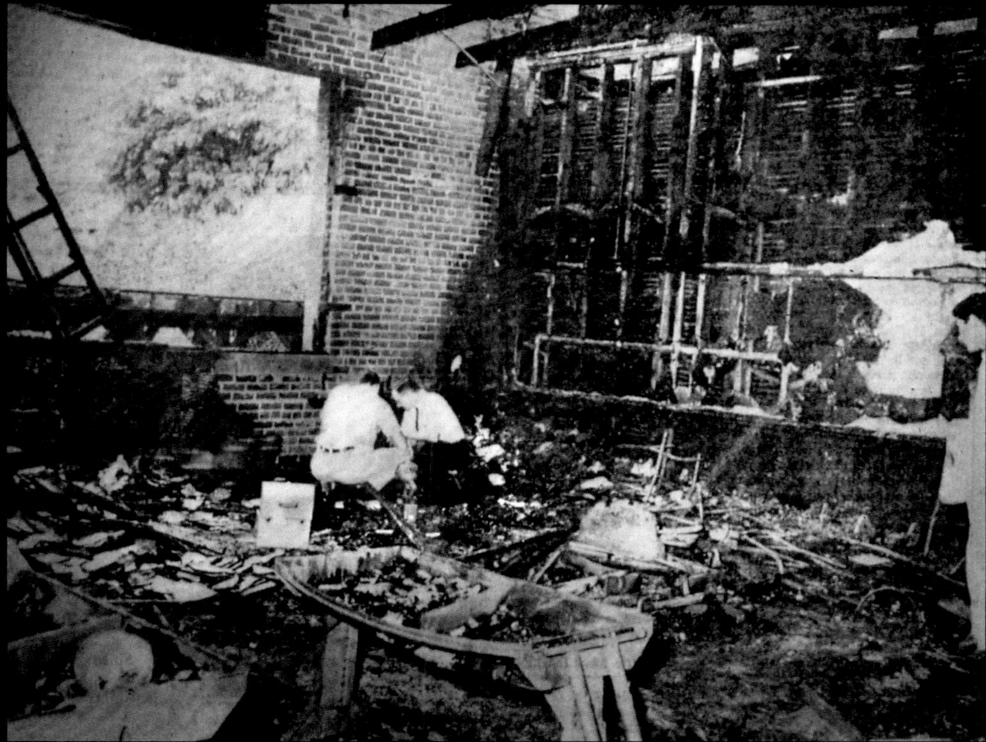

84.

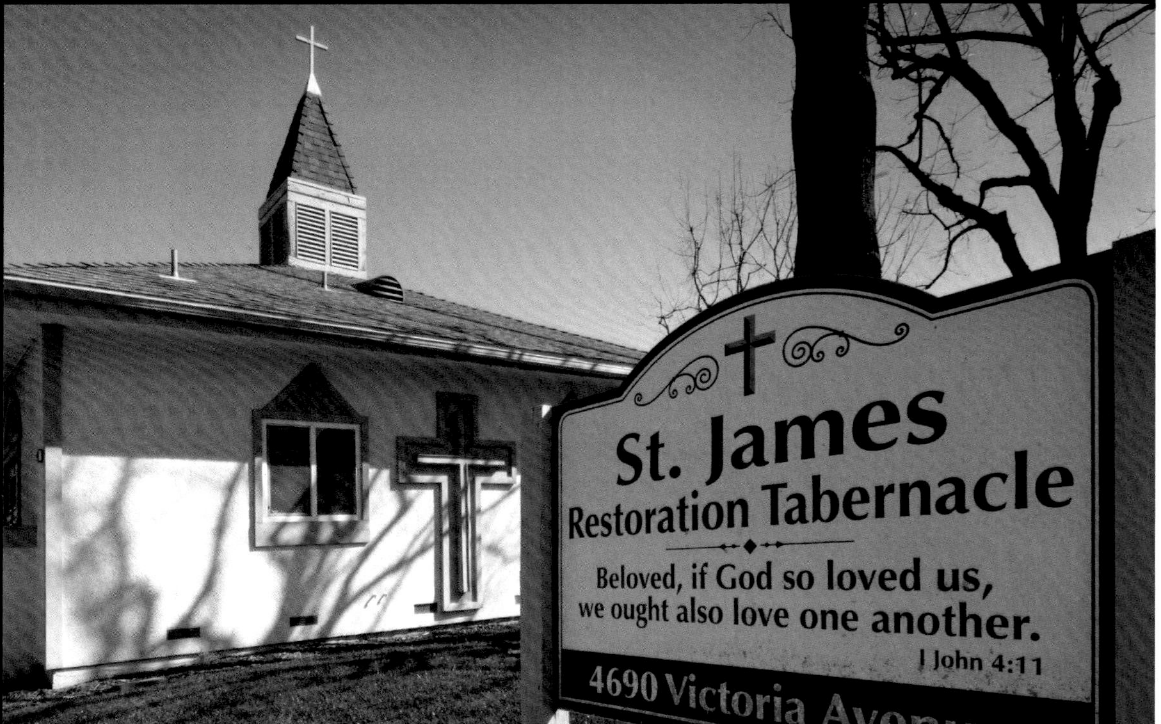

85.

The burned buildings were eventually cleared, and I remember seeing a ghostly forest on Victoria, towering eucalyptus with gleaming bone-white trunks near a lone building. That wood-frame building, with a bell tower at the front, was the kindergarten classroom.

A cross eventually crowned that bell tower. The land was bought by St. James Church of God in Christ, which had been worshipping in a small building on 11th Street since 1931. Pastor James E. Wall led the church, but it was his son Jesse who pressed him to buy the forest at Victoria and Cridge.

Jesse Wall was born in Mississippi in 1933. "I was three years old when I left there, thanks be to God, and we went to San Antonio, Texas until 1941. I came to Riverside to see my grandmother, on 11th Street." That was Margaret Henderson, a midwife who'd left Sunflower County in 1921. She was Daisy Carter's aunt. "My mother and I stayed with her. When it came time for me to go back, my mother wrote to my father, who was still in Texas: 'We're never coming back – Jesse will get his education here.' Solena Wall had plans.

Jesse and his mother worked with Daisy Carter and the four sisters, his cousins, at the Turkey House on Tenth Street. "The whole family would go down there and help the mothers pluck those turkeys – they came on the railroad cars every day. It was a competition, maybe 30 people. It was one of the few places we could work." Jesse Wall attended Longfellow, Riverside Poly, and got his degree at Cal State Los Angeles; he returned to Riverside to become the city's first Black teacher, at Ramona High, in 1959. By 1966, he was a school administrator, and when Lowell burned, he said, "It was an act of violence. Destruction of a school building. And I heard the board say, We need to do something about this eyesore." He went to his father with a plan to buy the 5.2 acres for a new church and a senior citizen housing complex.

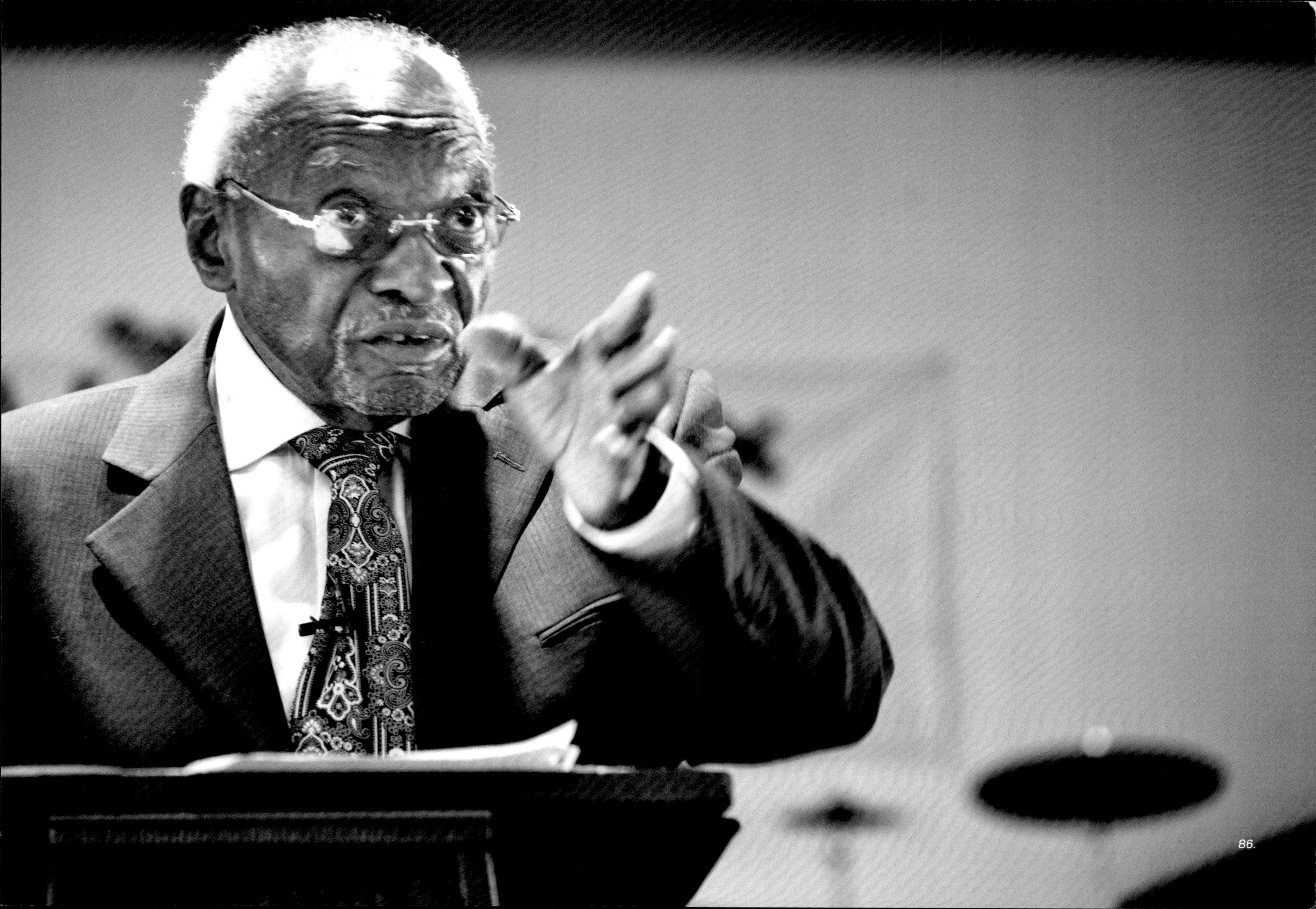

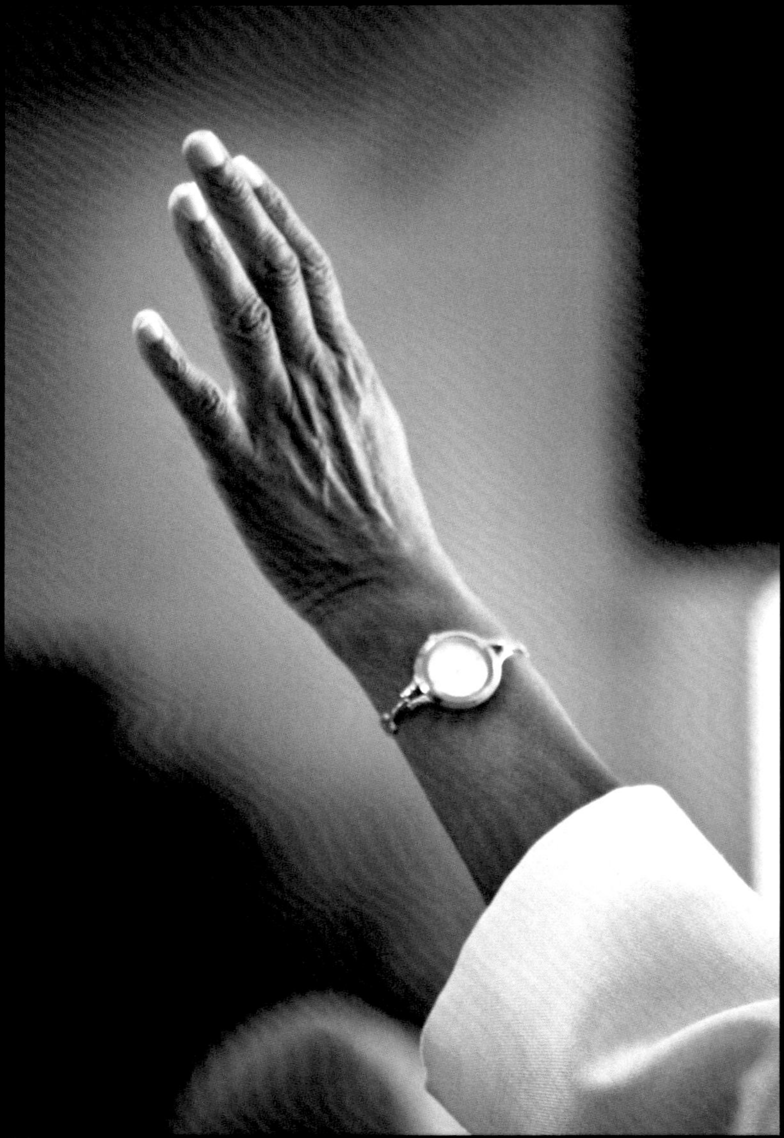

"My father said, 'It's too much. My mother got out of her bed and said, James, Jesse has a job, and white people listen to him. You should listen to your son.'" His voice rose as if he were still convincing his father, fifty years later. In 1967, historic cooperation for Riverside continued, with Truman Johnson, President of Sterling Savings, telling Jesse, "I will help you get this land – I will hold the paper." The school board accepted the offer – $36,000 – and the church paid off the mortgage in 1982.

Some of the century-old eucalyptus trees still stand among the two-story buildings, where the landscaping is eternally pristine and the apartments always renovated. Jesse Wall gestured around the paths where senior residents walked. "I was born to do this," he said.

Just vacant is the place where Stanford Samuels lived – a son of Myrtle Morris Samuels, cousin to Jesse Wall. Stanford passed away in 2012, and his neighbors visited around the corner from his apartment the other day. Connie Alvarez and her mother Aurora Perez, who is 93, have lived here for two years. "It's perfect, affordable, and I go to my Zumba class at Bobby Bonds," Alvarez said. Ella Stewart and Florence Carpenter talked nearby. "I've been here three years in August," Carpenter said. "I got myself settled the first week, then went to church right there" – she pointed at the old school building, where St. James holds services – "the second week." Where once rang the voices of children playing, the choir and Jesse Wall can be heard through the trees. Stewart said, "You know, before they built this, Pastor James Wall – the daddy – he walked the land and prayed over it and blessed it. He sure did. This is sacred ground." ■

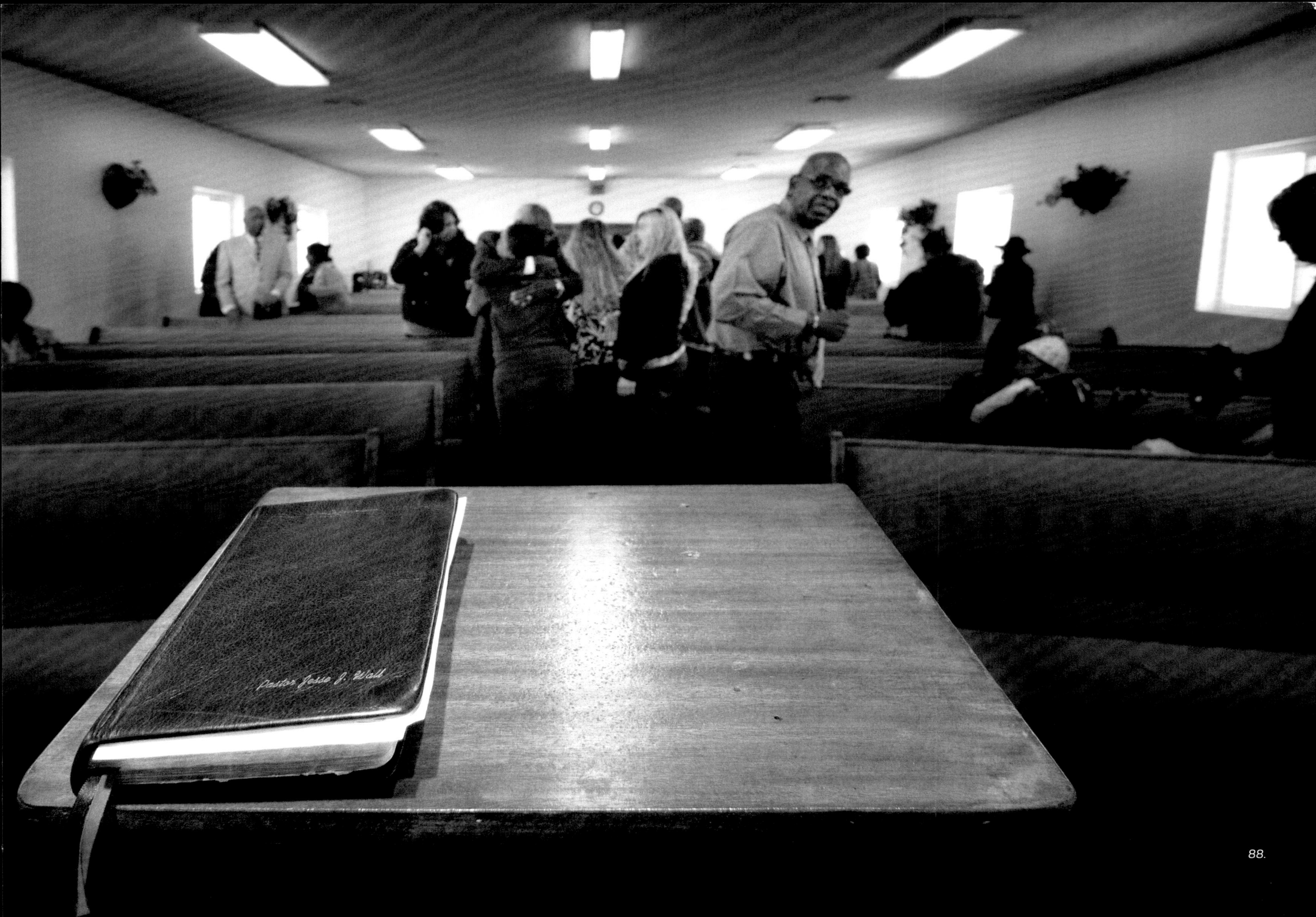
Pastor Jesse J. Wall

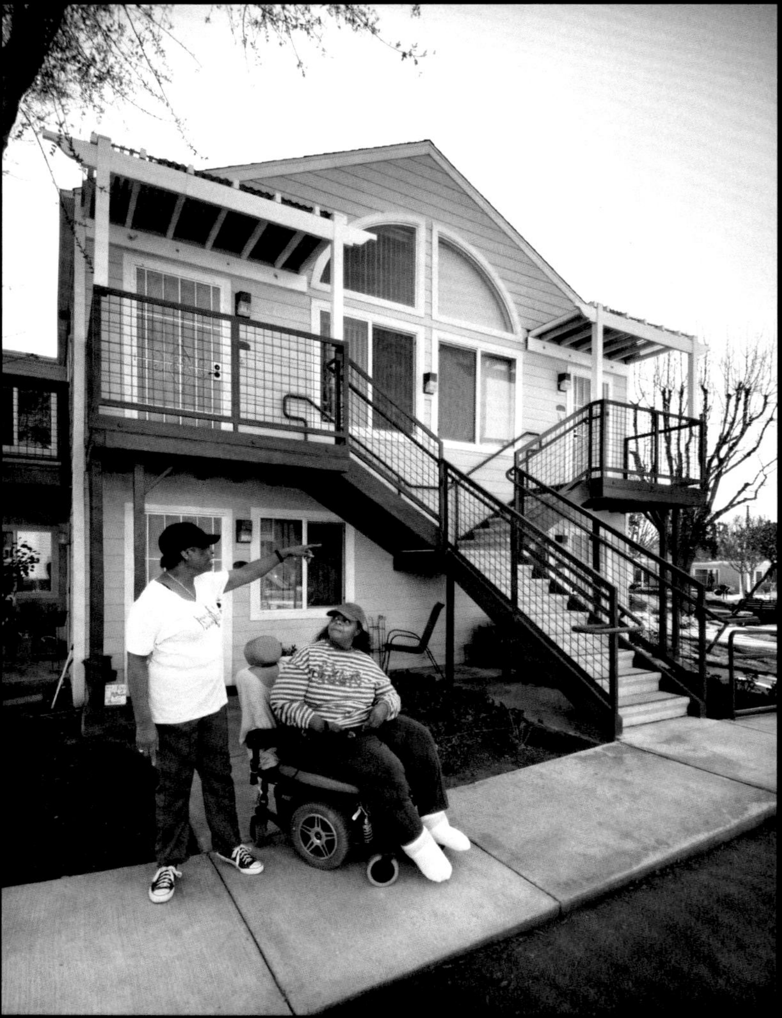

89.

81. *John Bennett at Orange Valley Lodge #13, where he attended a temporary Freedom School after Lowell School was burned in 1965, just before he began 1st grade*

82. *Arthur Littleworth, in his house on Victoria Avenue a few miles from both schools; as president of the Riverside School Board in 1965, he engineered the voluntary desegregation of schools after Lowell was destroyed by arson*

83. *Lowell School on Victoria Avenue, built in 1912 to allow white students to leave Irving School, only a few blocks away; very few Black or Mexican-American students could transfer there, date unknown*

84. *Arson investigators in the burned shell of Lowell School, published September 7, 1965, by Bob Ringquist, The Press*

85. *St. James Restoration Tabernacle, housed in the renovated kindergarten building of Lowell School, with the original 1912 tower*

86. *Pastor Jesse Wall at Sunday service, St. James Restoration Tabernacle*

87. *Faithful hand raised in devotion, St. James Restoration Tabernacle*

88. *Bible belonging to Pastor Jesse Wall on his pulpit, after services at St. James Restoration Tabernacle*

89. *Ella Stewart and Florence Carpenter, residents of J.E. Wall Victoria Manor, senior apartments built by Pastor James Wall and his son Jesse Wall on the site of the former Lowell School*

90. *Open Bible in the pews, St. James Restoration Tabernacle*

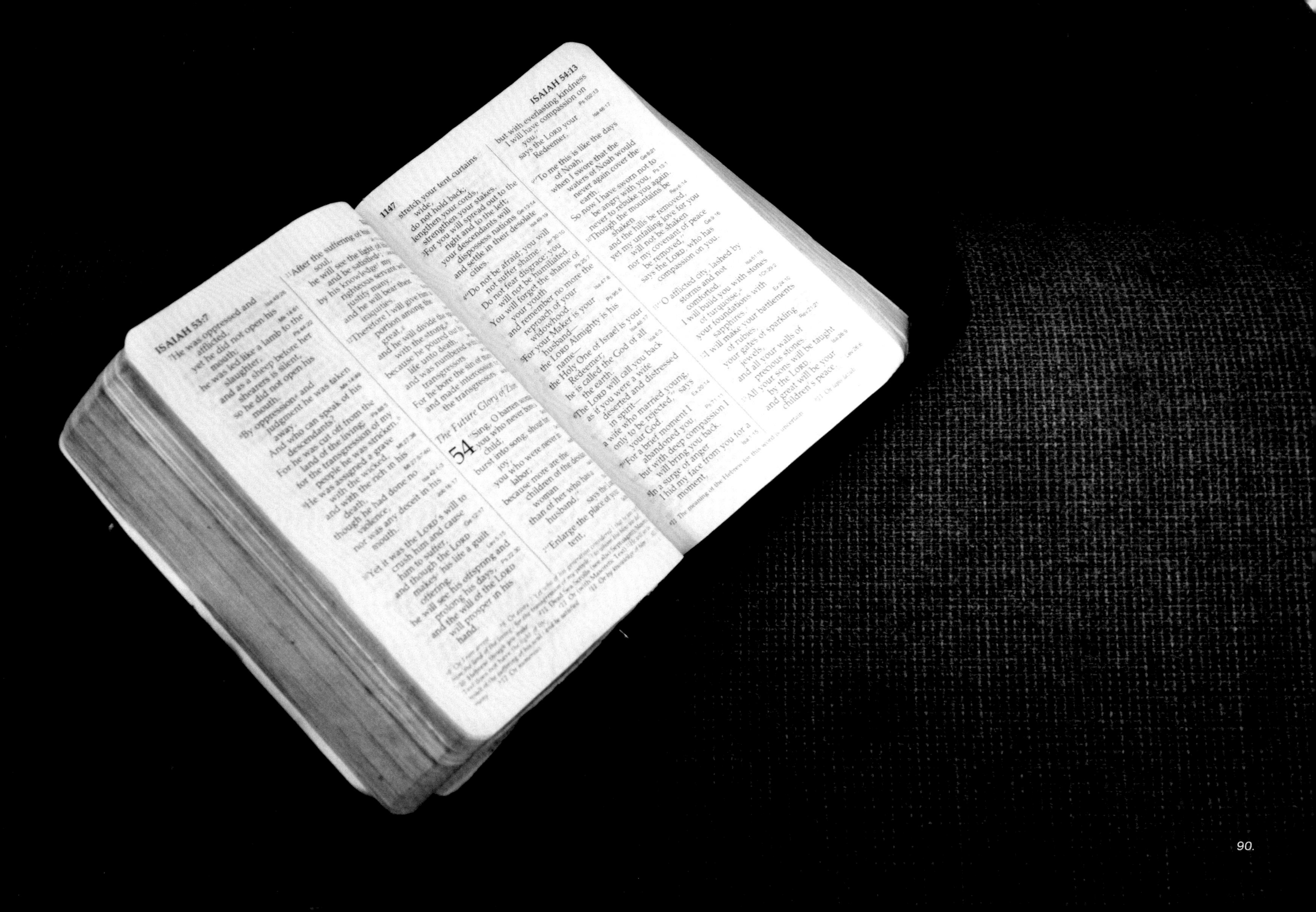
ISAIAH 53:7
1147
ISAIAH 54:13

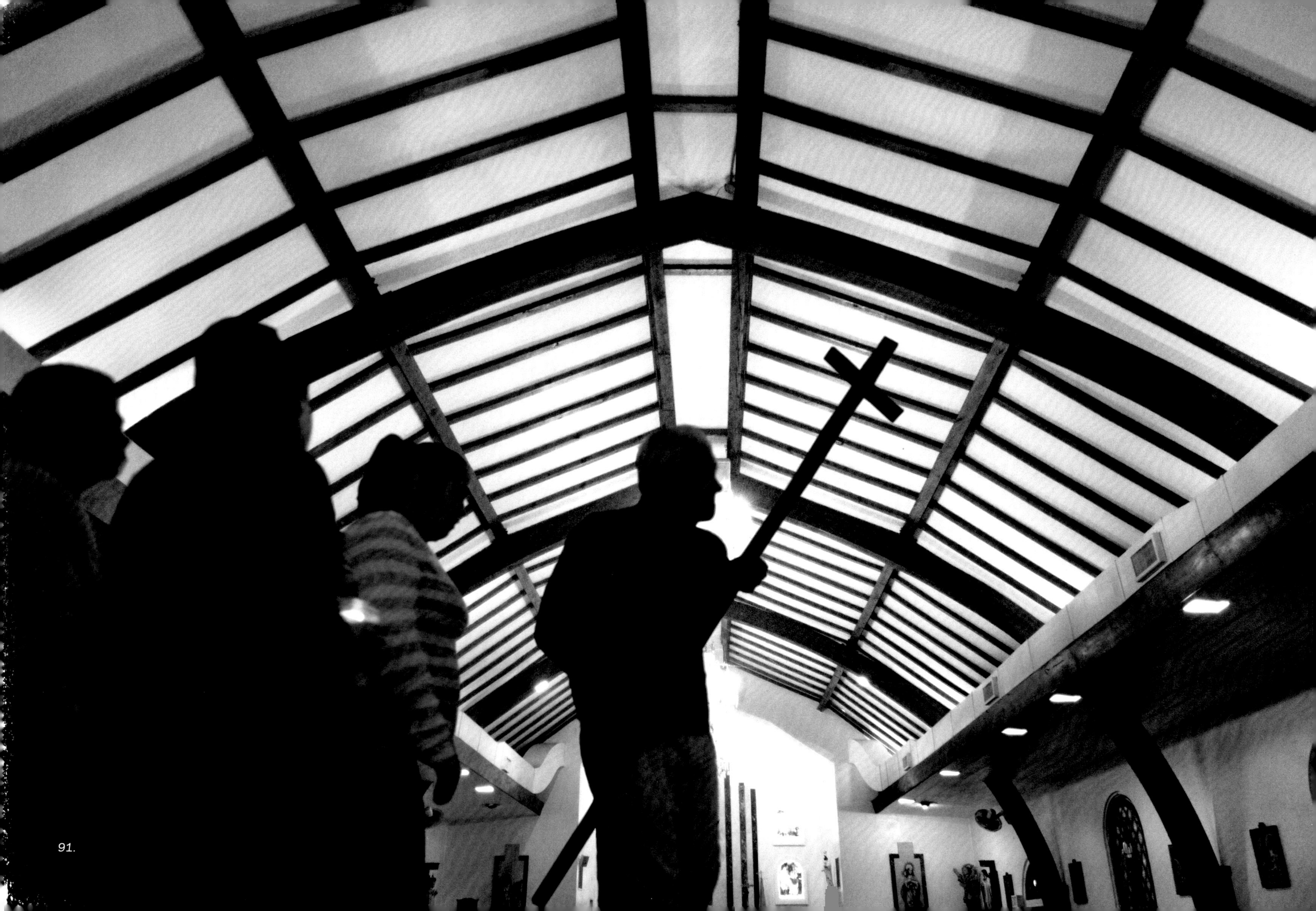

Tracing the Ashes, Ringing the Bells: The Shrine of Our Lady of Guadalupe

On Ash Wednesday, a steady stream of people came through the arched gateway of Our Lady of Guadalupe, headed down the sunlit center aisle, paused before the altar and received the cross of dark ashes on their foreheads. Babies whose skin had never been marked with soot, abuelas who had been coming here for fifty years, and some who had recently arrived from Central America. Tony and Sarah Lopez sat outside the church on the low rock wall near a statue of the patron saint, pointing down Ninth Street to where you could actually see the front yard of their house. "It's my father's house," Sarah said. "He bought it in the 1940s. He used to open the church in the morning, and close it at night. My mother used to bring him breakfast sometimes here, and dinner."

Sarah grew up on Eleventh Street, having come to Riverside when she was very small. Her father, Felix Vasquez, left Mexico to work for the Southern Pacific Railroad in the early 1900s, and as the family moved from Illinois west toward California, they would sometimes sleep in boxcars. But they stayed here. Sarah was a teenager when Our Lady held its first mass in 1929, before the roof was even on the building. She was 19, a soloist in the choir, singing in Latin, when Tony Lopez, who'd come from Guanajuato, Mexico when he was only 2, who lived on Fourteenth Street, became entranced. (They hadn't met at Irving School when they were children because, as Sarah put it, "You went to look at girls! I went to study!") But when he heard her voice that day, during a concert, he said simply, "I felt something."

They were married at that altar, only a few feet away from where they now sit with shoulders touching. "74 years in August," Sarah said. Tony added, "I walked up here for thirty, forty years. I rang the bells to call the people to Mass. When someone died, I rang the bells to tell the people. A family asked me, Why do you ring the bell when someone dies?" He gestured as if pulling down a rope, hard, and then laughed. "I said, They should have come when I rang the bells on Sunday!"

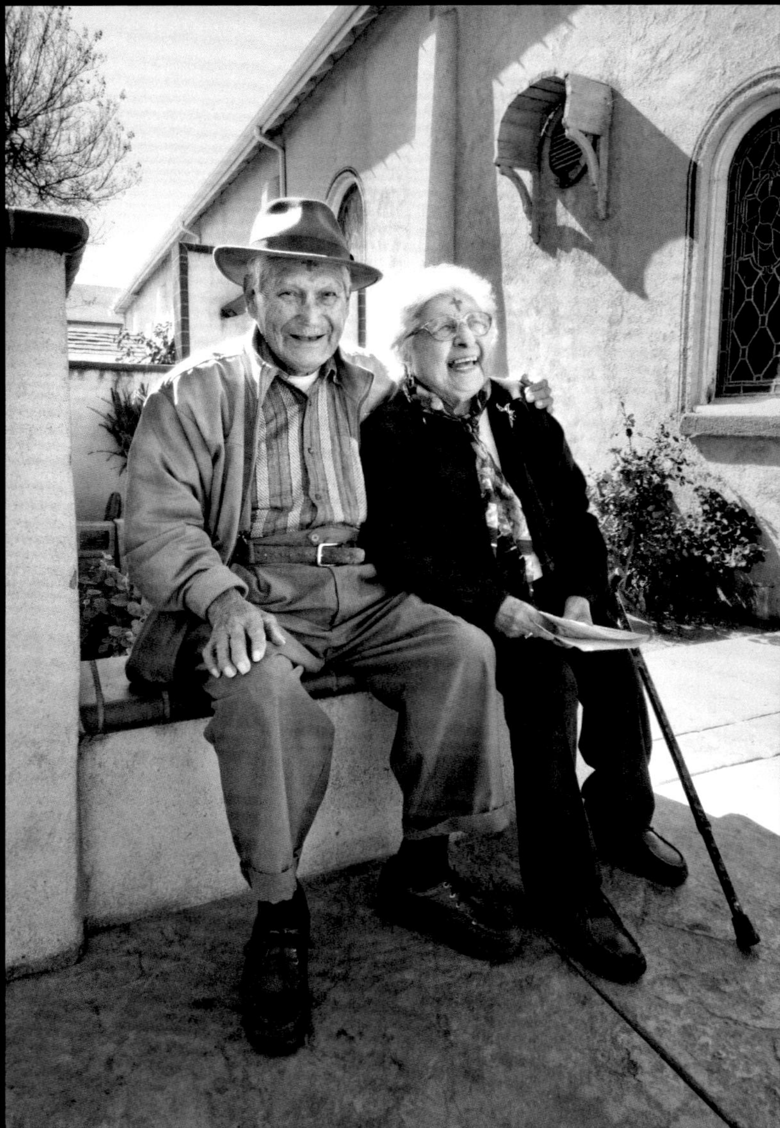

Robert Loya stopped to greet them, his forehead marked now. "I probably spent 50% of my life here, at Our Lady," he said, looking up at the bell tower. His father came in the early 1900s as well, and he remembered the small yellow house which used to stand nearby. For 30 years, the Loyas – including brothers Robert, Henry and Prax - were in charge of "La Gran Fiesta Ranchera," which helped raise the money to buy that land for "new hall" years ago. He took me up into the bell tower, where someone can actually stand in the wood-skeleton structure and see the rope dangling down to hand level, the bell's thick-flared edges high above. He has rung this bell, too.

Coming out into the sunshine, blinking under the first ever smudge of darkness on her forehead, four-month-old Nathalie Martinez is in the arms of her father, Danny Martinez, born on the Eastside, accompanied by his mother, Leticia Vargas, who was born in Mexico. Jasmin Perez, 18 months old, is with her mother Ana Ramirez and grandmother Julia Pinelda, both born in El Salvador. The Lopez's daughter, Theresa, arrives now, noting that for all these decades, new arrivals and natives of California worship together here.

Back in the 1890s, Saint Francis de Sales, in downtown Riverside, was the sole church for the entire parish area, and baptismal records show that 175 English-speaking families and 450 Spanish-speaking families attended. From the Eastside, which had strict residential boundaries then for Mexican-American and Black residents, families would walk downtown in large groups for mass. By 1925, parishioners received permission from the diocese in Los Angeles to raise money for a "mission church," and by 1929, that first mass was held outside the not-completed building, the two bell towers still only wood-framed.

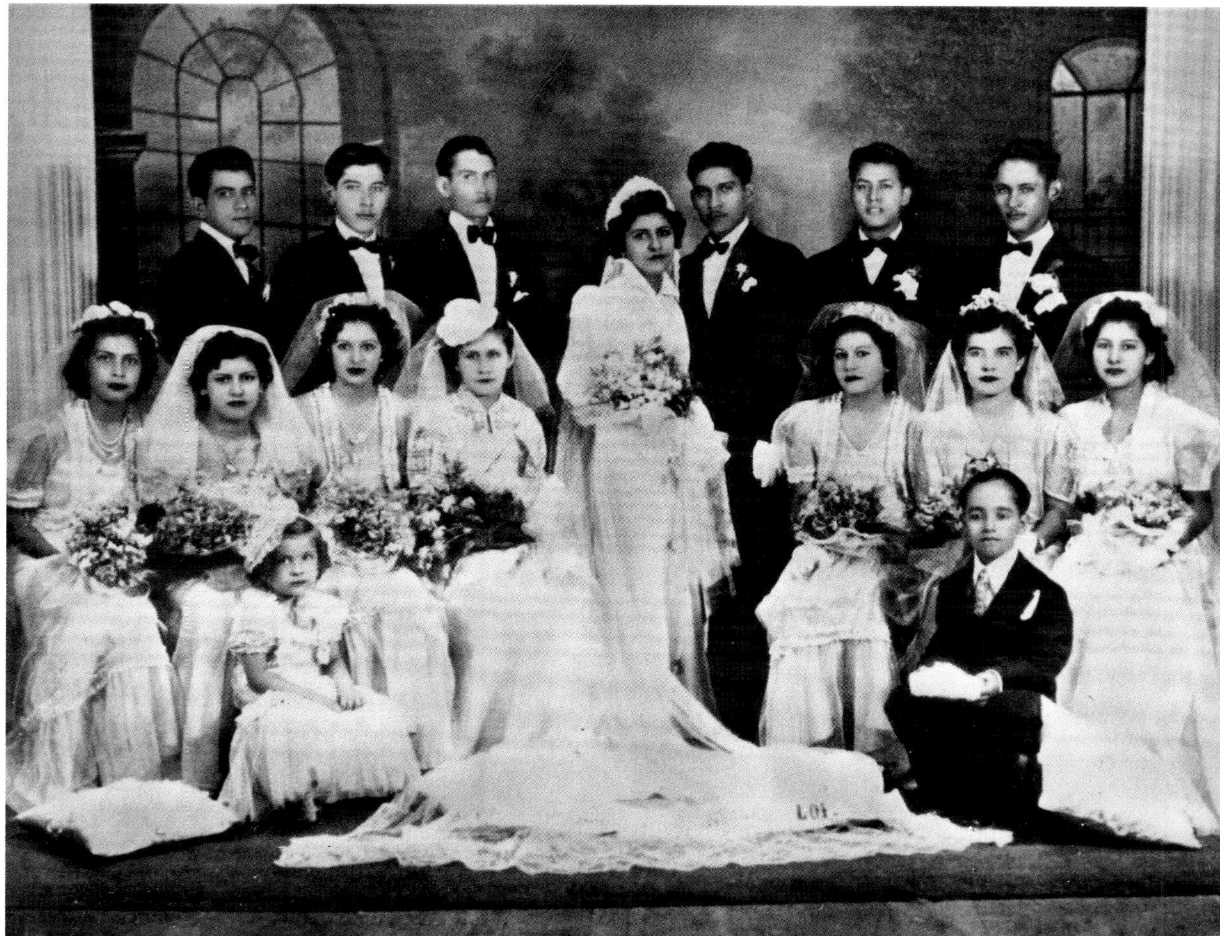

93.

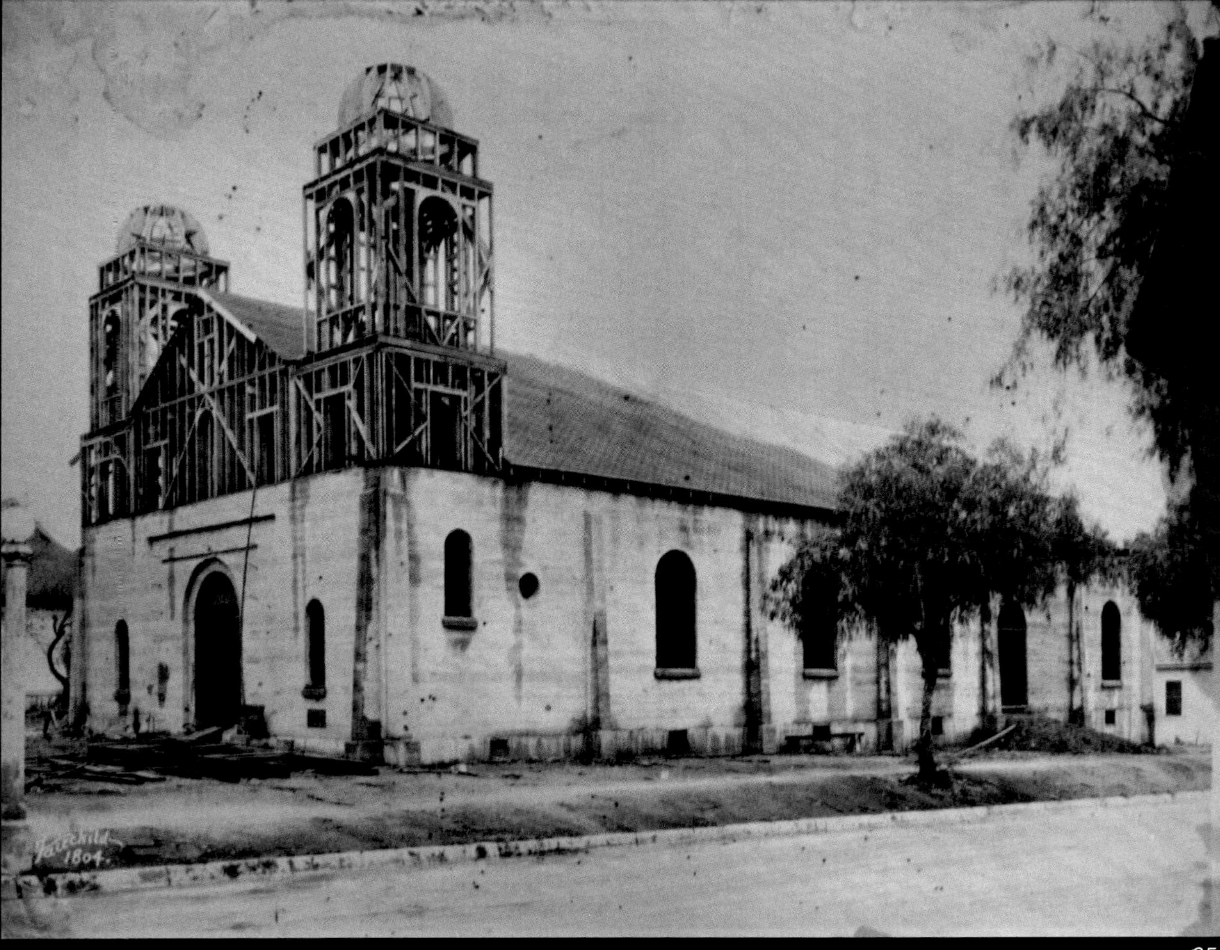
Fairchild.
1804.

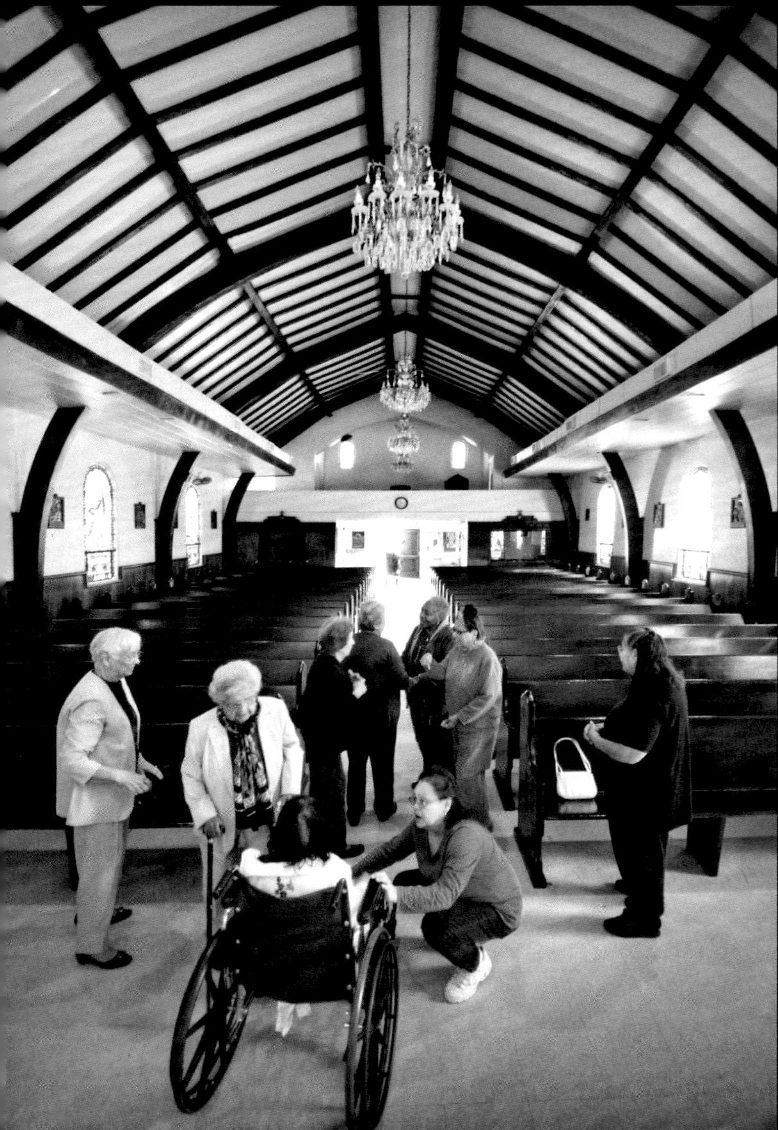

On March 1, 2013, Pope Benedict spent his last day in Rome as pontiff, and a helicopter flew him from St. Peter's to retirement at Castel Gandolfo. But the very next night, twenty people knelt and sang and prayed all the Stations of the Cross on a Friday in Lent at Our Lady. Their voices murmured the prayers in order as they moved about the sanctuary following the light of a white candle. Maria Fuentes headed Las Guadalupanas, which used to have around 30 members but now holds steady at ten women. They host the Blessing of the Sick and other masses, but Friday they are here, facing Christ at each of the moments depicted on the paintings. Their voices rise in sweet minor melancholy for each song, and they move onto the next illustration, kneel briefly, stand again, and continue on the journey.

And on a Friday, just after the morning Mass, the women of The Altar Society, led by current president Rose Calhoun, accompanied by past president Sarah Lopez, moved about the sanctuary completing the other vital part of keeping a church like Our Lady of Guadalupe alive – they cleaned the floors, restored the arrangement of the silver accompaniments on the altar, checked the pews and the sacraments. Rose Calhoun arrived in Riverside in the 1950s from Montgomery, Alabama, a devout Catholic who has worshipped here since, and now she led the rituals which are often overlooked. Tony Lopez happened to walk down the street with his wife, and so the women of the Altar Society fussed over him while they tended to the sacred, and the everyday, in the sunlight that shone through the stained glass windows donated by the old families of Riverside who wanted their own mission, their own Masses, their own devotion on Ninth Street and Park Avenue. ■

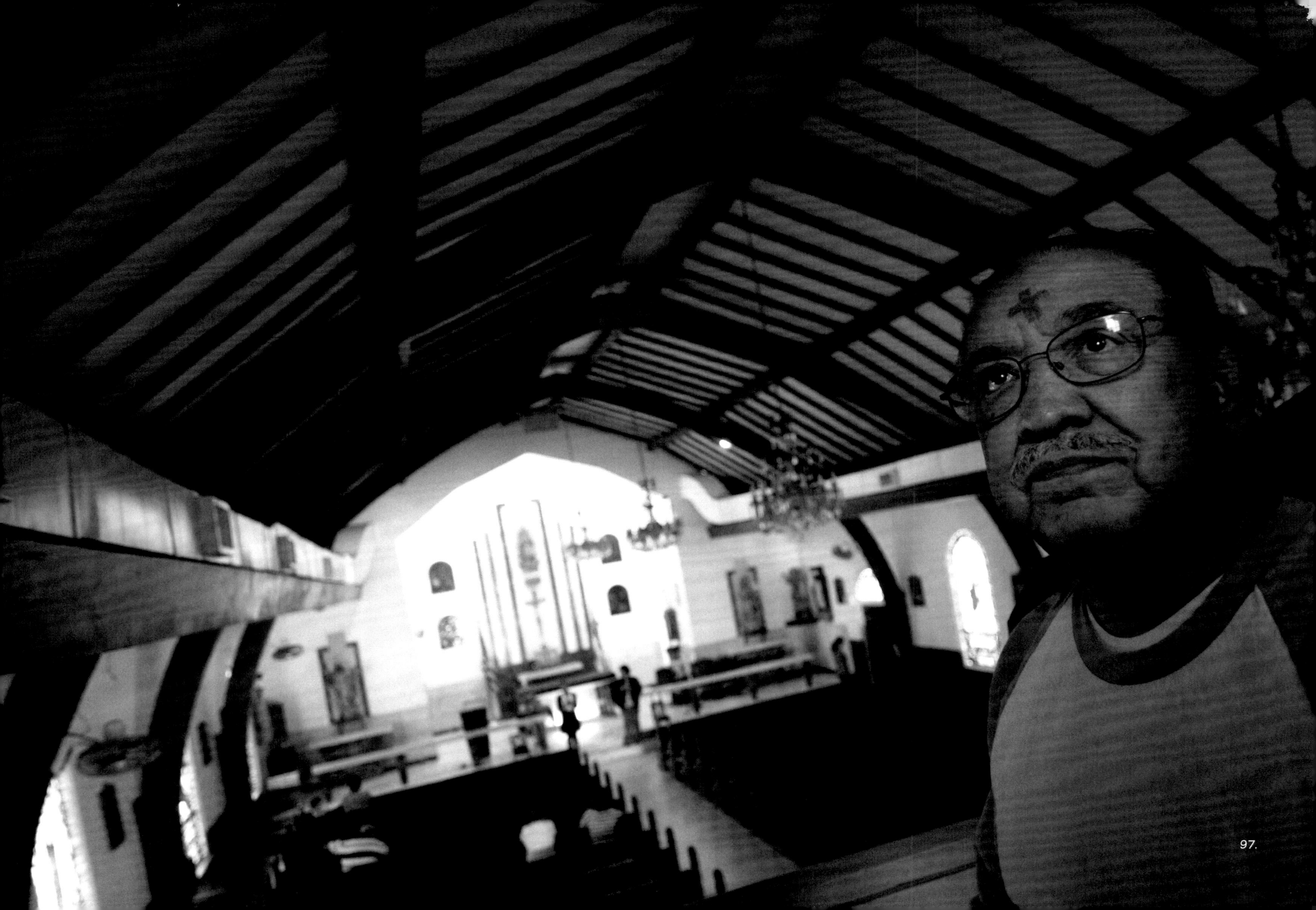

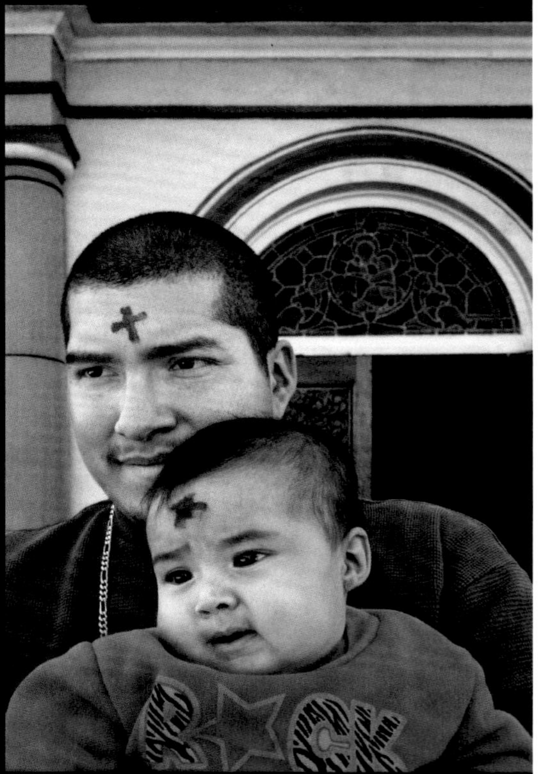

98.

91. *Parishioners at The Shrine of Our Lady of Guadalupe performing The Stations of the Cross with Maria Fuentes and Las Guadalupanas*

92. *Tony and Sarah Lopez, Ash Wednesday at The Shrine of Our Lady of Guadalupe*

93. *The wedding of Tony and Sarah Lopez, just inside the same doors, 73 1/2 years before*

94. *Robert Loya and others on Ash Wednesday at The Shrine of Our Lady of Guadalupe*

95. *Constructing the bell towers, 1929*

96. *Rose Calhoun, president of The Altar Society, Sarah Lopez, past president, and other members preparing to clean the sanctuary after Friday morning Mass*

97. *Robert Loya in the sanctuary – "I've spent 50% of my life here at the church."*

98. *Nathalie Martinez, 4 months old, having just received her first ashes, in the arms of her father Danny Martinez*

99. *Sunday services at The Shrine of Our Lady of Guadalupe, drop-offs at the curb*

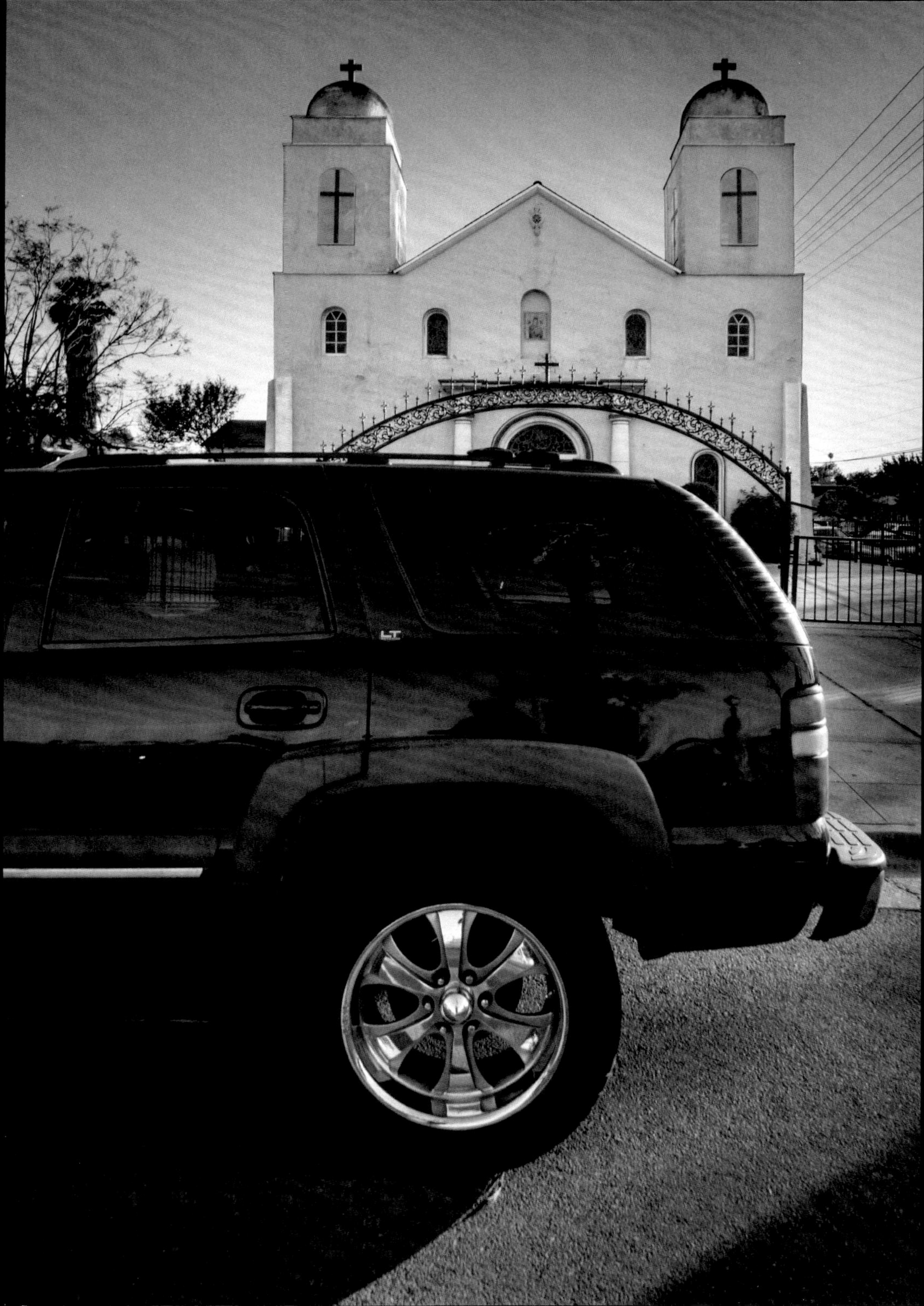

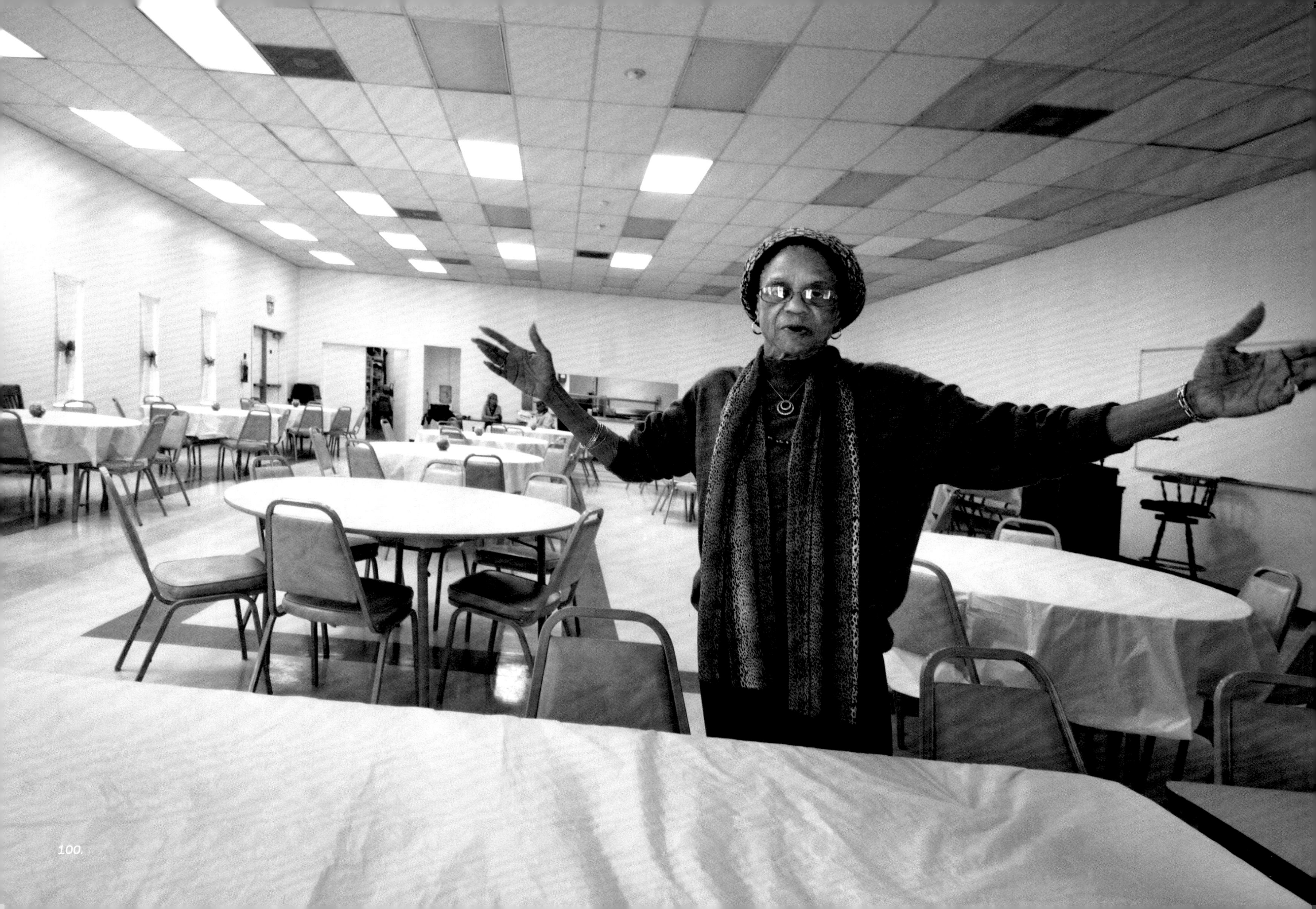

Keepers of the House: Rosaries and Secret Museums

"The past is always with us, in the form of our photographs, which we feel as we might a rosary, wearing them smooth with the fingering of our eyes."

—A.D. Coleman, writer and critic

If not for the living room of Dorella Anderson, where the light from a sliding glass door illuminates a floor spread with hundreds of photos, funeral programs, newspaper stories and announcements, this particular rosary would have few beads. Secret museums flourish in the houses of those willing to "curate" the life of a city. If not for the dining room table of Susan and Reggie Strickland, other chapters would remain unknown. If not for Tony and Sarah Lopez and their daughter Teresa, who placed baked goods and a vase of fresh flowers on their kitchen table before showing Doug historic wedding and Eastside photos, another set of lives might remain hidden.

One day, looking over a historic photograph of Riverside's Black pioneer families gathered at Fairmount Park, Susan Strickland put her finger on a woman's face and mused, "That's my aunt." Dorella Anderson said, "Girl, that's my aunt!" It was true. The woman belonged to both families, by blood and marriage.

Hundreds of stories. Centerpieces and cloths spread over tables. Songs taught to children at Lincoln Park, dances like The Funky Chicken and The Yolk (one before the other?) in the 1970s. Hats made, laps swum, thousands of shoes tied. Alphabets and sentences, bus rides. Meals prepared for church events, hymns sung, and photographs laid faithfully into albums. Dorella handed me another photo – herself, in leotard and tights – very 1970s – to teach dance class at the Settlement House.

On that same stretch of Park Avenue, Susan Strickland touched the fence at the house where she once lived. "My grandmother was making lunch, and my grandfather said, Oh, I couldn't eat lunch today! They're bringing the beams for the new church," Susan Strickland said, in front of Second Baptist, on Park Avenue just across the corner from Our Lady of Guadalupe. "It was 1957. Our house was right there, and we walked down here to see them."

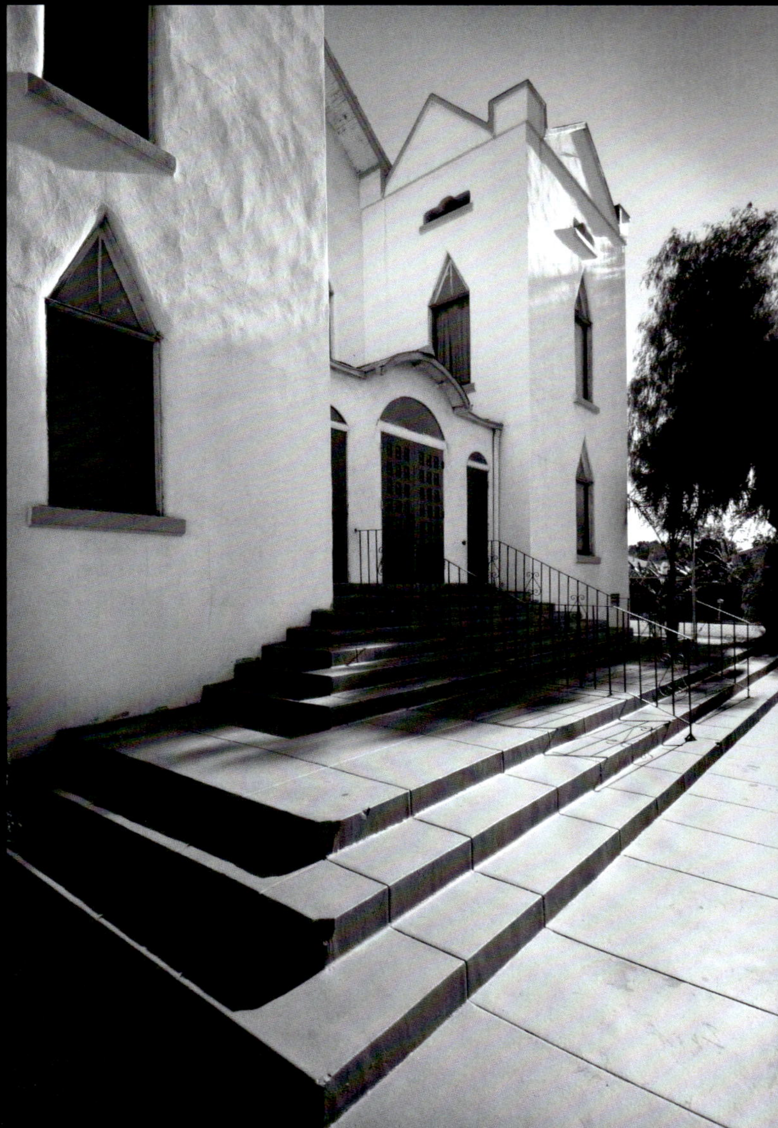

101.

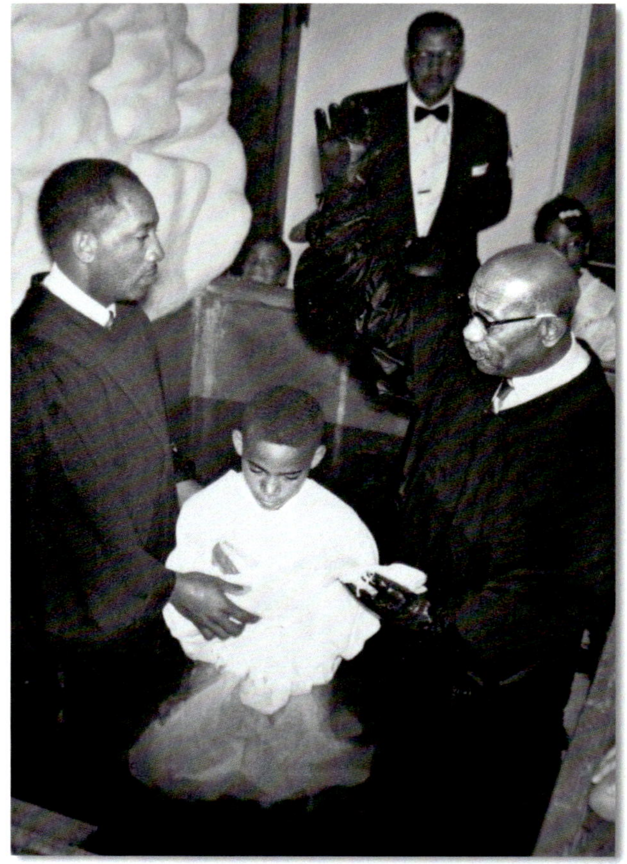

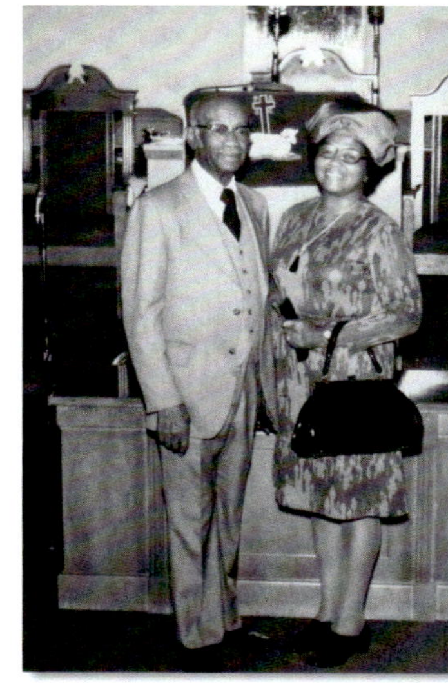

102.

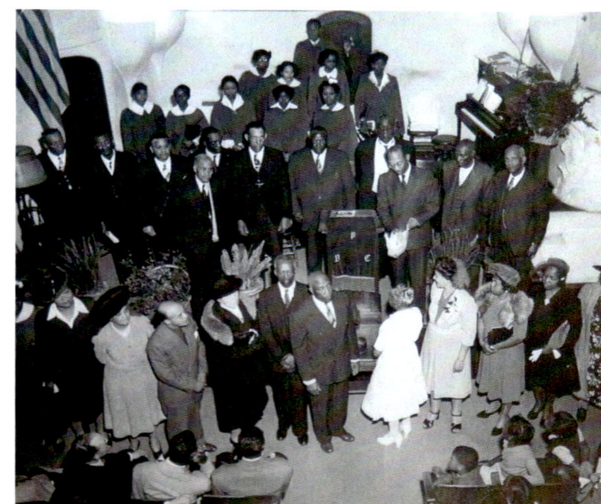

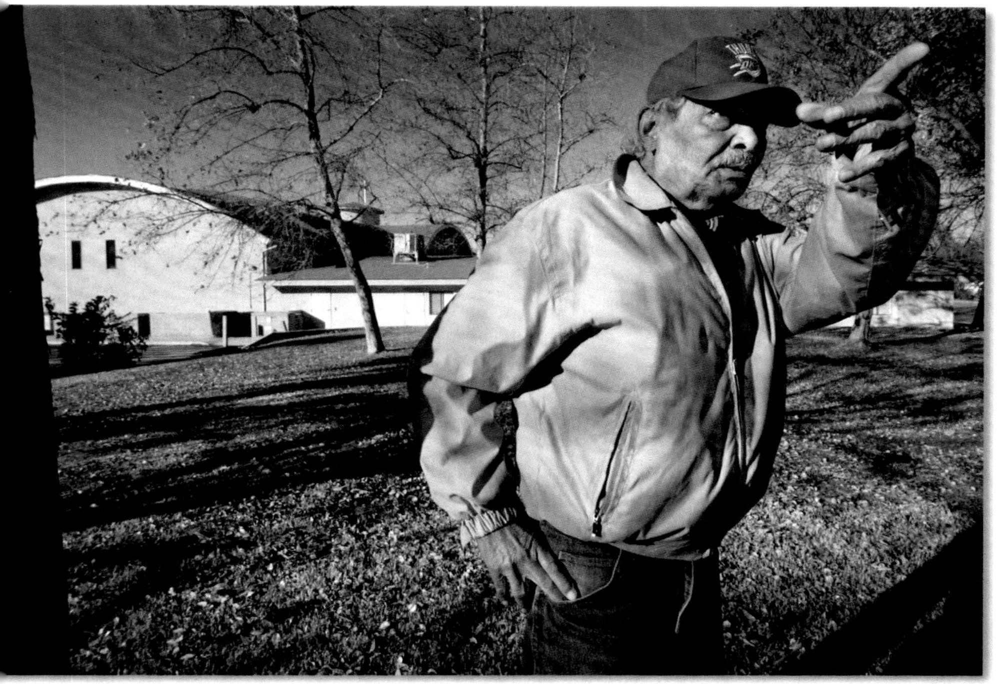

106.

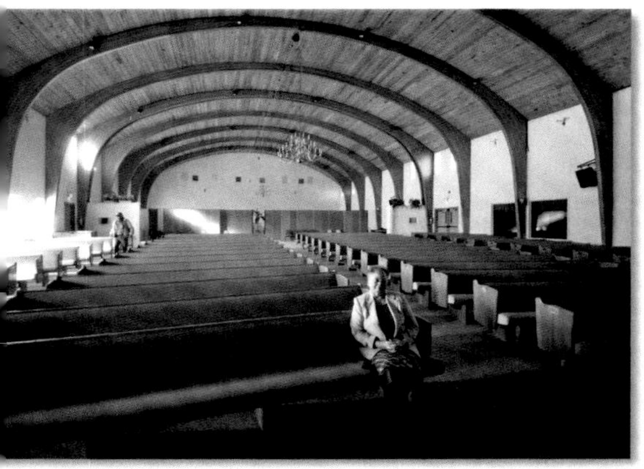

105.

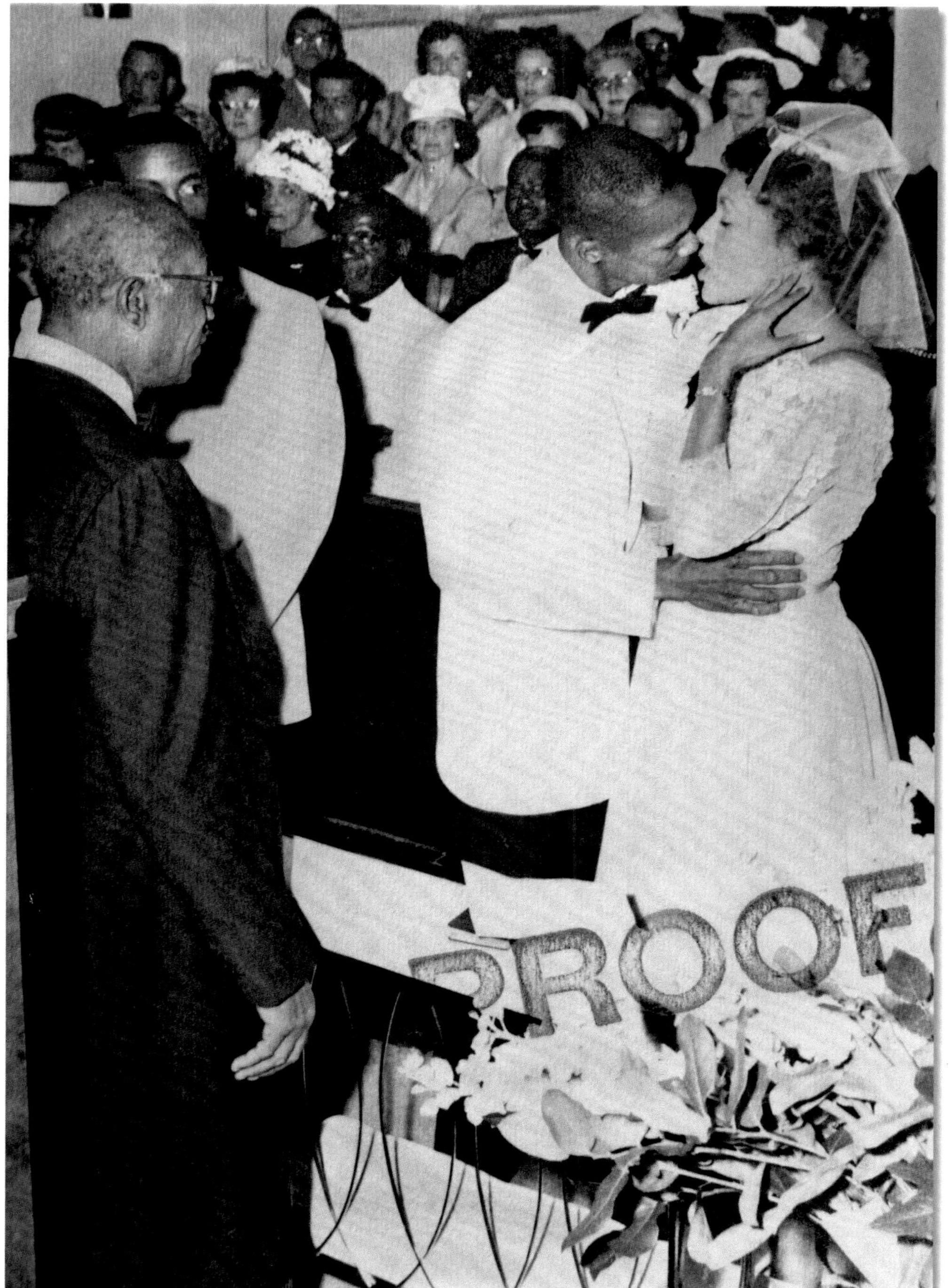

107.

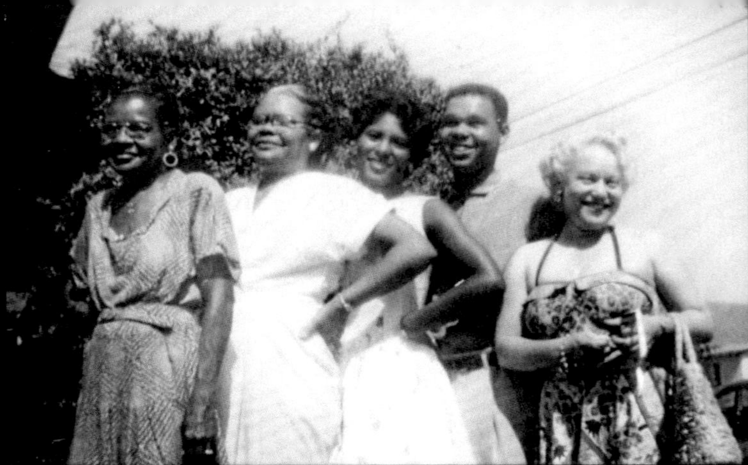

108.

109.

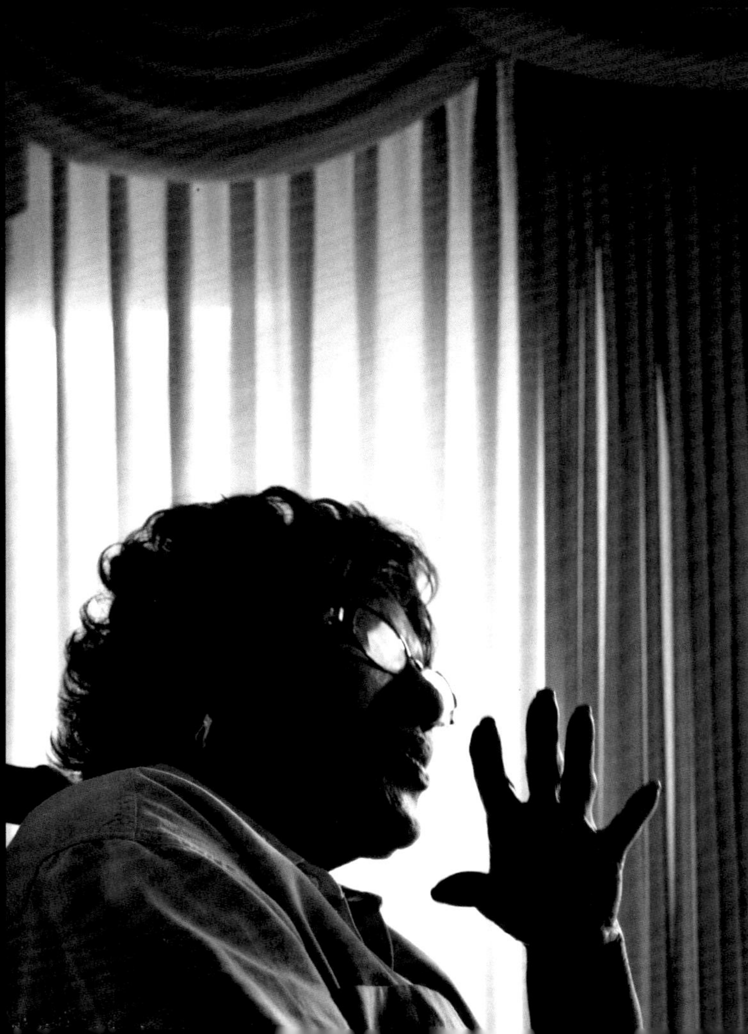

Back at her home, she lay on the polished walnut table a tinted photograph of six men formally dressed, formally posed, their faces grave. “This is my great-grandfather,” she said. “Edward Williams. He fought on both sides of the Civil War – he said they were both about the same.” Williams came to Riverside from Georgia with his youngest son Hayward in the 1890s to visit his sister, Janie Stokes, and his brothers, Walter, Robert and Mose. He came to Riverside permanently in 1926 – and died here when he was 105.

Reggie Strickland’s grandmother Cornelia, born in Rockmart, Georgia, arrived here in 1917. His mother was a singer – “she used to take me to clubs to sit in, and that’s how I learned to play the saxophone. I was only four years old. I started playing in clubs when I was 12 – Arthur’s in Colton, clubs in Los Angeles, San Bernardino, Riverside, all the way to San Diego and Blythe by the time I was 15, and I was making money.” He fanned out, on his side of the table, glossy black & whites of the musicians: Blinky Allen, a Riverside native, Edgar Hayes and the Stardusters, and others. Brothers: golfer Clifford Strickland, firefighter Ed Strickland who hosed flames one night in 1944 at the Victoria Country Clubhouse where he was not allowed to eat.

Another afternoon, Dorella Anderson handed me the Riverside City Basketball Champions, 1924, University Junior High. Twelve boys wearing heavy coats and soft caps. The handsome boy with almond-beige skin and fine features looked somehow familiar. “That’s Tony Lopez,” Anderson said. And there’s my father – George Williams.”

A couple facing each other in an orange grove, shiny black satin dress, shiny black patent shoes. “My grandparents. William G. Goodwin marrying Elizabeth – their wedding. He married me and Marshall, in my mother’s house.” Then a panoramic photo of Goodwins and Williams and Stokes – lawn bowling and croquet at Fairmount Park. “On the day when white people let them play there,” Anderson said. And a picnic. “See that small woman – just there at the edge? Parthenia Goodwin.” She lays

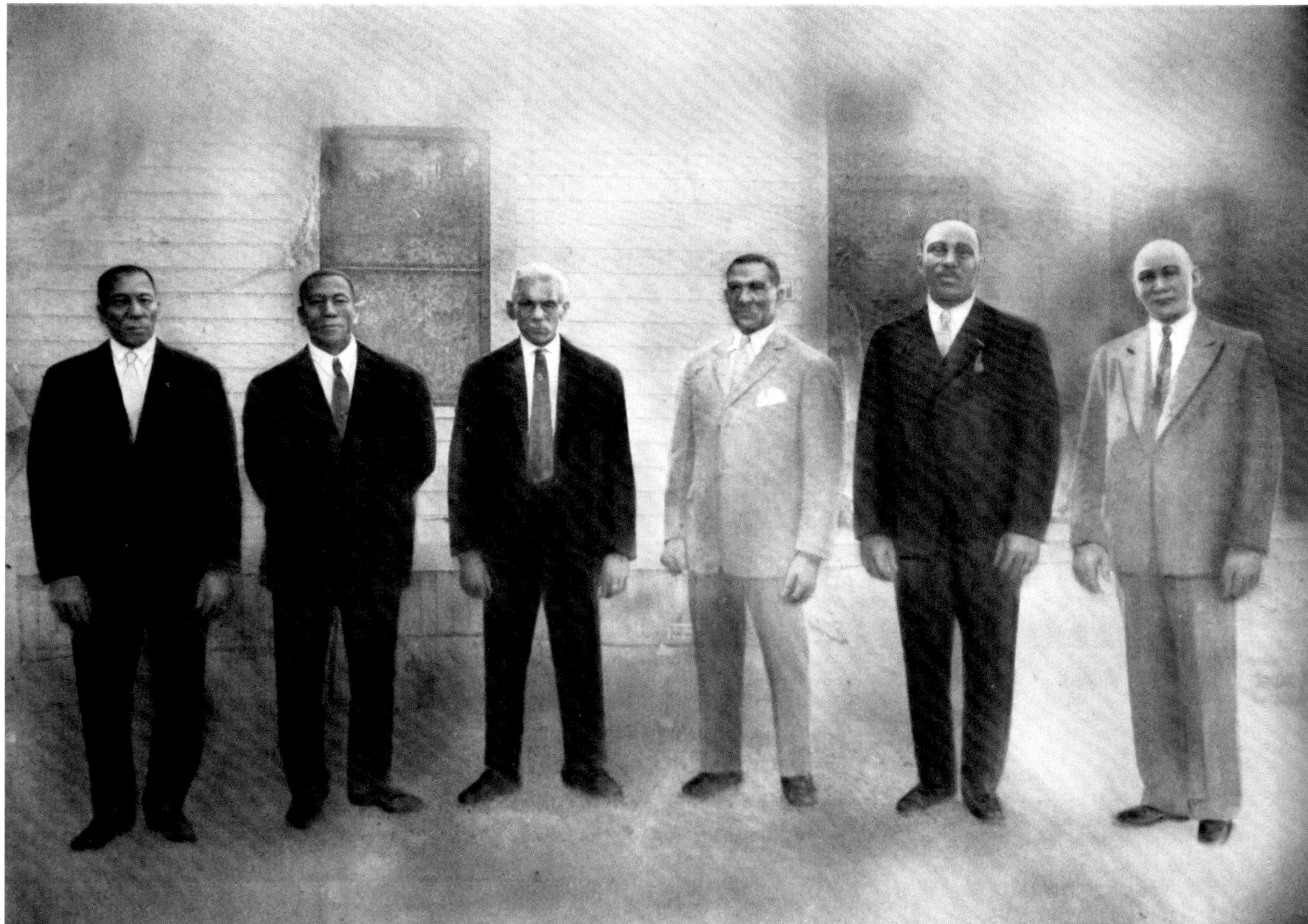

110.

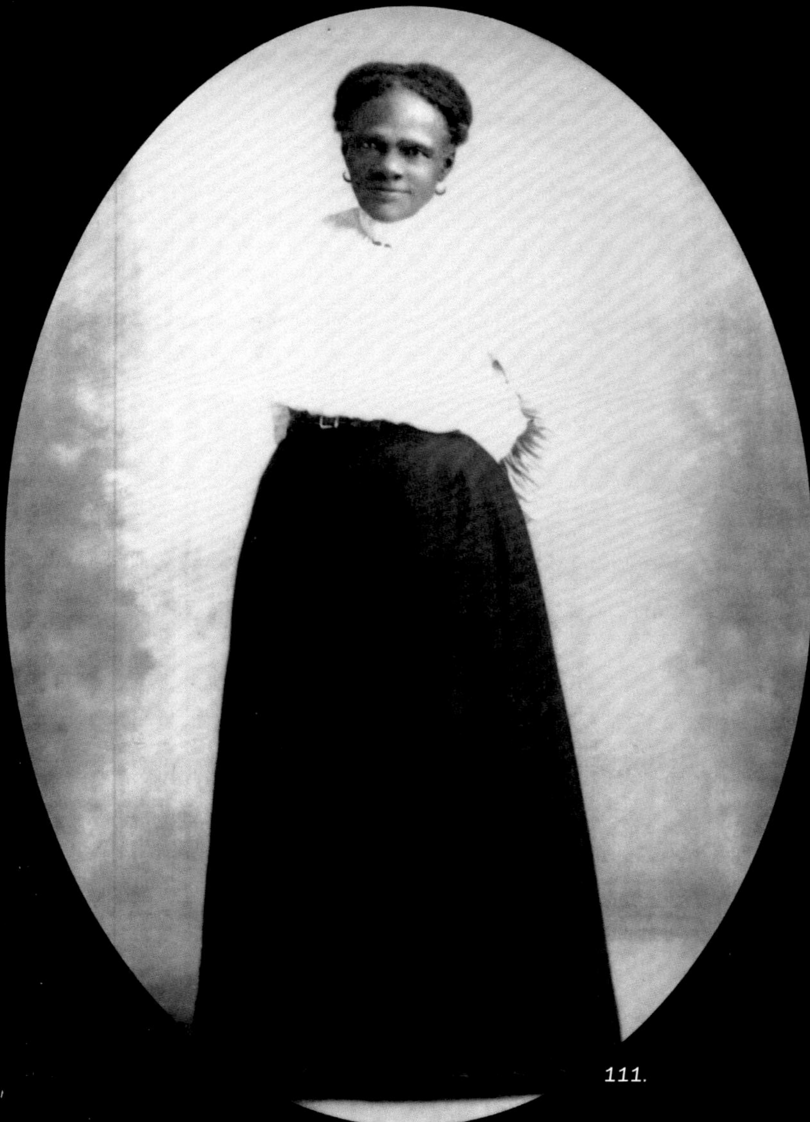

111.

another photo in my hand. Parthenia in the 1880s, in Tennessee, holding a gourd bowl of the kind made during slavery, wearing a headscarf and cotton apron. Back in the Riverside portrait, she seems child-sized, only up to the shoulders of the formally-dressed people at Fairmount Park. But she made it somehow across the country to visit her family – Reverend Goodwin who worked at The Mission Inn with the Tavaglione men.

Doug McCulloh, taking digital photos on the floor, in the light of the patio door, now has these images forever, inside inventions which no one imagined would exist when they put on black hats and bonnets and ventured down to Fairmount Park. A McCulloh quote seems appropriate: "Time past cannot be stopped, saved or regained. But a photograph allows you to borrow it."

Unless you reappropriate your history. Dorella sat back on her heels. "In school, they assigned us to do a paper on our family tree. When I got home, my mother was at work – she worked at the telephone company downtown – so I got on my bike and went down to the library. I asked the librarian for the Negro History section, cause I knew my family had been here forever. She took me over to a shelf, and there was one envelope" – she held out her fingers to indicate business-size – "and when I looked inside, there was one piece of paper. A letter with some official seal, said No Negroes had been born in the city of Riverside. None!" She cut her agate-gold eyes in classic Dorella fashion at me – the look she gave every person my age in Riverside, on Michael Street during barbecues, at Lincoln Park teaching wayward boys how to sit still. "Now I knew that wasn't true, because I was born here."

She rearranged more photos, handed me Park Avenue Baptist historic scenes. Then she mused, "You know what? I took it." She surveyed her work, all the neatly-bound photo albums, the folders and boxes, and then said, "That letter. It's probably somewhere in here." ■

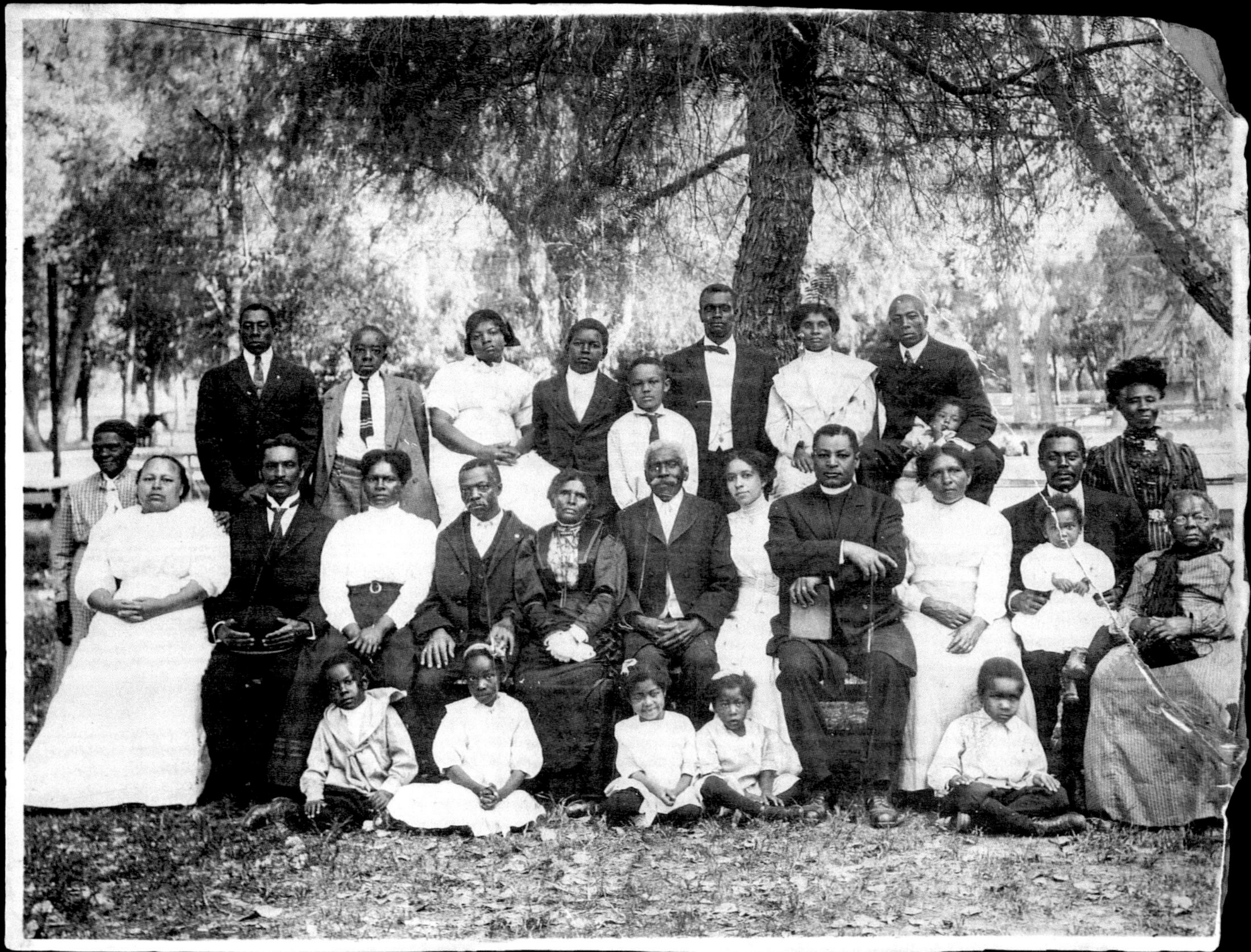

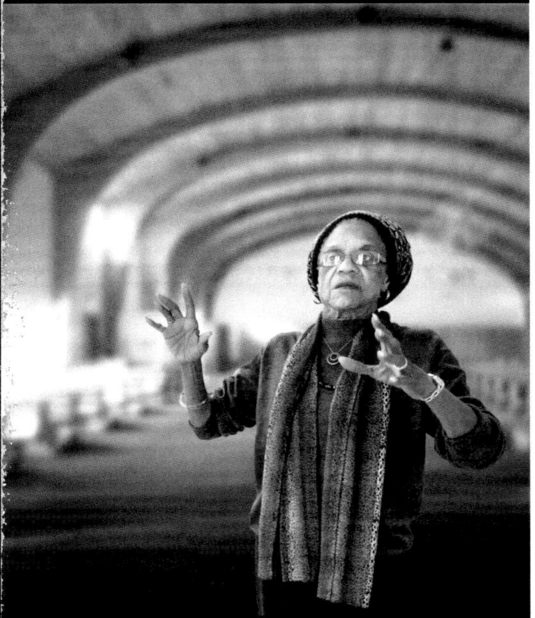

113.

100. Dorella Anderson preparing for a luncheon at Park Avenue Baptist Church

101. Historic Park Avenue Baptist Church whose cornerstone was laid in 1929, at 4192 Park Avenue

102. Reverend Leander B. Moss baptizing Andre Anderson, historic Park Avenue Baptist Church, 1967

103. Reverend Leander B. Moss and his wife Hattie Davis Moss, 1960s

104. Burning of the mortgage, historic Park Avenue Baptist Church, January 28, 1945

105. Park Avenue Baptist Church, moved in 1984 to Martin Luther King Avenue; Clarice Collins, church secretary and choir member, in the sanctuary

106. Jesse Lee Collins, groundskeeper, showing the sycamore trees he planted as saplings in 1984 when Park Avenue Baptist Church occupied its new location

107. Reverend Leander B. Moss officiating at wedding, historic Park Avenue Baptist Church, 1950s

108. Reggie and Susan Strickland with family in Riverside, 1950s

109. Susan Strickland, remembering her great-grandfather who fought on both sides of the Civil War – "He saw Abraham Lincoln, and he said how thin and old he looked" – in her living room

110. Eudell Williams, Trivell Williams, their father Edward Williams, Mose Williams, Walter Williams, Hayward Williams, at their house on Howard Street near Cottage; next door was Daisy Carter's first home, early 1900s

111. Parthenia Goodwin, born enslaved in Tennessee, circa 1880s

112. Iconic image of Second Baptist Church Sunday school picnic at Fairmount Park, Parthenia Goodwin on the far left, and members of Williams, Stokes, and other pioneer Black Riverside families well-represented, circa 1913

113. Dorella Anderson in the sanctuary at Park Avenue Baptist Church

114. Second Baptist Church, on Twelfth and Howard, including many members of the Stokes and Williams pioneer families, 1889

115. A treasured photograph from Dorella Anderson, three young daughters of the Williams family, historic Black residents, on an Eastside porch looking toward the future, circa 1900s

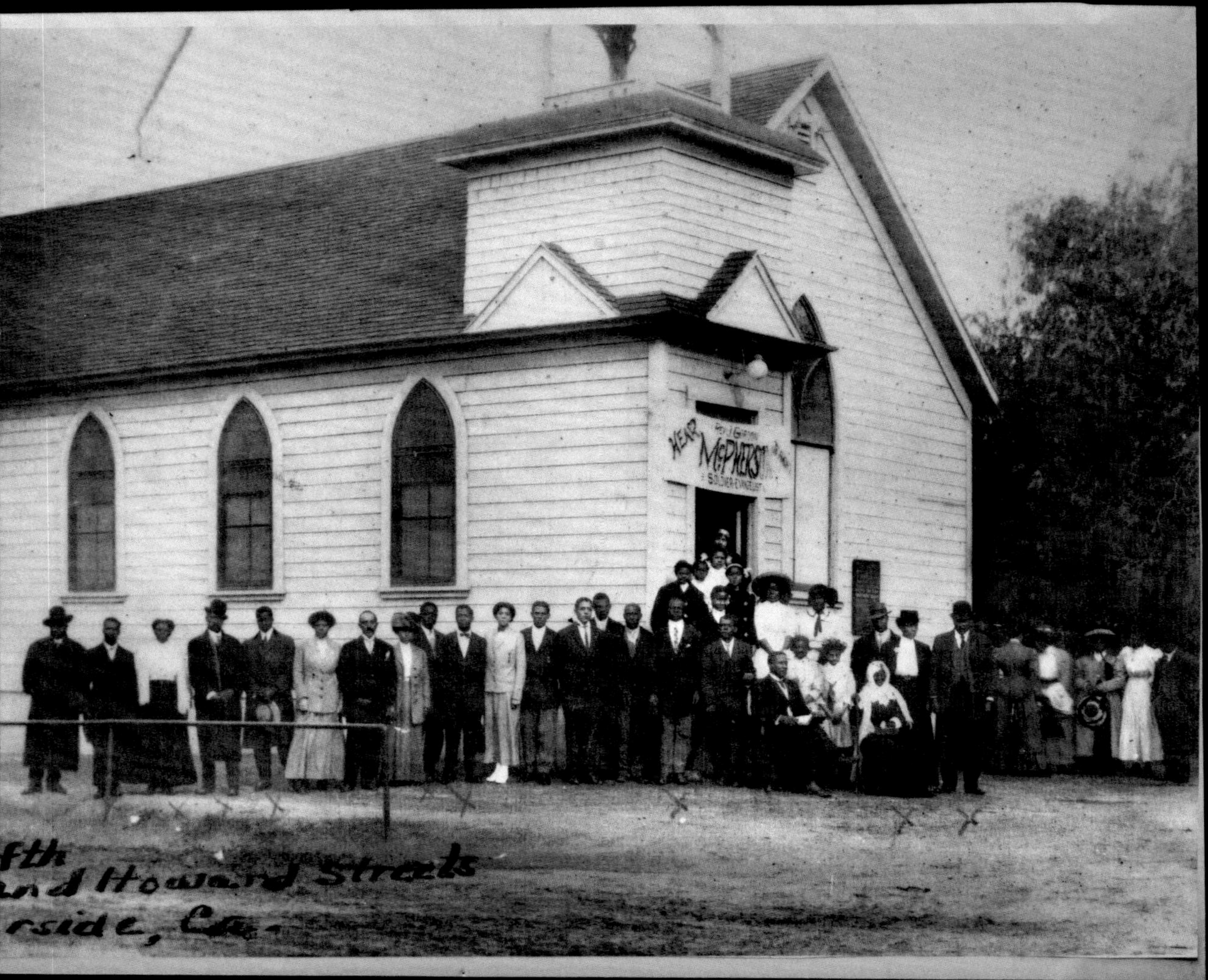
HEAR
McPHERSON
SOLDIER EVANGELIST
fth
and Howard Streets
rside, Ca.

114.

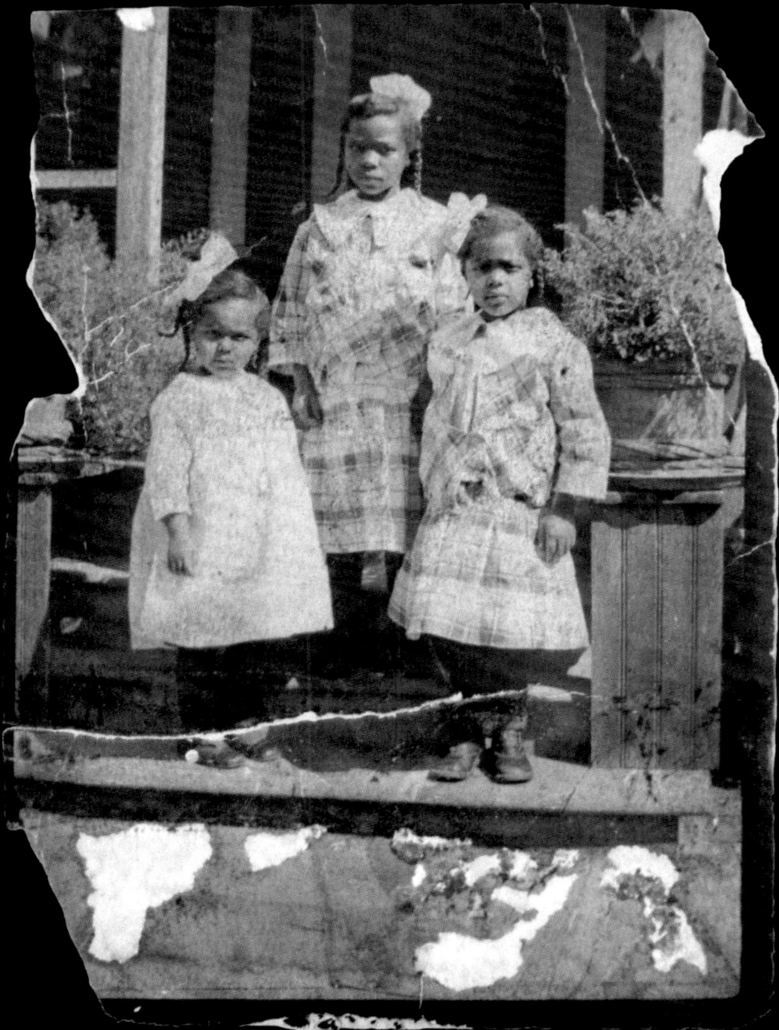

115.

Light Sensitive Metaphors from a (Freckled) Daughter of Riverside

DELPHINE SIMS

As with Douglas McCulloh and Susan Straight (my mother), when I wander under the southern California sun many unusual but welcome thoughts percolate. It was on one such walk that my mother and I were discussing the relationship between people, story, and photography, as we so often do, and she and I began to play with the theoretical intersections between freckles and family photography.

Freckles populate most of my face. Despite the fact that I have a freckled mother, the Sims family has always noted my spots and immediately designated me as the granddaughter of General Roscoe Conklin Sims II (photographs 12, 18, and 19). They called him Specks. His face and arms were truly a cosmos of small brown dots. He and I shared the frequent family comment, "You look like you got a tan through a screen door." We were light sensitive individuals. Grandpa General worked endless hours in the sun toiling in gardens across Riverside and at various outdoor hobbies with a spectrum of Riverside friends. I, as his granddaughter and the beneficiary of a hardworking family of migrants and immigrants, enjoy countless leisure hours in the sun, but in this labor of writing, another inheritance, I want to explore the collisions between photography, true to its origin as "writing with light;" skin freckles, or the sunlight-induced overproduction of melanin; and family images.

The family photographs in this book and exhibition are available to us because of those who cherished, protected, transported, and offered up their coveted family stories and images. But as we know, these are only snippets of long, epic, and intimate personal and familial narratives. Many others were culled over time, lost to various disasters (environmental and human) or curated through perspectives that historicized preferred or optimal stories and events. Freckles and photographs are both records of when and where a life has been lived — some disappear over time, some are lost then reappear, some record precise memories, and some record underlying life never exposed to the world. Freckles and photos also, however, encompass myriad actions in their surface presentation to the world. The bearer of the freckle and the photograph is able to determine the story that revolves around these markers. But these markers are not permanent, they are fragile and sometimes fleeting locales for experience.

Two beloved images in this show feature my grandmother, Alberta. In one she stands with her future sister-in-law, Loretta, and in the other she sits with her sisters, Mary, Rosie, and Myrtle (photographs 7 and 8). The final image in the catalogue features pioneer Black Riverside families at the Second Baptist Church (photograph 114). We might describe these photographs as damaged: edges are frayed and missing, emulsion is lost, and creases snake across the frame. Like my freckles, these family images are inherited – passed down from one generation to the next. However, just as there is a shift away from thinking of freckles as sun damage, we might understand these images not as destroyed but instead as lovingly preserved. We still have these images; indeed they are not solely a record of the moment the photograph was captured, but also a record of the life of the image itself. The fold speaks to the hands the photograph passed through, the locations it traveled, the times it was almost lost but miraculously continued to be saved, and finally its sheer singularity, for if we had more versions perhaps this particular print would not have lived such an extensive life.

The freckle and the photograph both require close looking. We might gloss over these visual objects but when we patiently observe, they offer exciting nuances and precious details reveal themselves. A school photograph might seem innocuous but an attentive viewer will examine the position, pose, and candor of a young group of students and begin to understand the wonders of an incredibly diverse place like Riverside. Here you might begin to constitute a world of co-existence (as my mother outlined) among the folks who attended Irving School (photographs 32, 33, and 34). If we are conscientious viewers can we begin to grasp the intricacies of life captured on these light sensitive surfaces – perhaps more simply that spectrums are not only possible but thrive in relation to one another. We might then think of Douglas's images in tandem with what the family archive offers. Only if we look closely do we begin to see the layered interiors that do indeed take on the reverence of a museum (photographs 2, 13, 19, 35, and 72). What fades into the background of our speedy lives suddenly takes on prominence when we are prepared to study what lies on the surface – even if that's an odd freckle or the small rectangular necklaces that connect sisters Roberta Tyson McClinton and Alicestyne Tyson Smith (photograph 24) beyond sisterhood, to recognition as sports ambassadors, honored as the essential "Team Cooks" behind a state championship.

We must be cautious however. While freckles and photographs are seemingly legible, ambiguity surrounds them. There are impediments to what is seen, both through deliberate opacity and the limits of exposure.

Freckles are often avoided, whether through prevention or concealment. There are those that populate the face only to be masked and there are those that never appear. Family photographs seemingly offer the promising arc of several generations – but just as the images present certain kinds of ideals, families themselves are messy, complicated, and disappointing. We learn of death and loss as well as harsh truths in violent moments of racism (photographs 1, 4, 83, and 84) but our access to an extensive archive of these types of events is limited for they are often too intense to have been strategically captured on film. We sometimes see the aftermath of these events, but what we see most frequently are posed episodes of joy – weddings, family portraits, sports teams, clubs, and church. Largely, we don't explicitly witness failed marriages and relationships, broken families and lost friendships, nor mental and physical harm. There are no pictures of life outside of heteronormative dreamscapes. That is not to say these parts of a more dreamers story have not been hugely important to family narratives, only that the curated archive of images and stories does not encompass or reveal them. This is an important acknowledgement both for those who collect, curate, and mediate the archive as well as the evolving ways in which community and family storytellers shape their stories, even given that some truths may seem too painful or too intimate to bring to the surface.

There are freckles that appear as singular marks — attracting attention to their appearance as an anomaly, but for many, freckles exist in wonderful constellations. This book is a testament to a kind of photographic constellation – some parts are in tandem and others exist on the edge – but ultimately all cohesively come together. There is an image that represents this coalescence – Douglas overlays dozens of images in an exquisite description of communion on Michael Street (photograph 15). Strewn on tables are the objects and remnants of hours spent together. Douglas stitches time into an overview of another extensive day in the driveway. When we begin to see such seriality, other constellations emerge offering panoramas of sites and events – suddenly you can experience multiple sides of the North gym or the flow from interior to exterior at the Orange Valley Lodge.

Finally, I implore us to continue to think about our tactile relationship to the photograph and the freckle. It's evident in the life of the family photograph that it has been touched incessantly, we see this in the remnants of oils and bends caused by eager hands. Recorded by the very presentation of the scanned digital images and the fabric prints of the exhibition, is the sense that a hand offered this photograph to Douglas, my mother, myself, and you, the audience. When we remember the touch upon the image we recall our most intimate ways of relating to photography in our own home and among our kin. Beautifully, the way an image responds to your body is alluded to in the installation of the show – the banners move with you as you walk amid visions of Riverside dreamers.

Exposure to the sun changes the way we see ourselves, see one another, capture experience, and record story. May we hold close those from whom we've inherited (freckled) dreams and the ways we are protected from, exposed to, and nourished by the golden California sun. ■

Portions of "The Red Sauce Equals Love at Zacatecas Café" previously appeared in different form in *The Los Angeles Times*. Portions of "People Who Stay: Friday Night Lights and the Gym of American Dreams," "Sacred Ground and Resolution on Victoria Avenue," and "Build Me a School: Queens of the Holiday Classic" previously appeared in different form in "SoCal Focus" *KCET, Los Angeles*.

Photographs by Douglas McCulloh with the following exceptions:

Courtesy of the Sims Family: 2, 3, 5, 6, 7, 8, 12, 13, 16, 17, 18, 20, 21, 22, 23

Courtesy of the Tyson Family: 25, 26, 27, 30

Courtesy of Dorella Anderson: 33, 59, 102, 103, 104, 107, 111, 112, 114, 115

Courtesy of the Medina Family: 66, 68

Courtesy of Robert and Mariko Anderson: 67

Courtesy of The Museum of Riverside: 74, 76, 95

Courtesy Riverside Public Library History Collections: 83, 84

Courtesy of Tony and Sarah Lopez: 93

Courtesy of Sue Strickland: 108, 110

SUSAN STRAIGHT was born in Riverside, California, where she still lives with her family. Her memoir, *In the Country of Women* (Catapult Books, 2020), was a national bestseller. It was a Best Book of the Year by NPR and CodeSwitch, longlisted for the Carnegie Medal for Excellence, and a Finalist for the Clara Johnson Prize for Women's Literature. Her new novel, *Mecca*, will be published by Farrar, Straus and Giroux in March 2022. She has published eight novels — *Highwire Moon* and *I Been in Sorrow's Kitchen and Licked Out All the Pots* were national bestsellers, and her trilogy of one family's journey from slavery to California includes *A Million Nightingales, Take One Candle,* and *Between Heaven and Here*. She has been a Finalist for the National Book Award and the National Magazine Award; she received the Edgar Prize for Best Mystery Story, the O Henry Prize, the Lannan Prize, and a Guggenheim Fellowship. Her fiction and essays have appeared in *The New Yorker, The Guardian, The New York Times, The Los Angeles Times, Harper's, The Believer, O Magazine, Real Simple, Alta, Reader's Digest, Family Circle* and other journals. She is Distinguished Professor of Creative Writing at UC Riverside.

DOUGLAS MCCULLOH is an artist, writer, and senior curator at the California Museum of Photography. His work has been shown nationally and internationally in more than 250 exhibitions including Victoria and Albert Museum, London; Central Academy of Fine Arts, Beijing; Centro de la Imagen, Mexico City; Art Center College of Design, Los Angeles; Contemporary Arts Center, New Orleans; and Smithsonian Institution, Washington D.C. McCulloh's most recent books are *In the Sunshine of Neglect* (Inlandia Institute), and *The Great Picture: Making the World's Largest Photograph* (Hudson Hills Press, New York). Exhibitions curated by McCulloh have shown in a range of venues including Kennedy Center for the Arts, Washington D.C.; Canadian Museum for Human Rights, Winnipeg; Flacon Art Center, Moscow; Center for Visual Art, Denver, Colorado; Manuel Álvarez Bravo Center, Oaxaca; Sejong Center, Seoul, South Korea; and, of course, UCR ARTS: California Museum of Photography. He is an honors graduate of the University of California, Santa Barbara and holds an M.F.A. from Claremont Graduate University.

DELPHINE SIMS is a Ph.D. candidate in the History of Art Department at UC Berkeley where she studies the history of photography in the Americas. In 2019, she was the Mellon Curatorial Intern at the Berkeley Art Museum and Pacific Film Archive (BAMPFA) during which time she helped organize the exhibitions *Unlimited: Recent Gifts from the William Goodman and Victoria Belco Collection* and *About Things Loved: Blackness and Belonging*. In 2018, she was a curatorial intern at the San Francisco Museum of Modern Art in the photography department. Previously, Delphine was a curatorial assistant at the Santa Barbara Museum of Art. She has worked on numerous museum exhibitions and contributed writings to several publications including *Laurie Brown: Earth Edges* (California Museum of Photography), *New Time: Art and Feminisms in the Twenty-first Century* (BAMPFA); "Sprouts from the Concrete" (*Matte* magazine), and "Where We Art" (*The Believer* magazine). Delphine, the daughter of Susan Straight, was born in Riverside, California.